Imbert de Saint-Amand

The court of the second empire

Imbert de Saint-Amand

The court of the second empire

ISBN/EAN: 9783337274122

Printed in Europe, USA, Canada, Australia, Japan

Cover: Foto ©ninafisch / pixelio.de

More available books at **www.hansebooks.com**

THE COURT

OF THE SECOND EMPIRE

BY

IMBERT DE SAINT-AMAND

TRANSLATED BY

ELIZABETH GILBERT MARTIN

WITH PORTRAITS

NEW YORK
CHARLES SCRIBNER'S SONS
1898

CONTENTS

CHAPTER		PAGE
I.	NAPOLEON III	1
II.	THE EMPRESS EUGÉNIE	13
III.	COUNT WALEWSKI	25
IV.	THE TREATY OF PARIS	33
V.	THE SPRING OF 1856	45
VI.	THE INUNDATIONS	54
VII.	THE BAPTISM OF THE PRINCE IMPERIAL	60
VIII.	THE BAPTISMAL FESTIVITIES	66
IX.	COUNT DE MORNY	72
X.	THE EMBASSY TO ST. PETERSBURG	82
XI.	THE CORONATION OF THE CZAR	92
XII.	THE FÊTES OF MOSCOW	101
XIII.	FRANCE AND RUSSIA	107
XIV.	THE PRINCE OF PRUSSIA	114
XV.	THE COMMENCEMENT OF 1857	121
XVI.	A BALL AT THE FOREIGN AFFAIRS	129

CHAPTER		PAGE
XVII.	THE GRAND DUKE CONSTANTINE AND THE KING OF BAVARIA......................	137
XVIII.	PRINCE NAPOLEON IN GERMANY..............	149
XIX.	THE INTERNAL SITUATION....................	159
XX.	THE QUESTION OF THE PRINCIPALITIES.......	166
XXI.	THE OSBORNE INTERVIEW....................	176
XXII.	THE OPENING OF THE NEW LOUVRE..........	186
XXIII.	BIARRITZ....................................	192
XXIV.	THE CAMP OF CHÂLONS......................	200
XXV.	STRASBURG AND BADEN......................	207
XXVI.	THE STUTTGART INTERVIEW..................	214
XXVII.	THE RESULTS OF THE INTERVIEW............	222
XXVIII.	THE BEGINNING OF 1858.....................	231
XXIX.	THE ATTEMPT OF JANUARY 14...............	240
XXX.	AFTER THE OUTRAGE........................	248
XXXI.	GENERAL DELLA ROCCA......................	257
XXXII.	THE ORSINI TRIAL...........................	269
XXXIII.	GENERAL ESPINASSE.........................	279
XXXIV.	COUNT DE PERSIGNY.........................	289
XXXV.	MARSHAL PÉLISSIER AS AMBASSADOR.........	301
XXXVI.	COUNT CAVOUR..............................	310
XXXVII.	PLOMBIÈRES.................................	318

CHAPTER	PAGE
XXXVIII. THE CHERBOURG INTERVIEW	326
XXXIX. THE TOUR IN BRITTANY	331

PORTRAITS

THE PRINCE IMPERIAL .... *Frontispiece*

COUNT DE MORNY .... *Face page* 74

ALEXANDER II, EMPEROR OF RUSSIA .... " " 216

VICTOR EMMANUEL, KING OF SARDINIA .... " " 266

THE COURT OF THE SECOND EMPIRE

1856–1858

CHAPTER I

NAPOLEON III

A SINGLE portrait of those who have played a great part in history is not enough; to represent them fairly it is essential to sketch the different phases of their career. In age and ill health they were no longer the same, morally or physically, as when young and strong. There is as much difference between the periods of a human life as there is between the seasons of a single year. Aided by the impressions and recollections of our contemporaries, we are about to attempt the reproduction of the historic figure of Napoleon III. as we saw him from 1856 to 1859, and we hope that those who lived in Paris at that period will find the likeness faithful.

On the morrow of the birth of the Prince Imperial the Second Emperor was a happy man and one who enjoyed his happiness. Neither on his countenance nor in his heart at that time was there a trace of melancholy. Appearing at Rome in the character of another Charlemagne, and throughout Europe as an arbiter and peacemaker, if he recalled the painful experiences of childhood and youth, it was only by way of contrast with his actual prosperity, and as yet he foreboded none of the calamities awaiting him in the future.

Princes born on the steps of the throne and who have never known adversity have not the same enjoyment of power as a man like Napoleon III., for whom the fortress of Ham was the vestibule of the Tuileries. If in earlier days he had been flouted, jeered at, contemned, in 1856 at least he was lauded to the skies. Foreigners courted him even more assiduously than the French. Take, for example, a telegram sent from Sebastopol, March 23, 1856, to the Minister of War by Marshal Pélissier:—

"Your despatch of the 16th announcing the happy delivery of H. M. the Empress and the birth of the Prince Imperial did not arrive until Sunday morning, the 23d. At noon the news was greeted by one hundred and one salvos of artillery fired simultaneously by the French, English, and Sardinian armies and by the fleets. At the same moment a *Te Deum* was chanted in every army corps in presence of all the troops. During the day the commanders-in-chief of the English and Sardinian armies came to offer their congratulations, which I beg you to lay with mine and those of the generals under my command at the feet of Their Imperial Majesties. Our soldiers have ended the day by continued cheering around a multitude of fires which give our camps the appearance of a splendid illumination. The Scotch and Sardinians encamped on the heights of Kamarak were able to build such enormous fires that the light from them could be seen at immense distances. And lastly, the Russians, taking part in our special manifestations, suddenly illuminated the whole line from Inkermann to Corolès, thus completing this unique spectacle."

As soon as Napoleon III. was made acquainted with Marshal Pélissier's despatch, he sent an aide-de-camp to Lord Clarendon, Count Cavour, and also to Count Orloff, thanking them for the demonstrations by which the birth of his son had been celebrated in the Crimea. The attentions he received from the powers, and the extraordinary respects paid to the cradle of his heir delighted him both as a father and a sovereign. He was particularly pleased at seeing the court of Russia display exceptional courtesy even before peace was concluded.

People forgave Napoleon III. his success because he used it in moderation and without conceit or violence. His past misfortunes had left behind them no trace of bitterness or rancor. Nearly all his ministers had formerly been Orleanists, and if the most advanced republicans had presented themselves at the Tuileries, they would have received a cordial welcome. Napoleon III. had forgotten the injuries inflicted on Louis Bonaparte. He left the salons which opposed him entirely undisturbed, and no such persecutions as those of which Madame de Staël was the victim under the First Empire occurred during his reign.

Invariably self-possessed, the former outlaw and captive was as tranquil in gladness as in sorrow. If his letters are ever published, as has happened in our day to those of Napoleon I., we do not believe they will be found to contain a single phrase, a single word of hatred or anger. M. Pinard, one of his ministers, has said: "He became familiar with those who had been his earliest friends without permitting them to cross the distance separating them. He was always the Emperor; but his voice at that time had inflections of great sweetness, and, I may add, of great power as well. The sovereign whom the political world sometimes called William the Silent had in private conversation a seductive charm which the firstcomer might not suspect, but of which women had an intuition."

The imperturbable apathy of the Second Emperor was only a mask. At bottom, no disposition could be more impressionable, ardent, or passionate than his. Naturally violent, it had cost him much to acquire that self-mastery which was afterwards the principal trait of his character. Madame Cornu, the companion of his earliest years, has said: "As a child he was subject to such fits of anger as I have never seen in any one else; while they lasted he knew neither what he said or what he did." Experience and misfortune taught him to control himself, and he succeeded in making his thoughts as impenetrable as his face. "When I met him again, in 1848," says Madame Cornu, "I asked what was the matter with his eyes. 'Nothing,' said he. I saw him again a day or two later. His eyes seemed still more singular. Finally I noticed that he had contracted a habit of keeping the lids half-closed and assuming a vacant and dreamy expression."

Napoleon III. has often been called a dreamer by those who judged him by his manners and facial expression. It would be much truer to say that he was a man of action, for there are few political personages who have had a hand in so many things or broached so many formidable problems. Not all of his attempts succeeded, but every one of them, in Asia and America as in Europe, was marked by an adventurous spirit and an audacity truly extraordinary.

The sovereign whom, in the final period of his career, we shall see timid and undecided, wavering between the most contradictory resolutions, and letting himself be dragged by a sort of fatality into a war to which he was averse, displayed in 1856 a coherency, a vigor, and energy which nothing could withstand. His power was essentially personal; his policy originated entirely with himself. He reigned and governed. Having succeeded in spite of the predictions of all others, he had no confidence in any opinions but his own, and no one ventured to advise him.

The powerful monarch applied when on the throne the programme which the prisoner had elaborated. His ministers were mere docile instruments in his hands. There was but one will at that time, and it was his. "If a minister," says M. Pinard, "developed an idea coincident with his, his eyes, ordinarily half-closed, lighted up in a singular manner, although the face still remained grave and almost impassible. If the speaker had not succeeded in convincing him, the Emperor maintained a significant silence which often disconcerted the most resolute; he seemed to forget those who were near him, and even him who had just been speaking. When he expressed his own opinion, the deliberate slowness of his speech was not unlike that of his gait: it seemed to indicate a man who was listening to an interior voice. At such times he appeared to be talking with himself."

Everything great and useful that was done during his reign bears the sign manual of the sovereign. Baron Haussmann, that prefect to whom grateful Paris ought to raise a statue, has admitted that he could have done nothing without Napoleon III. "Alone," he says, "I should never have been able to continue, much less to carry to a successful termination, the mission confided to me by the Emperor, and for the accomplishment of which his increasing confidence left me by degrees a greater freedom of decision. I could never have struggled successfully against the inherent difficulties of each operation; against opposing wishes, whether due to sincere convictions or to unavowed but implacable jealousies in the great governmental bodies, and even in His Majesty's immediate circle; nor against the open attacks of parties inimical to the imperial régime, which, not daring to censure the policy impressed on the country by the sovereign, endeavored to oppose him indirectly in the municipal enterprises due to his initiative and executed under his inspiration; if I had not been really the expression, the organ, the instrument of a great idea, the conception and merit of which I must in the first place attribute to him, and whose realization he invariably guarded with a firmness never belied." In reality, the transformation which has made Paris the capital of capitals is the personal work of Napoleon III.

The Second Emperor was a cosmopolitan sovereign. During his long exiles his character had assimilated somewhat from each country in which he had lived. From the Italian carbonari he had borrowed the inclination to conspiracy; from German philosophers the tendency to dream; from English statesmen the habit of combining business and pleasure. Humanitarian rather than patriotic, a citizen of the world still more than Emperor of the French, he may be accused of having entertained projects too vast, and of sacrificing the special interests of France to what he considered the general interests of civilization. His policy may have aimed too high, but its noble and chivalric aspects cannot be despised. To better the moral and material conditions of the majority, not merely in France but throughout Europe, to proclaim the principle of nationalities, to maintain the right of peoples to dispose of their own destiny, to unite them by commercial treaties, the multiplicity of exchanges, the rapidity of communications,—such was the object of his efforts. Never would he have vaunted the programme of blood and iron, nor have declared that force takes precedence of right. The policy of M. von Bismarck, his successful rival, was a survival from the Middle Ages. His own was modern, and it may be affirmed that if he had triumphed in 1870 as he did in 1855 and 1859, general civilization, instead of being retarded, would have advanced with giant strides.

It might have been believed in 1856 that Napoleon III., pleased with his unexpected successes and at the summit of his fortunes, would be contented tranquilly to enjoy the benefits of a peace which public opinion desired and which had been purchased by so many heroic sacrifices. But, on the contrary, his ambition as the apostle of nationalities sought new aliment, and he began conspiring to deliver the country of Machiavelli from Austrian domination as seriously as he had conspired to gain the throne of France. After the hecatombs of one of the most sanguinary struggles of modern history, all Frenchmen, with the single exception of the Emperor, longed for the maintenance of peace. Even at the moment when the signing of the treaty of Paris was causing universal joy and satisfaction, and when people supposed that the sovereign was definitively returning to the programme of the famous speech of Bordeaux and could once more say with sincerity, " The Empire is peace," he alone had an approaching war in prospect. His passion for military affairs, his youthful memories, his temperament as a political gamester, his adventurous spirit, his pretensions as the champion of the cause of nationalities, all combined to drag him into a path the end of which was an abyss.

Napoleon III. believed himself a military man of the first order, and nothing interested him so much as the army. His greatest amusement as a child was to play soldier. In Switzerland, as a young man, he had been the pupil of a great tactician, General Dufour. He was especially occupied with the artillery branch of the service, and had published works on this subject of which he was very proud. Full of confidence in his talents as a strategist, he had a presentiment of winning great victories. He had keenly regretted his inability to go to the Crimea, and when his troops returned triumphantly to Paris it afflicted him to think that it was not he who had conducted them to victory. But that, he told himself, was but a game deferred; the day would come when he would gain battles, and when his head on the coins would be crowned with laurels. Up to the present he had fought during a few days only, — in the Romagna, in 1832, — and then he had suffered a lamentable defeat. He wanted his revenge.

It has been said that Napoleon III. was more of an Italian than a Frenchman. That is an exaggeration, but it may be affirmed that he considered Italy as his second fatherland, and thought that he had duties toward it. He said it was the land of his ancestors; that Napoleon First had been crowned in the cathedral of Milan as well as in Notre Dame de Paris; that Italians, companions in arms of Frenchmen throughout the whole duration of the Empire, had shed torrents of blood for France under Murat, King of Naples, and Prince Eugene de Beauharnais, Viceroy of Italy. The insurgent of 1832 had made promises to Italian liberals which the powerful Emperor desired to keep. The recollection of that fatal expedition of the Romagnas, where he made his first campaign, was destined to exert the greatest influence over all his subsequent career. There his brother died, and he longed to avenge him.

Such were the thoughts by which the Emperor was obsessed. Persuaded that it was his providential mission to do away with the treaties of 1815 and assure the independence of Italy from the Alps to the Adriatic, he likewise believed that in so doing he would serve the interests of France, which, after a successful war with Austria and an accession of territory to Piedmont, would regain its own natural frontier on the southeast. Madame Cornu has written: "A war intended to drive the Austrians out of Italy, in which he should have command, has been his dream from childhood. He once said to me at Ham: 'I feel that I shall command a great army some day; I know that I shall distinguish myself; I am conscious of possessing all the great military qualities.'" A triumphant entry at Milan at the head of a victorious and liberating army, amidst a tumult of applause and under a rain of flowers, was a vision which delighted his ardent and poetic fancy.

But the realization of such a dream was by no means easy; in France the impediments were as many and as serious as in foreign parts. To surmount them Napoleon III. summoned in the first place cunning, dissimulation, mystery, to his assistance. He concealed his Italian schemes from his wife and his ministers just as he had concealed the Strasbourg expedition from his mother. He had had but two confidants at Ham: his physician, Doctor Conneau, and Charles Thélin, his valet. The confidants of his designs on Italy were hardly more numerous between 1856 and 1859. Whom will he send to Turin in May, 1858, to arrange his interview with Cavour at Plombières? Doctor Conneau, who was far more conversant with his plans than his Minister of Foreign Affairs.

Napoleon III. had relapsed into his inveterate habit of conspiring. The apostle of nationalities took good care not to prate about his programme. He never mentioned it during the Crimean War, for then he absolutely needed Austria; if that power had taken sides with Russia, it would have drawn all Germany in its train, and the Crimean War would have resulted in frightful disasters to France and England. Hence Napoleon III. was mute. It was not one of his own plenipotentiaries who brought up the Italian question at the Paris Congress, but Count Cavour, secretly supported by him. And as if to get his hand in while awaiting the day when he could openly concern himself with Italy, the Emperor sought to constitute a nationality: that of Roumania. The idea that Piedmont and Prussia might play a similar part in Italy and Germany, far from alarming him, was agreeable. He foresaw an agreement between Turin and Berlin, and made special advances to the Crown Prince of Prussia, the future Emperor of Germany, the man who was to be his deadliest foe. Under the most pacific appearances, amidst incessant festivities at Fontainebleau and Compiègne, at Biarritz and Plombières, at the Tuileries and Saint-Cloud, the crowned conspirator pursued his purpose patiently and mysteriously. The period we are about to retrace may be summed up in one phrase: preparation for the Italian war. The apostle of nationalities never suspected that he would be its martyr.

CHAPTER II

THE EMPRESS EUGÉNIE

THE Empress had just fulfilled her principal mission. She had given a son to her husband and an heir to the Empire. The child was born on Palm Sunday, a day of triumph. She did not forebode that he would end his brief existence by a calvary. What delighted the happy mother above all was that this longed-for child was not merely a son of France but a son of the Church, and that as a godson of the Pope, the benediction of the Holy Father had rested on his cradle.

There was not a cloud on the relations between the Empire and the Holy See at this period. French troops were on guard at the doors of the Vatican. Pius IX. had written to Napoleon III., February 8, 1856: "I feel bound to tell Your Majesty that God has inspired me with a pleasing hope. I flatter myself that He is about to shed abroad new mercies which will descend abundantly upon you, Sire, in proportion as you fulfil your promise to support and protect the Church in whose bosom you were born. As for me, my words and prayers have no object but the glory of God, the salvation of souls, the propagation of the faith and the honor of Catholic princes. ... Receive, Sire, the apostolic benediction which I give Your Majesty from the bottom of my heart, as well as to Her Majesty the Empress and the august infant she carries in her womb, and to all France."

The tidings of the birth of the Prince Imperial reached Rome just as the Pope was celebrating the Mass of Palm Sunday in the basilica of Saint Peter's. A salvo of one hundred and one cannon, fired from Castle Saint Angelo, announced it to the crowds assembled for the ceremonies of Holy Week. In the evening the palace of the French embassy, the academy of France, the national churches, and the military club were illuminated.

Count de Rayneval, French ambassador at Rome, wrote on March 29 to Count Walewski, Minister of Foreign Affairs: "I had the honor to present in person the letter by which the Emperor acquainted the Holy Father with the birth of the Prince Imperial. The Holy Father availed himself of the occasion to express in most affecting terms the extreme interest he takes in this auspicious event, the wishes he forms for the welfare of the young Prince and for the speedy restoration of Her Majesty's health. So evident a sign of the favor of Heaven cannot fail to have the best results. Security of the future will be a powerful assistance in overcoming the difficulties of the present. The prayers of His Holiness will never be lacking to Their Imperial Majesties nor to France. The Holy Father was very keenly affected by the mention in His Majesty's speech of the pontifical blessing which reached the young Prince almost at his birth. Aside from his personal interest in this display of the Emperor's sentiments, His Holiness greatly praised this striking testimony to the union of the two powers and their mutual sympathy. Under every aspect their cause cannot but be the gainer by it."

Count de Rayneval announced at the same time a piece of news which delighted the Empress Eugénie. " His Holiness," he added, " has decided that the golden rose which he blesses annually during Lent shall be sent this year to Her Majesty the Empress. This pious custom, the origin of which it would not be easy to discover, is not often carried out. The last occasion was when the golden rose was given to Her Majesty the Queen of Naples at the time the Holy Father returned to his States, in grateful recognition of the generous hospitality he had received at Gaëta and Portici during his entire exile." No gift could have been more acceptable to the Empress than the golden rose. Her ardent faith and her devotion to the interests of the Holy See made her deserving of it. Throughout her reign she acted like a faithful daughter of the Church, and the difficulties which sometimes arose between the Empire and the Papacy were the greatest annoyances of her life. But on the morrow of the birth of the Prince Imperial there was as yet no symptom of dissension between Napoleon III. and Pius IX. Their agreement seemed absolute and definitive.

The Empress showed herself as charitable as she was devout. The numerous foundations placed under her patronage received her constant solicitude. She took great interest in the Eugénie-Napoleon asylum, the first capital for which was the six hundred thousand francs intended by the city of Paris for the purchase of a necklace for the sovereign; the Sainte-Eugénie hospital, founded in 1854, and the orphanage of the Prince Imperial, created in 1856. The salvage society for the shipwrecked, like all other asylums, was placed under the protection of the Empress. Committees were organized in Paris and its suburbs to collect subscriptions for a testimonial of devotion to her at the time of the Prince's birth. The lists were speedily filled up in every quarter. More than six hundred thousand signatures were collected in a few days, and the sum raised exceeded eighty thousand francs. The amount received from each subscriber being limited to between one and five cents, the number of names proved that the working classes had been especially anxious to show their sympathy with the sovereign.

The presidents of the committees having inquired to what purpose Her Majesty desired this sum to be devoted, M. Billault, Minister of Internal Affairs, replied, May 20: "The Empress thanks you for herself and her son. She will gratefully accept the volumes of signatures, eloquent witnesses of the sentiments of the inhabitants of Paris, but as to the sums realized from the subscription, you will permit her to devote them to some benevolent work for the children of the people, as was done with the six hundred thousand francs voted by the municipality of Paris at the time of her marriage. Herself the patroness of the maternities and refuges, she wishes to place the poor orphans under the patronage of her son. She desires that the poor workman carried off prematurely from his family may at least have in dying the consolation of knowing that imperial benevolence will watch over his children. A gratuitous and permanent commission will seek out in Paris both orphans and families of honest workingmen, by whom, in consideration of an annual payment, these poor children will be taken, brought up, given a new family and apprenticed to a trade. . . . Thus the Empress will have realized the tender and pious desire of assuring to these poor little creatures, deprived by death of their natural supporters, not the shelter of an asylum but the aid, affection, and care of a new family."

We cite also this extract from the journal of M. Pinaud: "The rôle of a charitable lady who never tells her name to any one and who visits the sick and poor in person, was very attractive to the Empress. At certain dates she made discreet excursions to humble dwellings and climbed many pairs of stairs, accompanied only by a lady of the palace dressed as simply as herself. One day she was recognized and followed. From that time two agents were designated to assure her safety, but discreetly and without her knowledge, whenever these charitable pilgrimages were renewed."

The Empress was really popular at the time of the Prince Imperial's birth. People were pleased with her kindness and her beauty. To charm, to console, and to do good seemed to be her motto. People liked to fancy her as the Emperor's good angel and the Providence of the poor. As yet no trait of the female politician had been discovered in her. Her husband reserved to himself all the duties and responsibilities of power.

The Empress was really happy at this period. The clergy treated her as a second Blanche of Castile. If she entered a cathedral, it was beneath a canopy and surrounded by a cloud of incense. She enjoyed all the prestige of supreme rank without being subjected to the minute and fastidious details of antiquated royal etiquette. Her ladies of the palace were young, agreeable, and distinguished women. The château of the Tuileries had lost its sombre appearance and no longer suggested the terrible catastrophes which are a part of its history. The sovereign's apartments were a model of luxury and elegance. Instead of being imprisoned there as Louis Philippe and his family had been, she could walk in the private garden in front of the château without being exposed to the curiosity of the crowd. The palaces of Saint-Cloud, Fontainebleau, and Compiègne were delightful residences in which she quietly enjoyed the most agreeable pleasures of country life and according to her taste could choose between the pomp of an empress and the privacy of a simple châtelaine.

We would not guarantee that Napoleon III. was an absolutely faithful husband in 1856. But as to that, we remind our readers that where sovereigns are in question, certain weaknesses do not belong to history except when made so notorious by display — as during the reigns of Louis XIV. and Louis XV. — that they become public scandals. What may be affirmed is that Napoleon III. never ceased to display towards the companion whom his heart had chosen the most respectful and affectionate attention, and that he always professed profound love and admiration for her. In July, 1856, having left her at Saint-Cloud to go and take the waters at Plombières, he wrote: "You and the little one are everything to me. . . . It makes me happy to see the moment drawing near when I shall see you and our child again, and I am so contented about it that I torment myself with thinking that it is really too good to be true, and that between now and then one or other of you will certainly fall ill, or that they will not be careful enough when he goes near the pond. Be sure not to tire yourself too much. All these recommendations are stupid, perhaps; but when I am so happy I am frightened."

Barring a few escapades which never attained publicity and which were perhaps more excusable in a sovereign exposed to every sort of temptation than they would be in a private citizen, Napoleon III. was a very good husband. Madame Cornu said of him: "Under various aspects his temperament is feminine. His love for his son is rather that of a mother than a father." Gentle and kindly, affectionate and sentimental, he displayed in private life an affability, good nature, and equanimity that nothing disturbed. It pleased him to see the Empress play her part as sovereign so well, and he eagerly sought occasions to amuse her, bring her into prominence, and make her admired. The things of the mind entertained her more than those of art, and her husband was never better contented than when he saw her taking a brilliant lead in conversation and charming her interlocutors.

We have remarked already that Napoleon had forgotten the injuries done to Louis Bonaparte. We may add that the Empress Eugénie forgave the persons who had been inimical to Mademoiselle de Montijo. She bore no grudge against those who had opposed her marriage, although there was a spice of malice in her occasional allusions to that fact. M. Mesnard, for example, former vice-president of the Senate and at one time counsellor to the Court of Cassation, had not approved of this marriage. After reading the message in which the Emperor announced and gave reasons for it, he had said: "A fine discourse, but I like the sauce better than the fish." Not long afterwards M. Mesnard was dining at the Tuileries and sat very near the Empress. Just as he was accepting some turbot the sovereign addressed him: "Ah! senator, I thought you merely liked the sauce and not the fish." Surprised for a moment, M. Mesnard bowed and said that he had changed his mind.

The three prosperous and peaceful years we are about to describe were the happiest period of Eugénie's life. Anxieties about her future, the anguish of the Crimean War, the dread of remaining childless, had disturbed the beginning of her reign. But as a mother she touched the summit of her fortune as well as of her beauty. The Countess Stéphanie de Tascher de la Pagerie describes her at this epoch: "I have seen women as pretty as the Empress, but I have never known a finer or more distinguished beauty. It is perfection in the most minute details. And the most remarkable thing about this beauty is that it is peculiar to herself; she is no more like a Spanish woman than a French or English one. There is this about her, — that wherever she appears she takes the precedence by her brilliancy and distinction."

Hence at this time the Empress united the satisfactions of the heart with those of gratified vanity. She saw that France, and one might say the world, took a sympathetic interest in the birth of her son, that child whose advent had been made the occasion of so many amnesties, pardons, and favors.

There was at this time a journal whose editors had several times been sentenced to fines and imprisonment. It was the *Figaro*. Its sale had been forbidden on the streets, and its days appeared to be numbered when its editor-in-chief, M. de Villemessant, had the ingenious idea of addressing to the Prince Imperial the subjoined letter, dated March 20, 1856, the anniversary of the birthday of the King of Rome:—

"Monseigneur, forty-five years ago to-day a Prince was born at the Tuileries. A few days after this event, a solicitor presented himself at the palace with a petition addressed to the King of Rome. The Emperor, your great-uncle, ordered the petition to be handed to his heir in person. Then he said, smiling, to the petitioner: 'What did the King of Rome reply?'—'Nothing, Sire; but as silence gives consent, I am authorized to suppose that the Prince grants my request.'—Napoleon ratified the tacit promise of his son.

"Monseigneur, availing itself of this precedent, the *Figaro* presents its petition to you to-day. The one hundred and one discharges of cannon which saluted your birth permit us to hope; for we know that you came into the world with your hands filled with pardon and indulgence.

"Hence the *Figaro* has thought that, as an intelligent prince, you would say to yourself on entering the world: 'I come to dry many tears. *Figaro* is certainly much less guilty than many whom I have pardoned. Let us restore *Figaro* to life, so that he may learn from us to be indulgent even to vice and ridicule.' Behold our petition, then, Monseigneur, in your hands. Do not say no, and *Figaro* will be saved." *Figaro* was saved. The penalties it had still to undergo were remitted. Its sale on the public streets was once more allowed. The dead journal returned to life.

The public naturally supposed that the birth of the Prince Imperial would be the signal for an era of happiness and prosperity. Parisians are very fond of children. Whenever the little Prince appeared on the promenade, everybody praised his pretty ways and looks. The motherhood of the Empress had given her a greater prestige than the throne itself. Her husband took good care not to disturb her joy by hinting at his ulterior warlike schemes. In talking with her, he scrupulously avoided all that might afflict or disquiet her. If he referred to his Romagna expedition of 1832, he told her that he had never been affiliated to the Carbonari, and that his ideas were such as those which Pius IX. had himself entertained at the beginning of his pontificate. He insisted that the liberals ought not to be identified with the revolutionaries, and that his own policy, inspired by generous and civilizing principles, would always remain a policy of order and progress.

Before launching France into the adventures and perils of another war, Napoleon III. intended to allow her to enjoy for awhile the delights of peace. Hence the programme was to avoid all disagreeable forebodings and secure the confidence so essential to industry and commerce. 1856 was the best year of the Second Empire. Happy year, when the foreign policy was as calm as that of the interior; when the eyes of France, instead of being fixed, as in 1855, on the horrors of a terrible and sanguinary war, rested upon the cradle of an infant; and when the eagle's claws no longer grasped the thunderbolt, but an olive branch. This is the period which may be called the happy days of the Empress Eugénie.

CHAPTER III

COUNT WALEWSKI

IN 1856 the diplomacy of France was as brilliant and as much in vogue as its army and navy. People admired the heroic combatants of Sebastopol, and were grateful to the diplomatists who had arranged an honorable peace. The Ministry of Foreign Affairs, where the sessions of Congress were held, attracted general attention. Situated on the quai d'Orsay, beside the Seine and next to the Corps Législatif, this mansion, proportioned like a palace, whose first stone had been laid by M. Guizot, *Sic vos non vobis*, had replaced that on the boulevard des Capucines, under whose windows had been fired the fusillade of February 23, 1848, which ushered in the revolution of the following day. The new ministry had just been installed. There is nothing remarkable in the offices, which occupy the adjoining house, but the reception rooms and those of the Minister are superb and very well arranged.

The leader of French diplomacy in 1856 was Count Walewski, Polish by origin, but naturalized a Frenchman, who had served both his countries nobly. Alexander Colonna, Count Walewski, belonged to a very old family, related to the Colonnas who gave a Pope and several cardinals to the Church, and to Italy generals and diplomatists. Born May 4, 1810, at the château of Walewice, his mother was the woman, famous for her beauty and her patriotism, who inspired a passion in the First Napoleon, and he was reputed the son of the Emperor. At the time of the abdication, the Countess Walewska repaired to Fontainebleau to testify her devotion to the unfortunate sovereign. And when the Emperor of the French was merely the monarch of Elba, a woman and a child arrived mysteriously to console him. People supposed it to be the Empress and the King of Rome. It was the Countess Walewska and her son.

Still a child when he lost his mother, the young Count Walewski terminated his studies at Geneva and then went to France, where he made his entry into society during the winter of 1829–30. He was one of the handsomest men of his time. His lofty bearing, his head like a Roman medallion, his grand manners, his perfect tone, his origin, made him the fashion at once. Count d'Haussonville, member of the French Academy and father of the present Academician, tells us in his *Souvenirs*, as a singular thing and a sign of the times, that the entry of the young Polish nobleman into legitimist salons was effected under the auspices of all that was purest and most exclusive in the aristocratic society of Paris.

"It was," he says, "the order of the day, so to speak, among the most fastidious ladies of the faubourg Saint-Germain, to give the most cordial welcome to the young man whose features recalled in a striking manner, but with a prepossessing and gentle expression, those of the celebrated cast. Notwithstanding this feminine eagerness to please him, M. Walewski, to his credit be it spoken, remained perfectly modest."

After the Revolution of 1830 the man of fashion did not hesitate to detach himself from his social successes in order to seek more serious ones, and hastened to defend his country. He ardently embraced the cause of Polish independence, took part in the battle of Grochow, and was sent to London along with Count Zamoyski and Marquis Wielopolski to ask the intervention of England. When Poland fell, he returned to France, and thanks to the Orleans princes, who treated him as a friend, he obtained, August 10, 1833, the rank of captain in the foreign legion. Naturalized a Frenchman December 3 of the same year, he was a brilliant officer in the 2d African chasseurs, and afterwards in the 4th hussars. After performing a confidential mission to Abd-el-Kader, and acting as director of Arabian affairs at Oran, he quitted the military service in 1838 and returned to Paris, where, not contented with his social successes, he aspired to those of a publicist and dramatic author. Among other pamphlets, he published one entitled, *Un mot sur la ques-*

tion d'Afrique, and another called *l'Alliance anglaise*. Founder and editor of the *Messager*, he supported the policy of M. Thiers, whose friend he remained forever afterwards. At the same time he occupied himself with the stage. It is claimed that he collaborated with Alexandre Dumas *père* in the production of one of his best plays, *Mademoiselle de Belle-Isle*. He brought out at the Théâtre Français, January 8, 1840, a comedy in five acts, of which he was the sole author, the *Ecole du monde*, or the *Coquette sans le savoir*. Although admirably played by Menjaud, Mirecourt, Geffroy, and Madame Plessy, the piece was a failure.

Renouncing forever the hope of success as a dramatist, Count Walewski became a diplomatist and entered the path which led him to the highest positions. President of the Council of Ministers from March 1, 1840, his protector, M. Thiers, bought the *Messager* newspaper for him and sent him to Egypt on an important mission to Mehemet Ali.

At that time Count Walewski was sincerely devoted to the July monarchy, and though everybody believed him to be the son of the Emperor, nobody considered him an imperialist. Under the ministry of M. Guizot, he continued the career he had begun under that of M. Thiers, and he was directing the French legation of Buenos Ayres when the Revolution of 1848 broke out.

After the election of December 10, he rallied to the support of the Prince-President, who appointed him minister of France to Florence in 1849 and to Naples in 1852. The Grand Duke of Tuscany and the King of the Two Sicilies received him in the most flattering manner. Becoming the friend of both sovereigns, he always desired the maintenance of their dynasties, and if Napoleon III. had heeded his advice, there would have been no Italian unity. He married a pretty and very attractive Florentine, Mademoiselle Ricci, niece of Prince Joseph Poniatowski, minister of Tuscany to Paris, and subsequently a French senator. She managed her salon admirably. Made ambassador to London in 1854, Count Walewski and the charming ambassadress were the greatest success. This was the finest moment of the English alliance. When the Countess Walewska left London, the ladies of the aristocracy clubbed together to present her with a bracelet as a keepsake.

The Emperor was pleased with Count Walewski for the reserve and tact which he displayed under every circumstance. No one ever heard him allude to his mother's relations with the First Napoleon. Some one having said to him one day: "You who are the son of a great man," he replied: "I did not know that my father was tall." They say that Morny wanted to pose as the brother of Napoleon III. Never did Count Walewski take the attitude of a cousin-german to the Emperor.

M. Drouyn de Lhuys, having handed in his resignation on May 7, 1855, was succeeded as Minister of Foreign Affairs by the ambassador of France at London, Count Walewski. An experienced and conscientious diplomatist, laborious and devoted to his duties; solid rather than brilliant, and cloaking a natural timidity and an unalterable kindliness under a somewhat haughty bearing; calm, well balanced, full of tact and good sense; an honest man in every sense of the word, and possessing a noble character and generous sentiments, Count Walewski was a good minister. " In power and out of power," M. Pinard has said, "he never sought for money nor the affairs which lead to it. He thought the rôle of a financier incompatible with that of a statesman. He admired and wished to imitate those Corsicans who twice saw a Napoleon on the throne without increasing their patrimony under either Cæsar. He spent freely the large emoluments pertaining to the posts he occupied and was able to die poor. That is one of his titles to the esteem of all men."

I shall never forget that I owe my own entry to the diplomatic career to the kindness of Count Walewski. It was he who appointed me an attaché of the political department of the Ministry of Foreign Affairs, September 1, 1855. I recollect the prestige then surrounding the ministers of Napoleon III., and the impression they produced on their subordinates. It was my business at that time to write out the minutes of the committee on disputed claims, then under the presidency of Count Portalis. As the members of the committee had just completed the preparation of an arbitrament which the Emperor was to render, I was, to my great surprise, ushered into the minister's private office as soon as they had left it. I recall the emotions I experienced in crossing for the first time the threshold of this sanctuary of diplomacy; I remember what pleasure, what gratitude, were aroused in me by an encouraging word which the minister honored me by speaking.

The Ministry of Foreign Affairs was at that time as eminent from the social point of view as from that of politics. Nothing could be more brilliant than the balls and dinners given there. The Countess Walewski received every Wednesday evening, and the plenipotentiaries of the Congress and the élite of Parisian society were invariably present. No salon was more elegant than hers, and there was no Ministry of Foreign Affairs in all Europe as splendid and as much frequented as that of France.

This was the apogee of Count Walewski's career. He presided at the Congress of Paris with much authority and dignity. His imperturbable calm, his exquisite politeness, his perfect courtesy, his thorough acquaintance with the technical details and questions of every kind, were remarked by his colleagues. They appreciated his spirit of conciliation, his impartiality, his faculty of stating the points in litigation with precision, and of summing up the debates intelligibly. The foreign policy of France, which later on was frequently subjected to well-founded criticism, was at this time, one might almost say, uncensured by either the public or the press. With the exception of a few observers more prudent and perspicacious than the rest, people approved the Crimean War and considered its results not disproportionate with the sacrifices it had entailed. The work of the army and of French diplomacy was favorably considered not merely by imperialists but even by the older parties. This is the epoch when M. Thiers wrote in the preface to the twelfth volume of his *History of the Consulate and the Empire:* " The greatest compensation for being unimportant in one's country is to see that country all that it should be in the world."

CHAPTER IV

THE TREATY OF PARIS

WHEN the Congress of Paris resumed its sessions, interrupted for four days, on March 18, 1856, two additional members were present: the Prussian plenipotentiaries. Prussia had been neither a belligerent nor an ally of either Russia or the Western powers, and it seemed as if she ought not to figure in the Congress. Such was the opinion of England. Prince Albert had written to the King of the Belgians: "Great powers can take no hand in the great game of politics unless they put their money on the table." But in the end Napoleon III. contrived to make the opposite opinion prevail. Under pretext that the court of Berlin had concurred in 1841 with the stipulations concerning the closing of the Dardanelles, he obtained not merely that Prussia should be represented in the agreement relating to the straits, but that she should sign the general treaty of peace. Her two plenipotentiaries, Baron Manteuffel, Prime Minister of Frederick William IV., and Count Hatzfeldt, minister of Prussia at Paris, although introduced at the eleventh hour to the Congress, were treated on the same footing as the representatives of the other powers.

At noon on Sunday, March 30, the plenipotentiaries assembled in uniform at the Ministry of Foreign Affairs to sign the treaty. Peace was signed at one o'clock. Directly after the session they repaired to the Tuileries, where they were received by the Emperor. At two o'clock a salvo of one hundred and one guns from the Invalides announced to the people of Paris that peace was concluded. In the evening there was a dinner of sixty covers at the Ministry of Foreign Affairs to celebrate the great event. Count Walewski offered a toast to the duration of peace. "It will be durable because it is honorable to *all*."

On Tuesday, April 1, Napoleon III. held a review on the Champ de Mars in honor of the peace. Preceded by his equerries, aides-de-camp, orderlies, and followed by a numerous staff, among whom were seen Prince Napoleon, Prince de Reuss, General Count Orloff, and the Russian officers attached to his mission, Marquis Villamarina, the Sardinian minister, Marshal Narvaëz, Baron Seebach, minister of Saxony, Marshal Vaillant, General Prim, Marshal Canrobert, he traversed the garden of the Tuileries, the Place de la Concorde, and followed the Cours la Reine and the quays. When he came out on the Pont d'Iéna, the troops paid him military honors and joined their acclamations to those of the crowds that covered the rising grounds of the Champ de Mars.

The Countess de Damrémont wrote to M. Thouvenel, then minister at Constantinople: "I wish you could have seen Paris last Tuesday to get an idea of the public satisfaction. In the first place, the morning review was magnificent. An immense multitude of spectators had assembled at the Champ de Mars, and the weather was in unison with the prevailing sentiments. Everybody seemed happy, the head of the State especially, since by a firm and stable policy, full of moderation, he has raised the country to the rank from which it descended nearly half a century ago.

"The Emperor beheld himself followed by representatives of the greatest powers of the world, and at the summit of the most incontestable glory. These representatives were there, ten paces behind him, in brilliant uniforms, and witnessing by their presence to the sympathies which the wisdom and loyalty of his policy have inspired even in those who not long since were still his enemies. It seems to me that no finer or more amazing procession was ever known than that which accompanied him that day. Among others was seen — and everybody wanted to see him there — Count Orloff, the very man who, forty-two years ago, March 30, 1814, after the battle fought under the walls of Paris by the allies, had been the third to enter our capital, following Counts Nesselrode and Paar."

During the entire day of the review the people kept holiday. Their manifestations of joy were prolonged through the evening. The illuminations were general. As if to demonstrate their spontaneity, the public buildings remained dark, in striking contrast to the brilliancy of private houses. In the business quarters the crowd was so great that it was not easy to penetrate it. The sky glittered with stars. Every countenance shone with joy.

It was said that the treaty had been signed with the quill of an eagle, procured at the Jardin des Plantes by M. Feuillet de Conches, introducer of the ambassadors. Nemo — the pseudonym by which M. de Pène signed his articles in the *Nord* newspaper — wrote on April 6: "But this was a radiant week! A cloudless sky, joy in every heart, a pacific salvo of one hundred and one cannon which found an echo in the hearts of all mothers, windows draped and illuminated, satisfaction for all honest men, who, for once, were included in a single party! To write the chronicle of this happy week an iron pen would be too bellicose, a goosequill too stupid. As for an eagle pen, it needs a congress to procure such a thing and a M. Feuillet de Conches to dare to pluck it from the bird of Jove. We cannot sufficiently admire the courage displayed by M. Feuillet de Conches in his expedition against the dangerous penholder from which it was a matter of detaching a fraction of his plumage. No adequate details have been given of this bold larceny accomplished in honor of the Congress of Paris and its labors of pacification."

Ratifications of the treaty having been exchanged, it appeared with its annexes in the *Moniteur* of April 29, and the protocols were published April 30 and May 1. In drawing up these diplomatic instruments scrupulous care had been taken to avoid anything which might wound Russian self-esteem. M. de Bourqueney said to Herr von Beust: "One can read the treaty of March 30 without discovering which is the victor and which the vanquished." Not a word was said of the question of the Holy Places which had been the beginning of the quarrel between the cabinets of Paris and Saint Petersburg. The claim of the Emperor Nicholas to take the orthodox subjects of the Sultan under his protection was likewise passed over in silence. The principal stipulations of the treaty applied to all the powers, and their general character was not such as to offend the feelings of Russia.

The powers collectively received an official acknowledgment of the firman by which the Sultan improved the condition of his subjects without distinction of race or religion (Article 9).

The Black Sea was made neutral. Open to the merchant marine of all nations, its waters and its ports were interdicted to all ships of war, whether of the riverside or any other powers (Article 11).

Article 22 stipulated that no exclusive protection should be exercised over the Danubian Principalities by any one of the guaranteeing powers. By Article 23 the Sublime Porte pledged itself to ensure an independent and international administration to the Principalities. A committee was to be formed whose business it would be to learn their actual condition and propose the bases for their future organization.

Article 28 stipulated that the principality of Servia should preserve its independent and national administration, as well as full liberty of worship, legislation, commerce, and navigation.

Article 15 proclaimed the free navigation of the Danube. A permanent committee was to undertake the removal of existing impediments to this, and to enact regulations for policing the river.

The only clause in the treaty which offended Russia was that which took away from her a portion of Bessarabia and delivered it to the Moldavian principality. The territory ceded was insignificant, but it annoyed Russia to include no part of the Danube within her limits. It was Austria that insisted on the adoption of this clause, and the Russians were correspondingly bitter against the cabinet of Vienna. Count Orloff said to Cavour: " The Austrian plenipotentiary does not know what tears and blood this rectification of the frontier will cost his country."

The Russians might well have been vexed with Piedmont, which, although not in any way menaced by them, had gone to the Crimea to fight against their country and take part in a quarrel which concerned in no wise the house of Savoy. But their resentment against Victor Emmanuel was much less keen than their wrath against the Emperor Francis Joseph. Alexander II. was convinced that if Austria had not issued her ultimatum Russia would have been victorious in the Crimean War. To the Czar this conduct on the part of Austria, which Russia had saved at the time of the war with Hungary, was a monstrous ingratitude. Napoleon III. viewed with satisfaction the bitterness of Russian enmity towards Austria, intended to make use of it, and in 1856 was already making ready for what he was to accomplish in 1859. But, true to his instincts as a conspirator, he was careful not to alarm those whose interests were concerned and felt his way at first with much prudence. His Minister of Foreign Affairs, Count Walewski, was an essentially conservative diplomatist, and extremely opposed to a war in Italy. Yet it was he whom the Emperor charged to lay before the Congress what has since been known as the *Italian question.*

After signing the treaties the plenipotentiaries held several additional sessions. During that of April 8, Count Walewski remarked that it would be well if, before separating, the plenipotentiaries should exchange ideas on various subjects demanding a solution and sure to crop up later if not considered now. He added that Lord Clarendon would undoubtedly unite with him in declaring that while France and England awaited with impatience the moment when the present business could be concluded, yet to terminate it without considering important modifications in the existing condition of things in Greece would entail serious inconveniences.

The first plenipotentiary of France next reminded the Congress that the Pontifical States were also in an abnormal condition, and that the necessity of not delivering the country over to anarchy had decided both France and Austria to comply with the request of the Holy See, the former by occupying Rome with troops and the latter by sending its soldiers to the legations. On one hand, declared Count Walewski, the title of *eldest son of the Church*, on which the sovereign of France prided himself, made it the Emperor's duty to give aid and support to the Sovereign Pontiff. On the other hand, said he, it was impossible to deny the anomalous condition of a power whose maintenance depended upon foreign armies; adding that France earnestly longed for the moment when she could withdraw her troops without endangering the interior tranquillity of the country and the authority of the pontifical government.

Not content with formulating the *Roman question* in this manner, Count Walewski inquired whether it were not desirable that certain governments of the Italian peninsula, rallying to their support by well-devised acts of clemency minds that were misled but not perverted, should put an end to a system which instead of reaching the foes of order resulted merely in weakening governments and increasing the number of demagogues.

Lord Clarendon not merely abounded in the same sense but he put into the shape of a formal indictment what Count Walewski had expressed in very measured terms. The first Austrian plenipotentiary declared that it was impossible to discuss the internal condition of independent States not represented at the Congress. Count Orloff excused himself by alleging the absence of instructions. Count Cavour, however, developed and emphasized the grievances mentioned by Count Walewski and Lord Clarendon. The Italian question was formulated.

Protocol XXII. — that of the session of April 8, 1856 — concluded as follows: "The exchange of ideas which has taken place is not without utility. The first plenipotentiary of France establishes that there does in fact result from it: —

"1. That no one has disputed the necessity of maturely considering the necessity of ameliorating the situation of Greece, and that the three protecting courts have recognized the importance of a mutual understanding on this subject;

"2. That the Austrian plenipotentiaries join in the desire expressed by the plenipotentiaries of France to see the Pontifical States evacuated by the French and Austrian troops as soon as it can be done without inconvenience to the tranquillity of the country or the consolidation of the authority of the Holy See;

"3. That a majority of the plenipotentiaries have not disputed the efficacity of measures of clemency opportunely taken by the governments of the Italian peninsula and especially by that of the Two Sicilies;

"4. That none of the plenipotentiaries, even those who have felt bound to reserve the principle of the freedom of the press, have hesitated to blame emphatically the excesses to which the Belgian journals have gone with impunity, or to recognize the necessity of remedying the inconveniences resulting from the unbridled license so greatly abused in Belgium."

The members of the Congress completed their work by a declaration of principles concerning maritime law. It related to the four points subjoined: —

"1. Privateering is abolished;

"2. Neutral flags protect an enemy's merchandise with the exception of contraband of war;

"3. Neutral merchandise, contraband of war excepted, is not liable to seizure under an enemy's flag;

"4. Blockades to be obligatory must be effective."

Thus the labors of the Congress terminated by the proclamation of reforms in harmony with the progress of general civilization.

Public opinion was satisfied. Certain minds more perspicacious than the others alone foreboded the war of which Protocol XXII. contained the germ. With the exception of mothers who bewailed the loss of their sons, nobody thought of the torrents of blood that had been shed in the gigantic struggle just concluded. According to the statistics mentioned by M. de La Gorce (*Histoire du Second Empire*), the losses of France amounted to ninety-five thousand men, twenty thousand of whom were shot, and seventy-five thousand stricken down by illness. Of the English twenty thousand had succumbed, but only four thousand in battles or assaults. The Sardinians had lost only twenty-eight men killed at the battle of Traktir, but to these must be added more than two thousand who died in the hospitals, mostly from cholera. The losses of the Turks were reckoned at about thirty thousand men, nearly all killed in the battles of the Danube or struck down by epidemics in the bivouacs of the Crimea. As to the Russians, their losses were estimated at one hundred and ten thousand killed or dead, not counting the innumerable victims who had succumbed on the long Russian roads before reaching the Crimea, nor those who died of typhus during the second winter. During that winter old military men were worn out by fatigue and younger ones were not yet inured to the rigors of a terrible climate; more than forty-seven thousand men entered the hospitals of the Crimea, and nearly nine thousand died there.

The evacuation of that scene of combats and suffering began in April. It was over by the end of June. Nothing was left of those earthworks whose possession had been disputed with such bitterness. The treaty of Paris did not deprive Russia in the Crimea of an inch of her territory nor a stone of her fortresses. Kamiesch and the entire Chersonese plateau was given back to her July 4. Marshal Pélissier was the last to leave this region, from which he took his title of Duke of Malakoff as a souvenir.

What remains at present of the treaty of Paris? In 1871 Russia resumed her former place in the Black Sea. The treaty of Berlin restored to her that portion of Bessarabia the loss of which she had felt so keenly. The traveller who now visits Sebastopol and its environs finds there but one trace of the Crimean War: the cemetery.

In 1856 the victors did not ask whether the results of the struggle in which they had taken so glorious a part could be lasting. They returned home with a sentiment of legitimate pride, and knew that grateful France did them full justice. "Perhaps you will not believe me," wrote Captain Charles Bocher, "but I do assure you that notwithstanding the pleasure it will give me to see Paris once more, I shall regret leaving this famous plateau of the Chersonese where I have experienced many griefs and undergone many sufferings, but where I have also had the greatest joys in the satisfaction that arises from duties fulfilled and the spectacle of the great deeds I have witnessed." General Fay thus ends his *Souvenirs:* "Of course, we suffered; but we knew very well that these sufferings were not in vain, for we had cicatrized in part the wounds inflicted on our fathers, and replaced France in the rank which after such great reverses and such great victories had been taken from her for a day."

At present the Crimean War is the object of many criticisms. In 1856 the only sentiment which it inspired in Frenchmen was admiration.

CHAPTER V

THE SPRING OF 1856

ONE should have lived in Paris in 1856 to form an adequate idea of the brilliancy of the great capital, newly embellished and transfigured, in the springtime of that radiant year. In France nothing dries tears and blood so quickly as the sunshine of victory. People compassionate the sufferings and calamities of war only when they have not resulted in success. Nobody dreamed of blaming either Napoleon III. or Queen Victoria for the hecatombs of slaughtered men which had reddened the Chersonese plateau. Her national pride satisfied, although she had obtained neither a cession of territory nor any personal advantage, France told herself that she was the great nation, and that thought sufficed her. The journals persuaded the country that the world admired her, that the French soldier was the soldier of God, *gesta Dei per Francos*, and that the Crimean War had not merely saved European equilibrium but the cause of universal civilization. Military men forgot their sufferings in looking at the decorations and promotions they had so gloriously obtained. Civilians were proud of the army. The inhabitants

of Paris are never so happy as when their vanity is
gratified. Success is what they prefer before all
things. The great city is like a pretty woman.
What she wants is to be admired.

In the spring of 1856, Paris, full of admiration,
excitement, and gaiety, presented a fairy-like aspect.
More brilliant equipages, richer toilettes, more elegant
houses at the theatres had never been seen.
Pleasure was the order of the day. Official society
and that of the faubourg Saint-Germain vied with
each other in luxury and entertainments. Parisian
newspapers at this period paid very little heed to
anything but what are nowadays called worldly
vanities, *mondanités*. The Paris letters published
at Brussels by *Le Nord* and the *Independance Belge*
furnish the details of the social whirl.

The most brilliant of the legitimist fêtes was the
masked ball given April 2 by the Duchess Pozzo di
Borgo in her house on the rue de l'Université. It
was followed on the succeeding evening by a ball
at the house of the Prussian legation, on the rue
de Lille, occupied by Prince Eugene under the First
Empire, and at present by the German embassy.
Count Hatzfeldt and his wife, the daughter of Marshal
de Castellane, gave it in honor of the plenipotentiaries
of the Congress. The embassies and
legations were then a neutral ground where the
heads of the different parties met each other. At
the Prussian ball M. Guizot ran across Count
Walewski, Count de Montalembert, M. Rouher,

M. Dumont, and M. Achille Fould. As usual, the members of the Congress engrossed most of the attention. But the Princes de Reuss were also pointed out, and Marshal Narvaëz, M. Olozaga, Lady Clarendon, the Countess de Montijo, accompanied by a young and beautiful Spanish girl, Mademoiselle de la Paniega, who had just arrived in France, and who married the Marshal Duke of Malakoff two years later.

"The ball of the Prussian legation," wrote Nemo (Henry de Pène) in the *Nord*, "has brought to light a difficulty singularly embarrassing to the great personages who are here in an official capacity. They are confronted by a Parisian society divided into two very distinct camps: those who go to the Tuileries and those who do not. Personal sympathies, family affinities, mutual esteem, unite the representatives of powers friendly to France to a goodly number of recalcitrant Parisians. On the other hand, it is undeniable that their natural and indispensable place is at the court to which they are accredited."

The Turkish ambassador, Mehemet Djemil Bey, gave a ball to more than twelve hundred guests on April 10. And as the Sultan had attended a ball given by the French ambassador, the Emperor returned the courtesy by attending that of the Ottoman embassy. Two days afterward the Grand-Vizier, Ali Pasha, wrote from Paris to M. Thouvenel: "The Emperor deigned to honor our fête of the 10th by his presence. I cannot tell you how happy this great imperial favor has made me. It is an additional title to the hatred of the envious."

April 12 Napoleon gave a banquet at the Tuileries to the members of the Congress. The cardinals, marshals, presidents of the great bodies of State and grand officers of the crown were present with the foreign ministers. At the right of the Emperor, who sat at a table shaped like a horseshoe, was Lord Clarendon, and on his left Count de Buol. Prince Napoleon was opposite the sovereign, with Count Orloff on his right and Ali Pasha on his left. Towards the end of the dinner, Napoleon III. rose to his feet and said: "I propose a toast to the union so happily restored between the sovereigns. May it be lasting, and it will be so if it rests on right, justice, and the real and legitimate interests of peoples."

The relations between those who yesterday were enemies had become most cordial. General Duke de Mortemart, then commanding the division of Bourges, wrote to Marshal de Castellane: "This is a fine peace, and I can assure you of one thing, namely, that my old camp companion in the war of the Balkans in 1828, Count Orloff, is enthusiastic about our Emperor. He declares that he is the arbiter of what is just and true throughout the world."

Napoleon entertained especially friendly relations with Prussia and all Germany. In May the King of Würtemberg was his guest. Reaching Paris on the 3d, this monarch occupied the pavilion of Marsan at the Tuileries. The 5th he dined at the Palais-Royal with his brother-in-law, King Jerome. Prince Napoleon, the Princess Mathilde, Baron Waechter, minister of Würtemberg in France, and Baroness Waechter, Baron Fatenheim, grand equerry of the Würtemberg sovereign, were among the guests. On the 13th the King left Paris to return to his dominions, enchanted with the reception given him by the Emperor. The former quarrels of Germany and France seemed to be forgotten forever.

May 13, the Emperor and the Empress installed themselves at the château of Saint-Cloud with their son, who now left Paris for the first time. Just a month earlier, the Duke of Alba had brought the *Golden Fleece* from Queen Isabella to the little prince who, on the 28th April, the day when the treaty of peace was published by the *Moniteur*, had been inscribed as child of the regiment on the roll of the 1st regiment of grenadiers of the imperial guard. His baptism, which was to be celebrated with extraordinary pomp at Notre Dame de Paris, was fixed for the 14th of June.

Nor was it the court alone which was perpetually keeping holiday. The city seemed equally delighted. As people made a good deal of money, so they spent it with great readiness. All the industries of Paris, especially those of luxury, realized unexpected gains. The optimism of the financial world was imperturbable. Any one who had pointed out the least cloud on the horizon would have been treated as an alarmist and a coward. The transformation of Paris, effected as it were by the wand of a magician, coincided in the happiest manner with the conclusion of peace. The predictions of the great prefect, Baron Haussmann, were fulfilled. He had asserted that extraordinary disbursements are not injurious to the budget, but, if intelligently made, enrich instead of impoverishing, and bring about a general increase of the revenue. He had quoted the remark of Louis XIV. to Mansard: "Build, keep on building; we will make the advances and foreigners will repay them." Foreigners! they had come in crowds to admire the marvels of the new Paris, now the cosmopolitan city by excellence. The Parisian, critical at first of the work of transformation, began to applaud the moment it was completed. He halted in front of the squares which distributed light, air, and verdure so widely and in so doing restored or preserved the public health. He went with pleasure through the new streets. He looked at the Louvre, still surrounded by scaffoldings, but soon to display its splendid and majestic ensemble.

"When the weather was fine," says M. de La Gorce in his *History of the Second Empire*, "the Parisian was very willing to prolong his outing; he prolonged it by the Carrousel, finally purged from the shameful diversions which had obstructed it so long; those who were most courageous went further still, and found their way through the long avenues to the Champs-Elysées and even to the Bois de Boulogne, of which an art which knew how to avail itself of a graceful disorder had completed the embellishment, and which imitated the splendors of Hyde Park while surrounding them with a still more beautiful frame.

"As he went he admired the police service, reorganized and enlarged, the better organized street commissions, the macadamized roads substituted for the old pavements, the improved and developed water service, the public travel by means of the omnibuses beginning to traverse every quarter. Then when evening suggested his return, he wondered at the interminable lines of gas jets on either side of the regular streets, and, in the dazzling splendor of all those new things which it seems nowadays as if we had always enjoyed, the wisest, the most far-sighted, the least enthusiastic was allured into forgetfulness of present cares and admiration of this Paris of Napoleon III., so animated and so bright, and into the hope that, in spite of already visible signs to the contrary, the Second Empire would gain a renown for wisdom equal to the seductive prestige due to its brilliancy."

The Crimea, soon to be evacuated by the allied troops, sent none but joyous echoes to France. In a despatch from Sebastopol addressed to the Minister of War, Marshal Pélissier said: "For my part, Monsieur le Maréchal, I am delighted to affirm that no star ever shone so brilliantly as that of the Emperor. This peace signed above the cradle of a child is a most fortunate omen. If the Emperor and the Empress will kindly accept them I beg you to offer the respectful congratulations of the army and my own."

The Russians and the French had become real friends, true brethren in arms. One might have thought they had been fighting on the same side during the war instead of against each other. April 13, General Luders, the Russian commander-in-chief, went to meet the commanders-in-chief of the allied troops on the bridge of Traktir, and led them to the heights whence they witnessed a review of ten thousand men on the Makenzie plateau. After the review he offered them a banquet.

As a response to this courtesy Marshal Pélissier and General Codrington, the new commander-in-chief of the English army, invited General Luders to a brilliant review. This took place April 17, 1856, on a particularly fine day. The French army, with the redoubt of the Balaclava Pass on its right, its centre on the height of the monastery of St. George, and its left towards Karatch, presented a line of battle more than twelve thousand yards in length. There were in all one hundred battalions of infantry in massed battalions, thirty squadrons of artillery, and one hundred and ninety-eight cannon, in all fifty-five thousand French soldiers. "The Emperor," wrote Marshal Pélissier, "would have been delighted, as I was myself, at the fine appearance and martial bearing of our soldiers, to whom I had made known that very day the rewards of which His Majesty kindly authorized the bestowal in his name."

Now listen to an eye-witness, General Fay: "Marshal Pélissier," says he in his remarkable and interesting *Souvenirs of the Crimean War*, "did the honors to General Luders of those magnificent troops which he had so bravely fought, and who, notwithstanding their worn and patched uniforms, were as presentable as on a parade day in garrison. A considerable group of officers of all arms who were galloping in the rear of the commanders-in-chief looked extremely picturesque. The French flags, blackened by powder and torn by Russian projectiles, one after another bowed to the general, once our enemy, to-day our guest, saluting him with respect and applauding those who had rescued from the fight nothing but the flagstaff and some tatters. After the defile, the English army, amounting to some thirty thousand men, admirably disciplined, were in turn presented by General Codrington to the Russian commander-in-chief."

CHAPTER VI

THE INUNDATIONS

AS if to furnish a pendant to the luminous spring tableau of 1856, disastrous news reached Paris on the last day of May. The Rhone had overflowed both its banks, and at Lyons the quarters which divided it from the Saône were under water, as the Brotteaux, the Guillotière, and all the surrounding country were likewise on the opposite shore. It was learned the next day that several quarters of the city were in danger of total ruin; that the valley of Grésivaudan beyond Grenoble had disappeared from view; that the plain of Vaucluse was partly submerged; that at Aix the floods were beating against the faubourg of Trinquetaille, while beyond the Camargue they had swelled into the likeness of an immense lake. On hearing this, the Emperor left Saint-Cloud at once to direct in person the assistance given to the sufferers from the inundations. He was accompanied by his aide-de-camp, General Niel, General Fleury his first equerry, M. Rouher, Minister of Public Works, M. Franqueville, Director of Roads and Bridges, Captain de Puységur, orderly officer, and four troopers belonging to the hundred-guards.

June 1. Napoleon leaves Saint-Cloud and sleeps at Dijon.

June 2. He and his suite, in uniform, reach Lyons at half-past ten in the morning, and are received at the railway station by Marshal de Castellane and Senator Vaisse, in charge of the department. He breakfasts at the Hôtel de l'Europe. He mounts his horse at half-past eleven. Two gendarmes, followed by eight dragoons under the orders of a quartermaster, with an aide-de-camp of Marshal de Castellane at their head, precede the sovereign. He crosses the rue Impériale, the Morand bridge, the Charpennes, the Brotteaux, and the Guillotière. Surrounded by some sixty thousand workmen, who, with their wives and children, had been the victims of this scourge, himself pale with emotion, the Emperor distributes uncounted money from two saddlebags in a kindly manner which touches the hearts of all. Lavishing words of consolation and encouragement also, he visits the breaches made in the two dikes of the Rhone, and fords the roads where they are under water. Everywhere he is greeted with applause. As he passes the air resounds with shouts of "Long live the Emperor! Long live the Empress! Long live the Prince Imperial! Long live the Father of his people." According to Marshal de Castellane it was an ovation without a parallel.

At half-past three Napoleon III. repairs to the camp of Sathonay, with which he seems satisfied. He dines at the Hôtel de l'Europe. Every time he goes to the window before dinner he is greeted by thunders of applause.

June 3. The Emperor leaves Lyons for Valence and Avignon. He stops on the way at the towns which have suffered most. Valence is inundated. He arrives at the mayor's office on the back of a porter. As the railway between Orange and Avignon is cut off by the floods, he gets into a wretched boat, half staved in, and thus crosses a veritable lake which covers the plain as far as eye can see. He is on a level with the roofs of farmhouses scattered along the riverbanks, and the oars occasionally strike the tops of fruit trees hidden from view by the waters. Toward three o'clock he is received at the gates of Avignon by the flotilla of the city authorities coming to meet him. He enters the city on a boat so small that there is room for no one else except the mayor and the boatman.

General Fleury, an eye-witness, shall describe the scene : " The sights along the road had been painful enough already, but when we reached Avignon and saw the quarters where the houses were under water as high as the first story, and still others where nothing was visible but a multitude of roofs, they became still more distressing. Women with children in their arms were crying. Men, inert and powerless to struggle against flood and ruin, looked like images of woe. The Emperor, greatly affected, stood up in his boat and gave money by handfuls to these unfortunates, who blessed the prince who came at the risk of his life to share their dangers and their affliction."

At six in the evening, after visiting Tarascon, the Emperor leaves for Arles by the railway. On reaching the city he goes to the Arènes tower in order to get a bird's-eye view of the extent of the disaster. He sleeps at Arles.

June 4. He leaves Arles to return to Lyons by way of Avignon, Mortemart, and Valence. Everywhere he is received with popular acclamations. Everywhere he is affected by the sight of towns, villages, and country places in distress, harvests destroyed, houses cracked, submerged, thrown down. And everywhere he distributes abundant largesses, and stimulates the zeal of officials, the courage of soldiers, and the devotion of all the citizens by his example. On reaching Lyons, towards the close of the day, he reviews the troops under the command of Marshal de Castellane. They greet him with an enthusiasm shared by the entire population, who shout, "Long live the benefactor of the people!" At eight o'clock he leaves Lyons for Paris.

June 5. Arriving at Paris at seven in the morning he goes at once to Saint-Cloud. An address from the city of Lyons is waiting for him there. It is worded as follows: " Sire, it was in your heart that you found the happy inspiration to visit the scene of our sufferings. Not long ago you told the Lyonese to love you. Now you come to constrain them to do so. You have gained the coldest hearts; one cannot walk a step in our streets without hearing blessings on your name, without being moved by the touching expressions inspired by gratitude in the unfortunate and by admiration in all. These prayers will be granted, Sire; Heaven will continue to inspire you with great and generous thoughts, and will reward you in the imperial child whom it has given to France."

That very day, on entering Saint-Cloud, the Emperor learns that the same scourge which had afflicted the dwellers by the Rhone had likewise stricken those beside the Loire; that the river had overflowed at Orleans and Amboise, and that at Tours immense disasters had followed the simultaneous rise of the Loire and the Cher. Without hesitating for an instant, he sets off the next day to do for those regions what he had just done for those of the south of France.

June 6. The Emperor leaves Saint-Cloud in the morning to carry assistance and consolation to the inundated people of the Loire. Accompanied by M. Rouher, General Niel and General Fleury, he visits Orleans, Blois, and Tours. The streets of the latter city were so filled with water that they resembled the lagunes of Venice. The sovereign's presence produced a profound impression and his unexpected arrival in each city inspired equal gratitude and surprise.

Evoking the memory of the excursions when he had the honor of accompanying his master, General

Fleury speaks in his Memoirs of the fidelity with which Napoleon III. carried assistance to his subjects. "I always recur with emotion," he says, "to the circumstances of those bold and generous extremities to which the Emperor would resort when it was a question of exposing his life and distributing his benefactions. It was not the search for an idle popularity which moved him. What prince was more popular than he at that period? No; it was the love of goodness, it was the impulse of his heart which guided him."

June 7. In the evening Napoleon III. returned to the château of Saint-Cloud. He embraced most affectionately the child who was to be baptized at Notre Dame seven days later.

CHAPTER VII

THE BAPTISM OF THE PRINCE IMPERIAL

Saturday, June 14, 1856. The Parisians began their holiday at dawn. Their numbers increased by more than three hundred thousand visitors from the provinces and foreign parts, they thronged the squares and streets through which the imperial procession was to pass. Flagstaffs had been set up on the parvis of Notre Dame, from which waved banners with the arms of the Empire. Sanded, and strewn with foliage and flowers, this open space presented a magnificent appearance. A grand porch had been constructed outside of the cathedral.

The baptism of the Prince Imperial was not to be celebrated until six o'clock in the evening. Some hours earlier the four thousand invited guests, among whom I was one, wearing for the first time my diplomatic uniform, entered the resplendent basilica. I recall the impression of giddy surprise, the half-fantastic, half-religious effect which it produced, fully illuminated in broad daylight, its arches painted then in tender blue, sprinkled with golden stars, its hangings of red velvet, its ceiling covered with innumerable bees, from the height of which descended all along the columns the escutcheons of the great cities. The men were all in uniform, and the women in evening dress, with lace veils attached to their headdresses and falling back on their uncovered shoulders. At the back of the choir, illuminated by thousands of candles, a burning focus of light like melting gold shimmered over the platform, where were assembled all the archbishops and bishops of the Empire with their crosiers, mitres, and pontifical vestments.

Half-past four. The Pope's Legate, Cardinal Patrizzi, leaves the Tuileries in a carriage drawn by eight horses. As he is the personal representative of the Sovereign Pontiff, he receives the same honors as are paid the Holy Father. He is met at the entry of the church by the Archbishop of Paris, preceded by his chapter, the musicians the while executing the motet: *Thou art Peter.*

Five o'clock. The Emperor, the Empress, and the Prince Imperial leave the Tuileries to repair to Notre Dame. Cavalry are massed on the Place de la Concorde. The double row formed by the national and the imperial guards extends the whole length of the procession, which follows this route: the garden of the Tuileries, the Place de la Concorde, the rue de Rivoli, the Place de l'Hôtel de Ville, the bridge and rue of Arcola, and the Place de Notre Dame.

Six o'clock. Amid the noise of cannon and shouting the procession reaches the parvis of Notre Dame. This has been sanded so thickly that the eight horses are unable to drag the heavy imperial carriage any further, and it becomes necessary for the footmen to put their shoulders to the wheels. Alighting at the principal portal, the Emperor and the Empress are received by the Archbishop of Paris, who offers them holy water. After kissing the cross, they are conducted to their kneeling-desks under a canopy supported by canons. The ladies of the palace who have been appointed to carry the sacramentals of baptism, approach the table on which they have been laid, and receive them from an assistant master of ceremonies, in the following order: the candle is given to the Countess de Montebello, the chrisom-cloth to the Baroness de Malaret, the salt-cellar to the Marquise de Latour-Marbourg; those pertaining to the functions of the godparents, the basin, the ewer, and the napkin, to the Countess de Labédoyère, the Countess de Rayneval, and Madame de Saulcy, respectively.

I follow the details of the ceremony with extreme attention. In the middle of the transept a platform surrounded by a balustrade had been erected opening toward the nave. On this an altar raised three steps higher than its floor had been placed at the entrance of the sanctuary, opposite which, and at the same elevation, was the throne of Their Majesties with a kneeling-desk; the baptismal font, two steps lower, stood between the throne and the altar. It is said that the baptismal vase, which is made of damaskeened copper, in the Persian style of the twelfth century, was brought back from the Crusades by Saint Louis to serve as a baptismal font for the children of that pious king. The throne of the Cardinal-Legate, two steps higher than the platform, faced both the altar and the throne. In the middle of the sanctuary, behind the Legate's throne, were seats for the archbishops and bishops; a little to the left of the gospel side, on the platform, an armchair for the Archbishop of Paris and stools for the titular members of the metropolitan chapter. To right and left of the sovereigns' throne were ranged the chairs and hassocks intended for the Prince Imperial, carried by the governess of the children of France, and for the Dowager Grand Duchess of Baden, representing the Queen of Sweden, Prince Oscar (now reigning in Sweden as Oscar II.), and the princes and princesses of the Emperor's family. On the epistle side of the altar were chairs for the cardinals.

Napoleon III. and the Empress reach their throne overhung by a dais with hangings of purple velvet lined with ermine, and kneel down at their desk. The Cardinal-Legate goes to the foot of the altar to intone the *Te Deum*, which is executed by the orchestra. Meanwhile the ladies bearing the sacramentals lay them on the credence-tables near the altar. The *Te Deum* ended, the Legate proceeded to the ceremonies of solemn baptism, after which the governess remitted the Prince Imperial to the hands of the Emperor. A master of ceremonies advanced to the middle of the choir and cried three times: Long live the Prince Imperial! Standing with his son in his arms, Napoleon III., with a gesture very expressive of joy and tenderness, showed him to the spectators, the orchestra playing meanwhile the *Vivat* composed by Lesueur for the baptism of the King of Rome, and the shouts of the audience re-echoing beneath the venerable arches. Then the little prince was taken back to the Tuileries in a carriage drawn by eight horses, preceded by a squadron of guides. The Cardinal-Legate intoned the *Te Deum* and the *Domine salvum fac Imperatorem*, and then gave the Papal benediction, which concluded the ceremony. The Archbishop of Paris preceded by the metropolitan chapter reconducted the Emperor and Empress to the door of the church. Their Majesties entered the grand carriage, crossed the Arcola bridge, made their appearance on the Place magnificently decorated by the architect Ballard, and went to the Hôtel de Ville to be present at a banquet offered them by the Municipal Council.

Eight o'clock. The banquet took place in the great dining hall. All the high dignitaries of the State, as well as the bishops and archbishops, were included in the four hundred guests. Their Majesties, surrounded by princes and princesses, sat at a raised table from which all the other tables could be seen. While dinner was going on various pieces of music and cantatas were performed. The salons of the Hôtel de Ville were splendidly illuminated. The ovations of the day were to be renewed at night. For the return drive General Fleury had substituted demi-gala travelling carriages,—green, that is to say, with the underframe gilded,—drawn by six horses instead of eight. "The return having to be made at a trot," he says in his Memoirs, "these were the only sort possible. Still, nothing could be more richly elegant than these berlins with plate-glass windows, lighted from within and displaying the Empress and princesses resplendent with diamonds, to the admiration of the crowd. These berlins, with four lanterns, driven by gigantic coachmen and with four footmen behind, and drawn by immense horses, could vie on equal terms with gilded state carriages, moving at a measured pace, and advancing magisterially as if in a theatrical representation." Shouts resounded all along the passage of the happy father and mother.

CHAPTER VIII

THE BAPTISMAL FESTIVITIES

SUNDAY, June 15, 1856, was devoted to public rejoicings. At six in the morning salvos of artillery from the Invalides announced the beginning of the festivities. Free representations were given at one o'clock at the Opéra, the Théâtre Français, the Odéon, and the Opéra-Comique. Between two and four, on the Esplanade of the Invalides, four open-air theatres played military pieces and pantomimes; three hundred balloons ascended, scattering as they rose the christening sugar-plums. A similar programme was carried out at the barrier of the Throne. One hundred and twenty thousand commemorative medals, bearing on one side the double effigies of the Emperor and the Empress and on the other that of the Son of France, were sent to the pupils of the lyceums, colleges, and orphan asylums, and to the officers, subalterns, and soldiers of the army of Paris. Fifty thousand bags of bonbons were distributed among the children of the communal schools, and Napoleon III. signed numberless pardons for civil and military prisoners under sentence.

The night was given up to fireworks and illuminations in every quarter. The most notable took place in front of the Corps Législatif, the Emperor and the Empress being present under the colonnade of the Ministry of Marine. At a quarter past nine the Empress gave the signal for a magnificent piece of fireworks representing a Gothic baptistry. When it ended by the apparition of flaming cascades the air rang with applause. The crowd was so compact that the sovereigns were obliged to remain at the Ministry until eleven o'clock before they could get back to the Tuileries. The people, however, were in ecstasies all night over the illuminations. Those of Saint-Jacques tower, the Hôtel de Ville and its neighborhood, excited especial admiration. The Avenue Victoria was transformed into a vast garden, with sanded walks, fountains, reservoirs, cascades, and French and foreign flowers. Several large boats, draped and illuminated and carrying military bands in full swing, furrowed the Seine between the Pont Royal and the Pont de la Concorde. The weather harmonized superbly with this night of enchantments.

On Monday, June 16, Their Majesties were present with the princes and princesses at a grand ball at the Hôtel de Ville. The Cardinal-Legate was present for a time before dancing began. After presenting his respects to Their Majesties he withdrew, and the ball opened with a quadrille of honor in which the Emperor danced with the Baroness Haussmann and the Empress with the Prefect.

On Thursday, June 19, the ceremony of presenting the Empress with the golden rose took place in the chapel of the château of Saint-Cloud. During the Mass celebrated by Cardinal Patrizzi, Legate *a latere* of the Pope, the golden rose was laid on the gospel side of the altar. After the Mass, the Legate seated himself in an armchair in front of the altar, opposite Their Majesties. One of the prelates of his suite, Mgr. Monaco Lavalette, read in a loud voice the pontifical brief conferring on the Cardinal the necessary powers for remitting the golden rose to the Empress in place of His Holiness. This concluded, the Empress was invited by the master of ecclesiastical ceremonies to approach the altar, and the rose was presented by Cardinal Patrizzi with the usual formalities. The pontifical gift consisted of a golden rosebush issuing from a massive golden vase resting on a socket of lapis-lazuli with two bas-reliefs, one representing the birth of the Blessed Virgin, and the other her presentation in the Temple, incrusted with the arms of Pio Nono and Napoleon III.

After this ceremony, at which the Prince Imperial was present, the Cardinal-Legate presented the Emperor in the Pope's name with a fine picture in mosaic representing John the Baptist in the Desert, after Guido, and for the Son of France a reliquary adorned with enamels and engraved precious stones, containing a relic of the holy crib.

Cardinal Patrizzi returned to Rome much pleased with the reception he had had in France. M. Sampayo, chargé d'affaires at Rome in the absence of Count de Rayneval, wrote to Count Walewski: "Cardinal Patrizzi has arrived. I hastened to congratulate His Eminence on his happy return. He expressed to me in most feeling terms his gratitude for the welcome with which Their Majesties deigned to honor him. He has requested me to beg Your Excellency kindly to present to Their Majesties his sentiments of respect and attachment. The reception given by the French clergy to His Eminence, the sentiments of devotion to the Holy See expressed by all the bishops, the attitude and the earnestness of the faithful in the churches, have deeply impressed the Cardinal. He speaks to me with admiration of our numerous charitable institutions and the order and beneficence with which they are conducted. From what His Eminence says I cannot doubt that he has given the Holy Father a most favorable account of the religious situation in France. But for that matter such an appreciation could not have been unexpected by His Holiness, whom some persons do not scruple to accuse of a too partial leaning towards the Church of France."

June 28, the members of the committee which had organized the subscription in honor of the Prince Imperial's birth had an audience at the château of Saint-Cloud. M. Le Roy de Saint-Arnaud, brother of the Marshal, and mayor of the twelfth ward, approached the Emperor and the Empress, who was holding her son in her arms. "Sire," said he, "this humble sum of one hundred thousand francs, the rapid result of adding centime to centime, is the artless symbol of these affectionate and loyal populations where the individual is nothing, but where the unanimity of sentiments conceals treasures of love and strength. . . . May the Orphanage of the Prince Imperial, the noble inspiration of the Empress, linked to the souvenir of a thoroughly popular subscription, and enriched and perpetuated by the munificence of the Emperor, pass down the ages with the Empire and the dynasty which beheld its birth!"

Never had the Empress been so happy. The radiant springtime of 1856 had brought her nothing but joys and satisfactions. It is of this epoch that M. de La Gorce, the eminent historian who has not spared the Second Empire some deserved censure, has said: "Contemporaries had at last become convinced, some with pleasure, others with resignation, that the Napoleonic dynasty had assuredly been called to guide French society toward new shores and to develop democracy while restraining it. . . . The power of the Emperor found its completion in the impotence of all that was not he." At this moment the Empress was aware of none but favorable sympathies. The evidences of interest lavished upon her and her son by all classes of society both at home and abroad, charmed and reassured her. The benedictions of the Holy Father, her son's godfather, gave her confidence in the future. With what tranquillity, what pleasure, she reposed under the leafy shadows of Saint-Cloud, her favorite residence! How she would have shuddered had a prophet of misfortune predicted to her the end of that marvellous palace and of the pretty little boy whom she led through its alleys and under its great trees!

CHAPTER IX

COUNT DE MORNY

HAVING reached the summit of his fortune, Napoleon III. sought to assure its success by making the Emperor Alexander II. forget the unpleasant memories of the Crimean War, and by terminating at St. Petersburg the work of pacification so fortunately begun at the Congress of Paris. He had absolute need of Russia, whose benevolent neutrality, if not her armed support, was indispensable to his schemes concerning Italy, and whose resentment against Austria he was anxious to exploit.

General Fleury has written in his Memoirs: " A perfectly natural occasion presented itself for the offer of an act of courtesy. This was to send an ambassador to St. Petersburg at the time of the Czar's coronation. Count de Morny, the most notable personage of the Empire, seemed foreordained to represent France and Napoleon III. The notoriety attaching to his birth, his family resemblance, his distinguished manners, his experience of men, the very important part he had played with so much bluster on December 2, all contributed to put him in an exceptional position and concentrate attention on him." It is certain that his lordly bearing, his luxurious and ostentatious habits, his personal attractiveness, fitted the president of the Corps Législatif marvellously for the task of winning the good graces of Alexander II. By a decree of May 8, 1856, he was appointed ambassador extraordinary to the Emperor of all the Russias.

Count Auguste de Morny was born at Paris, October 23, 1811. He had not been recognized either by his mother, Queen Hortense, or his father, General de Flahaut. One Demorny, an obscure native of Auvergne, had given him a civil condition. He was brought up by a witty and intelligent woman, Adèle Filleul, who gained some literary success, and married in the first place Count de Flahaut, and secondly the Baron de Souza. Her first husband, a victim of the Terror, perished on the scaffold in 1793, leaving her a son who was a general of division and aide-de-camp of the Emperor under Napoleon I., a peer of France and ambassador at Vienna under Louis Philippe, and under Napoleon III. senator and ambassador at London.

The widow of Count de Flahaut married in 1802 the Baron de Souza, a Portuguese diplomat and literary man, who, after representing the court of Lisbon in Sweden and subsequently in Denmark, was at that time minister of Portugal at Paris, where he died in 1825. The Baroness de Souza published several successful novels, collected in six volumes in 1822. Elegantly simple in style, they chiefly depict the upper classes of society, — those in which the Count de Morny was destined to shine. From his infancy he had been remarkable for the vivacity of his intelligence; so much so that Prince Talleyrand said of him: "This little man will be a minister some day."

Having made a successful course of studies at the Bourbon College, young de Morny embraced the military career. Leaving the Staff School in 1832, he entered the 1st regiment of lancers as a sub-lieutenant. Finding no social distractions while in garrison at Fontainebleau, he set himself seriously to work. The Baroness de Souza said at the time to Sainte-Beuve: "You have seen the young man in whose future I take so much interest; what sort of books do you suppose he selects for his reading? Do you think he reads novels, fugitive verses, agreeable memoirs, Voltaire's stories? He prefers metaphysics and theology to that sort of thing."

The Count de Morny distinguished himself in Africa under the Duke of Orleans, who showed him great kindness. He made the campaign of Mascara under General Changarnier, and the first campaign of Constantine, where he was wounded. Having been mentioned several times in the bulletins, he received the cross of the Legion of Honor for having saved the life of General Trezel.

M. de Morny had gained in Africa the reputation of a brave and deserving officer. But for him the army was but the prelude to social and political

COUNT de MORNY

life. He resigned his commission in 1838, and went to Paris, where the dandy and the man of business replaced the officer. He had once been in garrison at Clermont-Ferrand, where he had made friends, and where he now found the source of his private fortune and that of his political rise. He bought a beet-sugar manufactory in the suburbs of the town, and in 1838 published a pamphlet on the question of sugars which gained his appointment, at the age of twenty-seven, as president of the sugar industry commission. In 1842 he became deputy from Puy-de-Dôme.

At this time M. de Morny was an Orleanist, and did not dream of the resurrection of the Empire. In the Chamber he occupied one of the right centre benches, and was a very energetic supporter of M. Guizot's ministry. He was thoroughly competent to handle the commercial and industrial questions to which he devoted himself. Among other reforms he asked for small bank-notes, and on the subject of the conversion of annuities offered a proposition which afterwards became the basis of the system adopted. He combined labor and pleasure. The Vicomte de La Guéronnière thus describes him at this epoch: "At the time when he made his appearance in Parisian salons, young Count de Morny was a medley of militarism and pure and keen intelligence, of positivism and careless unconcern, of good sense and chivalric audacity, of English stiffness and French politeness, of serious tastes and light ones, of the man of business and the artist. Brought up in a social circle both elegant and distinguished, feeling his own power, haughty without pride, confident without presumption, ambitious without egotism, shrewd but not crafty, amiable without levity, learned without pretence, firm without rudeness, he had every quality needful for success." A friend of the Orleans princes, he had created a very brilliant position for himself both at court and in the city. He showed his political sense at the beginning of 1848, predicting but too surely the coming storm. In January he published an essay in the *Revue des Deux Mondes* in which the imminent dangers of the social question were pointed out with singular perspicacity, and in February he made the most laudable efforts to bring about a reconciliation between the Opposition and the Ministry. His efforts were fruitless, but, as a convinced partisan of the July monarchy he had neglected nothing which might prevent parliamentary agitation from degenerating into revolution.

When the revolution of February broke out Count de Morny had never had any sort of communication with Louis Napoleon. It was only after the death of Queen Hortense, when examining the letters and papers she had left at the château of Arenenberg, that the Prince became aware of a filiation which caused him the most painful surprise. The future Emperor saw Count de Morny for the first time in London, in 1848, but the breadth of his political views struck him at once. From that day he resolved to make him at some time one of his principal collaborators and a great dignitary of his empire. Courteous relations were established between the brothers, but these never assumed the form of cordial familiarity. Each kept his distance.

Elected as its representative by the department of Puy-de-Dôme in 1849, Count de Morny maintained a conservative policy in the Assembly. Minister of the Interior, December 2, 1851, the part he took in the *coup d'État* is well known. Although he resigned January 23, 1852, in consequence of the confiscation of the property of the Orleans family, he speedily returned to favor. Elected deputy, he was made president of the Corps Législatif by the Emperor in 1854, and performed his new duties with tact and skill. Magnificently housed in the palace of the Presidency, he removed thither his fine gallery of paintings and led a princely life.

General Fleury paints a portrait of him which is somewhat less flattering than that of the Vicomte de La Guéronnière. It runs as follows: " Taller and more slender than his master, Morny was better endowed physically, but had not in so high a degree the gift to please and charm. He received you agreeably enough, but he lacked feeling. Under his laboriously gracious exterior you felt the sceptic and the blasé. Accustomed to being petted, flattered by a crowd of business beggars, it pleased him to be circumspect whenever he found himself once more among friends and well-bred people who made no demands upon him. He was a superior person, doubtless, under many aspects, but nobody could possibly have called him the best-bred man in France. Like the Emperor he was calm, imperturbable, and thoroughly energetic, but there was not in his glance that kindliness, that sweetness, that penetration which rendered the Emperor irresistible and fascinated all who approached him." In spite of these reservations, General Fleury does full justice to the eminent qualities of M. de Morny. His portrait terminates as follows: "Such as he was, Morny was an incomparable man, and his death was a great loss and detriment to both the Emperor and the country."

When we have to speak of a political man we like to invoke the testimony of those of his contemporaries who beheld him close at hand. This is why we cite the following extract from the journal of M. Pinard: " Whether at the private dinners of M. Benoît-Champy (president of the civil tribunal of the Seine) or the grand receptions of the Palais-Bourbon, M. de Morny, however different his surroundings, always seemed to me like a superior person taking the measure of his epoch and forcing the democrats to accept him. Really I ought to say that the democrats sought him more than he did them, and that they endeavored to do him credit and increase his renown. Everywhere at his ease, because he was always conscious of his importance, he was never in a passion, much less intimidated. More affable with his inferiors than with his peers, his attitude towards his adversaries had in it a suspicion of disdain rather than of pride. You felt that he could raise his voice but would not. Stupid people did not perceive this disdain, but the clear-sighted understood it, and that sufficed him. Nobody could preserve his dignity with less effort."

M. de Morny has been greatly blamed for occupying himself too much with business and financial speculations. On this head M. Pinard makes the following reflections: "The only point I am willing to point out in the brilliant and diversified career of M. de Morny — and this fault was serious — is that of driving politics and business abreast, four-in-hand, so to say. A substitute in the first chamber of the civil tribunal of the Seine, I heard his name very often when the list of trials was called at the opening of the session. M. Mathieu, whom I was afterward to meet in the Corps Législatif and at the bar, was his lawyer, and I said to him one day as we were leaving the palace: 'A man in M. de Morny's position ought neither to gain suits nor to lose them; he ought not to have any.' Still, there was an extenuating circumstance in M. de Morny's case: he had been in that line before he became a person of distinction. Having a good deal of use for money, he turned his attention to sugar, manufactures, and railways. Business is a wheel within a wheel; the manufacturer became a speculator. Too proud to ask anything from the Emperor's generosity, he relied on nobody but himself for the fortune which had become indispensable. The settling up of his estate — a long and arduous affair — revealed the secret of his labors and successes. The assets were large; so were the liabilities."

To sum up: M. de Morny, the son of a queen and the son of his own works, a self-made man, having found means to turn his birth, his mind, his courage, and his resolute and enterprising character to his own advantage, was the type of the modern and aristocratic statesmen who recall both the great nobles of the old régime and the heroes of Balzac. Demanding all possible brilliancy and charm from life, seeking money in order to spend it prodigally and with splendor, equal to any of the experts as a connoisseur of painting, and proving it by the possession of a gallery of superb pictures, all bought and selected by himself, fond of horse-racing and skilful in all manly sports, a lover of literature, journalism, business, and politics, a composer in his leisure moments of pretty little pieces, initiated into the secrets of all coulisses, those of the theatre and those of the Bourse, a frequenter of salons, a clubman, a dilettante, a speculator, a manufacturer, a statesman, as tactful as he was well bred, he had a hand in everything and succeeded in all. As seductive in politics as in love, as much at ease in the presidential chair of the Corps Législatif as in the boudoir of a fine lady, and turning an address to the deputies as neatly as a compliment to a pretty woman, he was in all things, and up to the day of his death, a successful and much sought-after man. Destiny granted him its last grace when it showed him only the fortunate period of a régime whose disasters he might have prevented had he lived but a few years longer.

Having glanced at the man, let us now consider the ambassador.

CHAPTER X

THE EMBASSY TO ST. PETERSBURG

ON his way to St. Petersburg Count de Morny stopped at Wildbad to pay his respects to the Dowager Empress Alexandra Feodorovna (formerly Princess Charlotte of Prussia), sister of Frederic William IV. and the Prince of Prussia (the future Emperor William), widow of Czar Nicholas I. and mother of Czar Alexander II. Plunged in profound distress the Empress Dowager, who believed that the vexations of the Crimean War were in part accountable for her husband's death, felt no great pleasure in seeing the envoy of Napoleon III. His reception was polite but cold.

Although not ill pleased on the whole with his welcome at Wildbad, Count de Morny could not shake off a certain impression of mistrust. A few haphazard words, caught by chance or repeated by unknown persons, gave him at first a suspicion that the existing friendly relations with France were a mere matter of convention, a prescribed attitude, in which confidence would easily be misplaced. It seemed to him that German affinities remained much as they had been, and that should the French government afford the least pretext for it, Russia would at once renew every tie of the old policy inimical to France. "In passing through Germany," he wrote to Count Walewski, "I have been able to ascertain that if we are not loved by a Russian, we are cordially detested by a Russian grafted on a German." This first impression of the ambassador disappeared as soon as he took possession of his post.

Count de Morny arrived in St. Petersburg during the night of August 5, 1856, and took up his quarters at the Worensoff-Daschkoff mansion, which he had hired some months earlier. His splendid style of living, his horses, the gallery of pictures he brought with him from Paris, at once attracted the attention of both the upper classes and the people. He was in luck from the moment he made his appearance. The Austrian ambassador, Prince Esterhazy, had arrived in St. Petersburg forty-eight hours before him, and in consequence should have had his audiences first. But, just as the Prince was on the point of asking them, he discovered that he had left his credentials behind him at Vienna, the result being that the French ambassador was first received and thus became the dean of the diplomatic corps. This little mishap of the representative of Francis Joseph amused Russian society, very badly disposed at the time toward Austria.

At Wildbad Count de Morny had found an old court still suffering under the weight of recent afflictions. At St. Petersburg he faced a situation entirely different: new men and a new policy. Prince Gortchakoff, Minister of Foreign Affairs, gave him a most cordial reception. The Prince concealed neither his tastes nor his aversions. He declared that he had always favored kindly relations with France, and professed great admiration and personal sympathy for Napoleon III. He added, that he had always been grateful for the manner in which Queen Hortense had treated him. And he proved, in the most precise manner, that being very independent both by position and character, he had consented to take the portfolio of Foreign Affairs only because the views of the Emperor Alexander II. agreed entirely with his own.

Born April 17, 1818, the Czar married a Hessian princess, April 16, 1840, who assumed in Russia the name of Marie Alexandrovna. He had succeeded his father, the Emperor Nicholas, in 1855, and from the moment of his accession had given evidence of his conciliatory dispositions. Intractable, inflexible, the Emperor Nicholas, whose indomitable energy and extraordinary tenacity were the mainspring of his dictatorial and imperious nature, would doubtless never have made the concessions decided on by his successor, and if death had not snatched him from the struggle he was carrying on with unbending obstinacy, he would have resisted the four powers indefinitely, even though Austria had assisted them. Alexander II. adopted another policy. Anxious to cicatrize the wounds of the war, and dreaming already of the humanizing and civilizing reforms which were the glory of his reign, he was inclined to peace, and very seriously desired a reconciliation with France.

Count de Morny had his audience August 7, at the château of Peterhof. The Czar came to meet him, holding out his hand with kindly condescension. "I am delighted to see you here," said His Majesty. "Your presence marks the close of a situation happily ended, and one which ought not to be renewed. I am much obliged to the Emperor Napoleon, and will never forget the friendly influence he has exercised on our behalf over the entire body of negotiators. Count Orloff has also told me what reason he has to be satisfied with Count Walewski, whom I beg you to thank for it."

The Russian sovereign added: "The Emperor has a very warm friend in Count Orloff, who has come back from Paris completely under his spell. Moreover, I would be at a loss to make you understand how deeply I am affected by the kindness shown all the officers whom I have sent to Paris by the Emperor and the Empress. My brother, the Grand Duke Michael, has just written·me from Wildbad that he is enchanted with a letter accompanied by a small model of a twelve-pound cannon which the Emperor has sent him through M. Favé. I cannot sufficiently assure you how pleased I am with all these marks of renewed friendship, and, if the war has any good side, it is that of showing us what natural esteem and sympathy exist between the two nations."

The ambassador replied that the Emperor Napoleon was of the same mind as the Emperor Alexander, and that if he had selected military men who had been in the Crimea as attachés of an extraordinary embassy, it was because they had been able to form their own estimate of the stubborn courage of the Russians. It had seemed to Napoleon III., that by making this choice he would manifest the most sincere courtesy.

Alexander II. replied: "That was the way I understood it, and we have all been delighted to see these officers here. In the choice of you, M. le Comte, to represent the Emperor Napoleon at my court, I discover a new proof of his feelings toward me. I know that the position you occupy in France does not seem to point you out as destined for a foreign mission, and I am all the more affected by your being sent here. I acted as the Emperor Napoleon has done, on that matter, in sending him Count Kisseleff. He was one of my father's oldest friends; for a long time he has been mine; he is in charge here of one of the most important departments of the empire; his age and inclinations, no less than his position in Russia, seemed to imply the impossibility of a foreign mission, and in order to induce him to accept it I was obliged to insist on my wish to see myself represented near the Emperor Napoleon by a man in whom I have thorough confidence."

The Czar afterwards laid stress, in the most friendly way, on his intention to remain on good terms with France and Napoleon III. "That was, at bottom," said he, "the policy and aim of my father, and I have sincerely regretted the misunderstanding between him and you. As for me, I give you my word of honor that you can rely on the loyalty and sincerity of my intentions, and, M. le Comte, if ever a doubt arises in your mind, come direct to me and you will always find me ready to explain myself and come to an agreement with you."

By the exceptional favor on the occasion of presenting his credentials, Count de Morny was invited, with all the members of his embassy, to spend the 7th and 8th of August at Peterhof. The 8th was the birthday of the Empress. The Grand Duke and the Grand Duchess Constantine, the Grand Duke Michael, the Duchess Marie of Leuchtenberg, the Dowager Grand Duchess of Saxe Weimar, the Grand Duchess Catherine, and the Grand Duke of Mecklenburg Strelitz, who were at Peterhof for the fête, willingly made an exception to the rule of etiquette requiring an ambassador to ask to be received by these personages in their private residences, and paid their respects to him after Mass in the château. In the evening he was present at a family ball given by Their Imperial Majesties. That same day he wrote to Count Walewski: " To sum up in accordance with the favorable dispositions I encounter here, I find Russia a real mine to be exploited by France. It pertains to the

Emperor's government to decide what advantage shall be derived from it."

In another despatch, dated August 15, the ambassador added: "I feel justified in repeating my first assertion, to wit, that we are on excellent terms with everybody here. I do not think I am in error in saying so, for all who surround us are of the same opinion."

Up to this time the court of Russia, which favored the Carlist cause, had refused to recognize the government of Queen Isabella in Spain. In a drawing-room talk Prince Gortchakoff said something to Count de Morny about the intention of the cabinet of St. Petersburg to recognize that government as soon as Spain should have recovered a little from the crisis she had just passed through. It seemed to be his purpose in introducing this subject to pay a certain homage to the Emperor Napoleon's influence, and he gave it to be understood that the Emperor Alexander, who was still anxious for the evacuation of Greece, would be glad to see it occur coincidently with the sending of a Russian Minister to Madrid.

This made the ambassador say in his despatch to Count Walewski: "Little gifts keep up friendship, as you will appreciate. I did not try to repel the insinuation of the Prince, thinking that it might be advantageous to France to serve Spain while at the same time pushing Russia into a path totally opposite, on this point, as on many others, to that which the Emperor Nicholas followed so obstinately."

August 15, the feast of the Assumption and of Napoleon's patron saint, Count de Morny caused to be celebrated in the Catholic church of St. Catherine with a splendor which that feast had never before received in Russia. He was present, with all the members of his embassy, at a Mass followed by a *Te Deum* and a *Domine salvum fac Imperatorem*. The Catholic Bishop of Riga presided. The ambassador had confined himself to notifying the diplomatic corps that places would be reserved for those who wished to be present. All the heads of delegations came in uniform with their secretaries and attachés. Just as he was about starting for the church M. de Morny received an aide-de-camp of the Czar, General Ougaroff, bearing the congratulations and good wishes of His Majesty for the Emperor of the French.

On arriving at the church the ambassador found M. Tolstoy, the deputy Minister of Foreign Affairs, who had been specially commissioned by the Emperor Alexander to represent him at the ceremony. General Count Kisseleff had joined M. Tolstoy of his own accord. The church, brilliantly illuminated and served by a large body of priests, was entirely filled by a part of the French colony and a great number of Russians. Count de Morny wrote to Count Walewski the same day: "The fine appearance of the members of my embassy, greatly set off by the uniforms of the military delegation, and, if I may be allowed to say so, by my handsome carriages and liveries, seemed to me to produce a very marked impression in St. Petersburg, the effect of which cannot but react favorably on our claims to consideration. In the evening I had the principal façade of my house illuminated. It faces the Neva quay, a stone's throw from the imperial palace. These illuminations drew a great crowd below my windows. . . . I enter into these details because they derive importance from our situation in this country, and because the splendor with which I have surrounded the Emperor's fête seems to me to respond worthily to the position which our sovereign occupies in Europe."

The ambassador having presented the broad ribbon of the Legion of Honor to the Emperor Alexander in the name of the Emperor Napoleon, the Czar said: "Acquaint His Imperial Majesty, until I can do so myself, how sensible I am of this attention." M. de Morny afterwards introduced to the Emperor and the Empress the military delegation and the newly arrived attachés of the embassy. August 18, he wrote to Count Walewski: "Our Crimean officers have had a great success, and all of them, generals, officers, and attachés, were invited with me for that very day to dinner with the Emperor, who showed us much attention in the evening also. An aide-de-camp of the Minister of War was placed at my disposal and that of the generals to show us the public and military establishments of St. Petersburg, and the Grand Duke Constantine sent me a verbal message that he would expect us to-morrow at Cronstadt, where we should be shown the fortress. In a word, we find ourselves the recipients of very marked, very exceptional favor, which causes as much astonishment, I almost said jealousy, to the Russians themselves as to foreigners."

The ambassador set off for Moscow, August 22. He met the same success there as in St. Petersburg. The ceremonious entry of the Czar into the holy city was fixed for August 29, and his coronation for September 7.

CHAPTER XI

THE CORONATION OF THE CZAR

MOSCOW had resumed the festive appearance laid aside since the coronation of the Emperor Nicholas in 1826, when the Emperor Alexander made his formal entry, August 29, 1856. The houses disappeared behind garlands, flags, and hangings. Squares and open spaces were adorned with gigantic columns. The entrance to the streets through which the procession was to pass was marked by triumphal arches. A double line was formed by the Pawlowski regiment on the right and the regiment of grenadiers on the left. The diplomatic corps occupied the windows of the Princess Kotchoubey's mansion. Count de Morny appeared in a carriage with six windows and gilded panels, lined with white silk embroidered in red and gold, and drawn by six magnificent bays. In Paris, the son of Queen Hortense, restrained by the reserve imposed on him by Napoleon III., did not brag of his origin. In Moscow one might say that he advertised it on the blazon which decorated his gala carriage. In the centre of this appeared a hortensia with this motto underneath: *Tace, sed memento;* Be silent, but remember.

All the officers attached to the embassy, — Generals Lebœuf, Frossard, Dumont, Colonel Reille, M. Piquemol, Prince de Bauffremont, Count d'Espeuilles, Marquis de Gallifet, — rode in line at the doors of Count de Morny's carriage. Concerning this, General Fleury writes in his Memoirs: "I have heard the somewhat exaggerated military pomp of the ambassador criticised rather severely. Being neither a marshal, nor an army commander, Count de Morny ought not to have displayed such a wealth of officers around him. . . . The fault was not Morny's, however, but that of the War Minister, who did not know how to observe moderation."

The ambassador's carriage was followed by three others containing the civil members of the embassy, Count Murat, deputy to the Corps Législatif, Viscount de l'Espine, second secretary, Viscount Siméon, Count de Lavalette, the Duke de Gramont-Caderousse, attachés. The magnificence of the equipages, the brilliant uniforms of the French officers, the elegant white, red, and gold liveries of the outriders, coachmen, and footmen, excited the admiration of the crowd.

At half-past two a cannon announced that the procession was starting from the imperial residence, Petrowski, outside of Moscow. The bells of 480 churches and monasteries began to ring and did not stop until sunset. The clergy of the churches in the line of the procession awaited the Emperor with banners and holy pictures. At four o'clock the

Cossacks of the guard made their appearance in the Tverskaïa, a long street which crosses the city between the gate of St. Petersburg and the Kremlin, with their red uniforms, their long spears, their fur caps; the representatives of the nobility on horses, and the deputies of Asiatic hordes subject to Russia in glittering costumes. Then came a long file of gilded carriages drawn by six or eight horses. Then the cavalry guards, the cuirassiers, the dragoons, the hussars.

And now the Emperor on horseback, preceded by several of his staff. At the door of every church he halted before the clergy, who incensed him, and, taking off his hat, he kissed the cross. In passing in front of the Kotchoubey mansion he bowed graciously to the diplomatic corps. Behind the Czar rode his son the hereditary Grand Duke, his brothers, the Grand Dukes Constantine, Michael, and Nicholas, Prince Frederic of Prussia, betrothed to the Princess Royal of England, the Princes Frederic of Würtemburg, Frederic of the Low Countries, Nicholas of Nassau, and Frederic of Hesse. A long file of footmen in the green and gold imperial livery preceded the two Empresses. The Empress-mother was in a carriage dating from the eighteenth century, the panels decorated with pictures by Boucher, drawn by eight bays, caparisoned with gold and garnet velvet; the reigning Empress in a carriage with eight grays harnessed with silver and blue velvet. Behind her, in three more gilded and painted carriages, were the princesses of the imperial family, escorted by equerries at the portières and pages behind. On arriving at the Kremlin, Their Majesties and Their Imperial Highnesses alighted from horse and carriage, to enter the churches of the Assumption, the Annunciation, and the Archangel Michael, where they kissed the holy pictures offered them by the holy synod, and afterwards prayed above the tomb of the former emperors.

In the evening the Princess Kotchoubey gave a dinner of two hundred and twenty covers to the diplomatic corps and several distinguished foreigners. As dean of the ambassadors extraordinary, Count de Morny proposed the health of the Czar.

September 1, Alexander II. reviewed the entire body of troops assembled for his coronation. Count de Morny and the English ambassador, Lord Granville, were on horseback. During the review, the Grand Duke Constantine devoted himself especially to the officers of the French embassy, to whom he had already given a cordial reception at Cronstadt.

September 5, in the morning, took place the procession of heralds-at-arms proclaiming throughout the city the accession of the Czar. Wearing red and gold musketry caps with black, orange, and yellow plumes, doublets of cloth-of-gold, and carrying their maces in their right hands, they were preceded by a squadron of mounted guards and four masters of ceremonies. Their white horses were led by lackeys in rich livery. On the Kremlin Square the trumpets sounded; the spectators took off their hats; the heralds-at-arms raised their maces; then, after the reading of the proclamation, they scattered copies of it amongst the crowd, who seized them with a sort of fanaticism and preserved them among the sacred pictures in their houses.

September 7 was the great day: that of the coronation. The beginning of the ceremonies was announced in the morning by the church bells and salvos of artillery. At the signal given by the Kremlin cannon, all those who were to occupy seats either in the tribunes erected around the inner court of the palace or within the church, betook themselves to their places through a crowd, part of which had been waiting in the streets since midnight. The diplomatic corps assembled at the palace of the French embassy; a company of mounted gendarmes guarded the approaches, and it was from there that it started for the Kremlin. At the head of this procession moved the state carriage of Count de Morny.

Never was there a grander or more imposing ceremony. Moscow is the holy city, the *holy mother* of which no Russian speaks without filial respect. Moscow is the heart of Russia. The Kremlin is the heart of Moscow. The church of the Assumption is the heart of the Kremlin. The sanctuary is not vast; but how resplendent it was with its walls gilded and decorated with Byzantine paintings, its extraordinarily magnificent iconostasis, its priests in chasubles of cloth-of-gold and cloth-of-silver, overloaded with fine pearls and precious stones! It was in this church, the object of universal veneration, that Alexander II. was to be crowned.

The Empress-mother was the first to make her appearance. A superb dais was awaiting her at the foot of the red staircase. Under the parvis the Metropolitan received her and presented the cross and holy water. Entering the sanctuary she took her place on one of the three thrones on a platform in the middle.

Then came the Czar and the Czarina, advancing processionally beneath a canopy of crimson velvet embroidered with gold and surmounted with white plumes, which was upheld by thirty-two superior officers. After bowing reverently before the holy pictures, Their Majesties seated themselves on two thrones of equal height overlooking the entire assembly. Then the coronation ceremony began. The Czar vested himself in the imperial mantle with the diamond chain of the order of St. Andrew. The Metropolitan made the sign of the cross, imposed his hands while reciting a prayer and presented on a cushion the diamond crown surmounted by the finest rubies that exist. The monarch took the crown and set it on his own head. Then, with his right hand he seized the sceptre, and with his left the globe with its glittering cross. Afterwards, seating himself on his throne and laying down the sceptre and the globe, he called the Czarina, who kneeled before him. Lifting the crown from his head, he touched the forehead of the Empress with it and replaced it on his head. Finally he put a smaller crown upon her forehead and vested her with the mantle and chain of St. Andrew. At this moment all the bells rang throughout the city, and one hundred and one guns were fired.

The Empress-mother, supported by the Grand Dukes Michael and Nicholas, left her throne, advanced towards her son, who made several steps to meet her, and fell into his arms. The emotion was indescribable. The other members of the imperial family then approached; they embraced the Emperor on the shoulder and kissed the hand of the Empress. They were kissed in return upon the forehead.

Wearing the crown and the imperial mantle and holding in his hands the sceptre and the globe, the Czar descended from his throne and — all others remaining on their feet — fell on his knees and prayed aloud for his people. Then he rose and all the spectators kneeled. The choir intoned the *Te Deum*. When this was ended the Metropolitan took the cup of Constantine containing the holy chrism, and dipping into it a gilded branch, anointed the Emperor on the forehead, eyes, nostrils, mouth, ears, breast, and hands. One hundred and one discharges of cannon and all the church bells of the city announced the holy unction. Then the Emperor went inside the iconostasis, a part of the altar which only the priest has the right to enter, and after prostrating himself three times, received Communion under both species according to the rite observed in the case of priests, while the Empress received at the door of the iconostasis in the same manner as the faithful generally.

Before returning to the palace, the Czar and the Czarina, in coronation costume and under the dais, went to visit the other two churches which likewise form part of the Kremlin, that of the Archangel St. Michael, which contains the tombs of the former emperors, and that of the Annunciation. They left the dais after this visit and ascended the steps of the red staircase. On reaching the top, the Czar, having the Czarina on his left side, turned and thrice saluted the enthusiastic crowd.

The ambassadors breakfasted in one of the apartments of the ancient Kremlin, and again assembled, to be present, according to usage, at the Emperor's dinner. A pillar, erected in the middle of the hall where this repast was to take place, was ornamented with old cups and pieces of gold and silver ware dating from very remote periods. A table with three covers had been prepared on an estrade covered with red velvet, for the Emperor and the two Empresses. Not far from the imperial table, another, which ran all round the hall, had been made ready for the Metropolitans of Moscow, St. Petersburg, Kieff, Novgorod, and the members of their clergy who had been present at the coronation ceremonies. Some moments after his arrival the Emperor lifted a glass to his lips; this was a signal for the ambassadors to depart, and they withdrew.

In the evening the city was like a scene of enchantment. The rue Tverskaïa, the Place of the Grand Theatre, and the palace of the ambassador of France, glowed with lights. The illuminated Kremlin seemed like a magic palace. Multicolored fires wound around the high crenellated walls and reached the summits of innumerable towers. The giant of the steeples, that of Ivan Veliky, dominating radiant cupolas, threw out sheaves of fireworks in all directions. The crowds massed on the quays of the Moskowa were in transports of joy. In the evening the Emperor drove out in an open carriage, greeted on every side by acclamations that were almost frantic. Oh how magnificently and joyously opened a reign which was to close in so tragic a fashion!

CHAPTER XII

THE FÊTES OF MOSCOW

THE grand traditional banquet offered to the people by the Czar, in a plain just outside of Moscow, was to take place September 20. During the preceding days, one saw police officers in the streets inviting all the moujiks whom they met *to dine with the Emperor*, and the latter charging them in turn to convey their thanks to the sovereign. On the day appointed, in the plain of Petrowski, an infinite number of tables, with mountains of meat, bread, and cakes, covered a space of more than one square verst. Fountains springing from the heads of lions, shed each into its own basin floods of wine, kvass, and tea. A Moorish pavilion had been erected for the Czar, who was to preside at the people's banquet after the fashion of his ancestors. Behind this pavilion were eight covered galleries, intended for great dignitaries of state and the members of the diplomatic corps. The Emperor arrived on horseback, surrounded by grand dukes and followed by a numerous staff. He alighted, and after talking for a few minutes with the princesses and the ambassadors, remounted and rode over the plain. Then he returned to the imperial pavilion and presided at the gigantic banquet, which was succeeded by many diversions: circuses, swings, Russian mountains, and gratuitous theatrical representations of scenes of national history.

The next day, September 21, the distribution of food and drink and the games began anew in the plain of Petrowski. Rain poured in torrents, but nevertheless, the Emperor returned and was received with lively enthusiasm. Just as he arrived a balloon filled with bonbons was sent up. On leaving, the sovereign invited the ambassadors to meet him at breakfast in the castle of Petrowski. Until night the crowds, though wet to the skin, made the air ring with their shouts of pleasure as they amicably disputed the way to the provisions and the fountains.

September 22, the Emperor offered an entertainment in the Kremlin to the citizens, the merchants of the three guilds, and the different working classes of Moscow. It was what was called a "bal masqué," although there were neither masks nor dominos. According to an old custom, suppressed by the Emperor Nicholas, the Czars and the members of their families wore, in similar circumstances, a small silk mantle over their usual dress. This disguise no longer existed, but the name of masked ball had been retained. There were no dances properly so called at this ball, but there were *polonaises*, a sort of ceremonious marches executed to the accompaniment of the orchestra by the Emperor, the Empress, and the personages of their court. Fifteen thousand invited guests assembled at the fête of September 22. The Czar wore his uniform as commander of the national militia. The two Empresses, the Grand Duchesses, and the court ladies were all in national costume, the Russian *kakochnik* or headdress, overloaded with diamonds, pearls, emeralds, rubies, and streaming veils of tulle or lace. Robes of gold and silver brocade were trimmed with furs. Corsages glittered with jewels. Immense embroidered trains swept the parquetted floor. During the polonaise the Emperor escorted the Empress first and afterwards the Grand Duchesses, and shook hands with the ambassadresses and several noble ladies. He subsequently visited all the halls of the palace. A marble staircase, which divides the building in two, leads to the hall of St. George, in which the names of all knights of this order who have been rewarded for brilliant deeds on the battlefield are inscribed on white marble tablets inserted in the walls in letters of gold. The hall of St. Catherine forms a pendant to this one. The order from which it borrows its name is one instituted for ladies. The Empress presides at the meeting of its chapter. In the long gallery, whose decorations recall the emblems of the order of St. Andrew and include the black eagles of Russia bearing the imperial escutcheon, the throne was set under an enormous cloth of gold lined with ermine. On the left had been placed a console on which lay the imperial insignia under the charge of a guard of honor. The throne had been separated from the spectators by a gilded balustrade like that before the bed of Louis XIV. in the château of Versailles, which the ambassadors had been authorized to cross. Around the sides of the throne-room tables had been placed which were hidden from view under salt-cellars and dishes in precious metals, offered with bread and salt by the numberless delegations. The fête terminated by a supper of two thousand covers, for which the court of the Kremlin served as a hall.

Three grand balls were given by the English, Austrian, and French ambassadors in that order. At the mansion of Lord Granville, a white and red tent adorned with flowers recalled a naval fête on the deck of a vessel. At that of Prince Esterhazy, a white and gold salon, refreshed by a large fountain, was like a salon from the palace of Vienna transported to Moscow. Every one was wondering what Count de Morny's ball would be. It was a marvel.

The ball took place September 29. The front of the embassy was illuminated by colored lamps: red, blue, and white. On every step of the staircase, adorned with green foliage and flowers, stood powdered footmen in white, red, and gold liveries. The great ballroom was magnificent with its azure decoration, its gilded trellis tapestried with natural ivy, and, springing from a parterre of flowers, its medallions representing Loves holding bunches of roses, its immense mirrors apparently increasing the extent of the hall and reflecting its lights, its six chandeliers, its great cupola diffusing a brightness still further increased by lamps placed at intervals in vases of flowers, its estrade garnished with blue silk curtains and armchairs of gold brocade and white for the Emperor and the imperial family, and its orchestra on a sort of terrace with a gilded balustrade. A door in the ballroom led to other salons. One of them had been transformed into a picture gallery for the fine pictures brought from Paris by the ambassador. Another, a charming boudoir in white muslin lined with blue silk, was intended for the Empress. In a third was an immense buffet with stewards ranged behind it in violet and gold liveries, white breeches, and silk stockings.

At ten o'clock the arrival of the sovereigns was announced. The ambassador and all his delegation went to receive them at the foot of the stairs. Preceded by footmen carrying candelabras and followed by the ambassador, Their Majesties entered the grand ballroom. The orchestra played the Russian national hymn. Then came a polonaise, led by Count de Morny, with the Empress on his arm, followed by the Emperor, giving his hand to the Baroness Seebach, daughter of Chancellor Nesselrode, and wife of the minister of Saxony at Paris. Count de Morny, being a bachelor, had begged this lady to do the honors of the fête with him.

The ambassador himself shall finish the description of his ball. He does so in a despatch addressed to

Count Walewski on September 30: "The Emperor and the imperial family were present last week at balls given them by the ambassadors of England and Austria. I had yesterday the honor to receive in my turn the Emperor, who came to the embassy accompanied by the Empress, the Grand Duke and Grand Duchess Constantine, the Grand Dukes Nicholas and Michael, and all the foreign princes now in Moscow. The Emperor wore the white uniform of the mounted guards and the broad ribbon and star of the Legion of Honor. He said to me on entering: 'M. l'Ambassadeur, to-day I have for the first time the honor of wearing the broad ribbon sent me by the Emperor Napoleon through you, and I am charmed that it should be in your house.' Throughout the evening the Emperor and the Empress testified the utmost kindness and cordiality. They did me the honor to remain from ten in the evening until two in the morning, and did not retire without partaking of supper. I had assembled around Their Majesties the diplomatic corps and the élite of St. Petersburg and Moscow society, as well as the principal military and civil functionaries of the Empire. It does not become me to praise my own ball, but it is permissible to say in accordance with what I have heard of the general impression, that although the last of the fêtes of the coronation it was not the least brilliant."

Indisputably, Count de Morny had been the most prodigal of the ambassadors.

CHAPTER XIII

FRANCE AND RUSSIA

THE hour had come when a durable and definitive alliance might be concluded between France and Russia. By a concurrence of providential circumstances the enemies of yesterday had become friends of to-morrow. The Russians bore a grudge against the English and the Austrians, but none against the French. They said that the war between the Emperor Nicholas and Napoleon III. had been simply a fatal misunderstanding, and that France in the Crimea had played England's game instead of serving her own interests. People were grateful to the Emperor of the French for his attitude during the Congress of Paris, and fully resolved to reward him for it. Count de Morny's great political good sense assured him that the psychological moment had arrived for an accord which might be equally useful to both nations. A shrewd observer, he perceived at Moscow, perhaps still more than at St. Petersburg, that not merely the official circles but all classes of Russian society were actuated by good dispositions towards France.

Every one said that England would have liked to

continue the war until all the Russian fleet had been destroyed, and that Napoleon III. had been the sole obstacle in the way of her doing so. September 3, 1856, M. de Morny wrote from Moscow to Count Walewski: "They say to us: 'You have been fierce enemies, but generous and humane ones. You have never warred on us like savages, and we are aware that we owe it to the moderation of the Emperor Napoleon that peace has been concluded; which is more than we can say of your allies.' So say officers, merchants, and the people." In the same despatch he adds: "The more closely I study Europe, the more I become convinced that the reputation for great moderation and perfect loyalty is at present what can give the greatest moral force to a government. Moreover, I can assure you that people here have a very real respect for the Emperor of the French, as well as a great admiration and absolute reliance on his word. Prince Gortchakoff is inexhaustible on this subject; he speaks of it openly; he says that his policy of thirty years is triumphant, that he has always considered an alliance with France as the most natural and the most advantageous for Russia: 'France,' says he, 'not a revolutionary comet, but a planet directed in its course by a firm and able sovereign.' This language, under every variety of expression, is that of everybody, and is addressed to all of us in every rank. We are cordially welcomed everywhere, and not merely at the official receptions; our officers are treated with a friendly distinction; our ears are constantly filled with words of admiration and sympathy for France. Is it only a watchword? So be it, but watchwords so well given and so generally accepted and repeated end by becoming a public spirit. I repeat what I have said to you, that with prudence, we may do many things here without wounding any one."

There was no cloud on the relations of the two governments. It might have been thought that the title of Duke of Malakoff given by Napoleon III. to Marshal Pélissier would excite some ill feeling in Russia. But it did not. Count Walewski had addressed the following telegram to M. de Morny, August 14, 1856: "The Emperor has named Marshal Pélissier Duke of Malakoff. We hope no one at St. Petersburg will be offended." The ambassador replied two days later: "I am continually forgetting to tell you that when I received your telegram announcing the creation of the duchy of Malakoff, I wondered by what clever arguments I might best gild this pill for the Russian government. I was even getting ready to call attention to the choice as a delicate attention, because the name of Sebastopol would have been more logical, greater, and more glorious, but also more displeasing to Russia, whereas Malakoff is no longer in existence, is merely a point, recalls nothing but a brilliant action, etc. Once armed with these arguments, I concluded not to say a word on the subject to anybody, nobody has mentioned it to me, and it is thus that I have conducted this thorny negotiation. I am rather disposed to employ this method often, and I believe that in many cases it would be almost infallibly successful. To forestall an objection is often to beget one."

Count de Morny saw clearly that the painful memories between France and Russia might be forever effaced. "I cannot avoid," he adds, "recurring to our situation in 1815. Let us remember that several of the Powers then set their foot on our throats. Others, more generous, extended their hands. The first have left behind a feeling of bitterness; for the others, in spite of their hostility and our humiliation, we are conscious of no rancor. The situation is nearly the same for the Russians. . . . To show ourselves equitable and benevolent on unimportant points is to obtain their gratitude very cheaply. . . . Hence my opinion is that, without doing anything calculated to alarm England, we ought to take serious note of the friendly dispositions, the preferences shown for us by Russia, to neglect none of the petty details which become matters of reconciliation, — commercial treaties, exchange of courtesies and of politeness, in a word, all those little means of being mutually agreeable which governments possess and which it is so easy to make use of. When the time arrives, without dignity being compromised on either side, I am convinced that I shall receive here open and public testimonials of a still closer union. I have taken care not to allow my desire for it to become visible; I have not breathed a word, but I should be very much amazed at not succeeding were I charged to arrange a result of that sort." M. de Morny's despatches do great honor to his memory. They speak the language of a skilled diplomatist, a clear-sighted patriot, and a real statesman.

M. de Morny had a singular comprehension of the present and read the future like a prophet. He was thoroughly aware that France excited great jealousy; that she could not preserve her preponderating situation except by the aid of some powerful alliance like that of Russia, and that in order that this alliance might be fruitful it must take an active character without recoiling from initiatives. "The European continent," said he, in his despatch of September 5, "seems to me a composite of chemical elements of different species. By agitating it in a certain way, by adding certain substances, one may produce new combinations there; but if these are left to repose quietly and with indifference, the ancient affinities will be seen to regain their attractive forces, and some fine day we may be surprised to find all the former ties renewed and old Europe against us. We must not delude ourselves; the triumph of our arms, the success of our policy, create more envy than admiration." The conclusion of the ambassador was that, to neutralize the effects of this jealousy of the powers it was necessary for France to unite itself to Russia by solid and indestructible ties.

M. de Morny was right in believing that no government but the Russian could render ineffectual the suspicions and bitter feelings of the Germans concerning France, and that Napoleon III. would obtain tangible results only through the friendliness of the Czar. He was affirming undeniable truths when he added in the same despatch: "In spite of its recent disasters, Russia still retains a great prestige in Germany. On the day when the latter believes that a serious accord exists between the two Emperors of France and Russia, she will go through the eye of a needle. If ever the map of Europe needs to be peacefully changed, it is very plain that no modification in favor of France could be made with the consent of Germany, nor would be possible without the concurrence of Russia."

In the forty-two years that I have been in the Ministry of Foreign Affairs, many despatches have passed through my hands. I have read none better than those of M. de Morny. No trained diplomatist has surpassed this improvised one. I have just been looking over the mass of his correspondence, and I tell myself that if his counsels had been followed our misfortunes would have been averted. What was lacking to the diplomacy of the Second Empire was a quality which M. de Morny, both before and after his elevation to the title of Duke, possessed in the highest degree: steadiness of mind. To the end of his life, too short, alas! he remained the convinced partisan of the Russian alliance, the friend and admirer of the Emperor Alexander II. He made in vain, but with the most laudable frankness and energy, the greatest efforts to prevent his sovereign from embroiling himself with the cabinet of St. Petersburg by an imprudent and fruitless intervention in the affairs of Poland. But for this unlucky intervention, which was a snare laid for France by Austria and still more by England, and which had no results but to people Siberia with exiles and break the Franco-Russian agreement, the two Empires would have remained indissolubly united, and Germany, obliged to watch her oriental frontier instead of being able to disgarnish it completely would not have dared to venture on the war which was so fatal to France. It may be affirmed that if the relations of Napoleon III. and Alexander II. had been still in 1870 what they were in 1856, we should have been spared all our disasters. But in 1870 the Duke de Morny was no longer there to tell Napoleon III. the truth.

I

CHAPTER XIV

THE PRINCE OF PRUSSIA

THE close of the year 1856 was made noticeable at the Tuileries by a princely visit to which Napoleon III. attached great importance, that of Prince Frederic William of Prussia, the future Emperor of Germany. The Prince was in his sixtieth year and had retained great vigor both of body and mind. Born March 22, 1797, he was the son of Frederic William III., and the brother and heir of Frederic William IV., who had no children and whose health was precarious. The Prince of Prussia already took an active interest in politics, and Napoleon III. fancied that he might some day find in him a distinguished collaborator in his designs on Italy. The Prince was destined to play a part, alas! still greater than that which the Emperor believed to be in store for him. As a youth he had invaded France, as an old man he was to invade it again. He remembered that when scarcely seventeen he had gone to Malmaison with his father, Frederic William III., his brother, the future Frederic William IV., and the Grand Duke Nicholas of Russia, the future Emperor Nicholas I. All three had been under the charm of the Empress

Josephine and Queen Hortense. The Queen had sung some songs of her own composition, glancing sympathetically meanwhile at the handsome Grand Duke Nicholas. So the Emperor William told one of his aides-de-camp some time before his death, and the conversation was reported to me. In 1856 he could remind Napoleon III. of the souvenirs of Malmaison. But he took good care not to evoke those of his own mother, Queen Louise, whom the victor of Jena and the conqueror of Berlin had wounded deeply, and whom the Prussians longed to avenge.

It is curious to note that of all the princes who came to France during the Second Empire, he who had the greatest success at the Court of the Tuileries was probably the future victor of Sedan. No one was more attentive to the Emperor, more gallant towards the Empress, whose respectful and enthusiastic admirer he claimed to be. His princely and military bearing, his kindly aspect, his simple and familiar conversation, assured him a specially courteous and cordial welcome.

December 11, 1856, Frederic William, Prince of Prussia, coming from Osborne in the Isle of Wight, arrived in Paris accompanied by Baron von Schreckenstein, commander in chief of the 7th Prussian army corps, and by an officer destined unfortunately to become very celebrated, General Moltke. Colonel Marquis de Toulongeon, orderly officer of the Emperor, and Count de Riencourt, equerry, went to Calais to meet the Prince. Prince Napoleon received him at the Gare du Nord, where a battalion of the guard and another of the line were drawn up. Four court carriages, escorted by a platoon of guides, awaited the Prussian Prince and conducted him and his suite to the Tuileries, where he was received at the foot of the grand staircase by the grand chamberlain and the grand master of ceremonies; at the head of the staircase by the Emperor, surrounded by his officers on duty. The sovereign afterwards presented him to the Empress, who was awaiting him in the white salon with the officers and ladies of her household, and afterwards conducted him to the apartments prepared for him in the pavilion of Marsan. In the evening the Prince and all the members of his suite and those of the Prussian legation dined at the table of Their Majesties.

December 31, at one o'clock, the Emperor reviewed in the court of the château nine regiments of the line and three battalions of infantry, all of whom had made the Crimean campaign. The troops were commanded by Marshal Magnan. Napoleon III., escorted by Marshals Vaillant, Baraguey d'Hilliers, Pélissier, Canrobert, and Bosquet, had the Prince of Prussia at his side. The Empress, surrounded by the officers and ladies of her household, was on the balcony of the hall of Marshals. After passing in front of the troops, the Emperor, stationing himself in front of the pavilion of the Horloge, caused the flags of all the companies to be united; then in the presence of these glorious ensigns, torn by shot and shell, he distributed the crosses and military medals with his own hand. During the review the Prince Imperial, coming from the palace of the Tuileries, passed through the line of soldiers, who cheered him heartily. Could one then have dreamed that he in whose honor this fine review was given would be so fatal to both the father and the son?

December 15, the Emperor and the Prince of Prussia set off in the morning for Fontainebleau, where they were to spend two days at the château. In the evening the city was illuminated. The next day the Emperor with the Prince reviewed the lancers of the guard. The Empress arrived at eleven o'clock in the morning. There was a hunt with hounds in the forest. At six in the evening Their Majesties started for Paris with the Prince of Prussia.

December 17. Review of the entire imperial guard in the court of the Tuileries and on the Carrousel. The Emperor wore the broad ribbon of the Black Eagle, and the Prince of Prussia rode at his side. He was accompanied by Marshals Magnan, de Castellane, Baraguey d'Hilliers, Pélissier, Canrobert, and Bosquet, and the Prussian generals of the Prince's suite, the Marquis de Villamarina, Sardinian minister, and a numerous staff. He passed in front of the lines, with the Prince of Prussia next to the troops, and frequently conversed with him. Then he stationed himself before the pavilion of the Horloge. At this moment he summoned the colonel of the 3d grenadiers of the guard and gave him the eagle of this newly formed regiment. The colonel uttered some enthusiastic words and carried the flag to his grenadiers. The march-by then began in perfect order. In spite of the cold, the Empress was on the balcony of the hall of Marshals. Among the ladies surrounding her were Lady Cowley, ambassadress of England, and the Countess Hatzfeldt, daughter of Marshal Castellane and wife of the minister of Prussia at Paris.

In the evening, the Count and Countess Hatzfeldt gave a grand dinner at the house of the legation, rue de Lille, in honor of the Prince. Marshals Vaillant, Magnan, de Castellane, Baraguey d'Hilliers, Pélissier, Canrobert, and Bosquet, all the ministers, all the great officers of the crown, and General Renaud de Saint-Jean d'Angély, were present at this repast. One of the guests, Marshal Castellane, wrote in his journal: " The Prince of Prussia talks well and freely; he discussed military matters in a way that showed he knew and had studied his trade; he is a tall, fair, handsome fellow, very polite, and with distinguished manners; everybody speaks well of him."

December 18. Ball of five hundred persons at the Tuileries. Their Majesties made their appearance at ten o'clock with the Prince of Prussia, and remained until three in the morning. The ball took place in the hall of the Marshals. The men were in dress coats with knee breeches and silk stockings. The Emperor and the Empress danced the cotillion, which lasted more than an hour, with much animation. The supper was served on small tables in the playhouse.

December 19. The Prince of Prussia visited the school of Saint-Cyr. Received at the chief entrance by General de Monet and all the staff of the school, he requested that no change should be made in the order of exercises. Two platoons of cavalry, composed of pupils of the second year, executed all the platoon movements. Shortly before leaving Saint-Cyr, the Prince passed in front of the pupils assembled with arms and baggage, who afterwards executed the manual and other exercises. His Royal Highness expressed his satisfaction to the general commanding, and went in the evening to the Opéra, where the ballet of the *Corsair* was given. Rosati was greatly applauded.

December 20. The Prince dined at the imperial table and afterwards went with Their Majesties to the Comédie-Française. Hardly had the Countess Hatzfeldt entered the box that had been offered her than the Emperor and Empress sent for her to come to theirs. The Prince was charmed with the courteous reception given by Napoleon III. and his court, not merely to himself but to the members of his suite and the Prussian legation. At this period no government maintained better relations with the Emperor than did the Prussian.

December 21. The Prince was to quit Paris at eleven in the evening with the Marquis de Toulongeon, orderly officer of the Emperor, and Count Riencourt, equerry, both of whom were to accompany His Royal Highness as far as Strasbourg. Before departing he dined at the imperial table. The Count and Countess Hatzfeldt had also been invited. The Countess wrote to her father: " We have again been invited to dine at the Tuileries; they kept us to the moment of the Prince's departure for the train. He has left Paris, and I think he was pleased with what he saw there; moreover, everybody here is well pleased with him. The men and my husband had gone, and then the Emperor, after a long consultation with the Empress, came to say that a table was to be arranged for a lottery. There were magnificent prizes, and, which was not quite a matter of chance, I won a charming gold bracelet with the word *Souvenir* written on it in diamonds. This was a very amiable way of making me a present. No one could be more charming than both of them were to us on this occasion, for, while being most polite, it would have been easy to show us less attention."

Very well inclined toward the Prince, whom he thought he could induce to enter into his projects for the changing of the map of Europe, Napoleon III. highly appreciated the Countess Hatzfeldt, whose chief aim it always was to bring about a sincere reconciliation between her two countries. Who knows? — if the worthy daughter of Marshal Castellane had been ambassadress to Prussia in 1870, the Franco-Prussian War might never have taken place.

CHAPTER XV

THE COMMENCEMENT OF 1857

THE year 1857 opened amidst an internal and external peace which it seemed that nothing need disturb. There was a reception of ladies at the Tuileries in the evening of January 2. Everybody wore a court mantle and a train. Preceded by the great officers of the crown, Their Majesties went to the throne-room, where they seated themselves with the princes on their right and the princesses on their left. All others stood. The grand chamberlain having received the orders of the Emperor, the reception began. Each lady was led to the Emperor by the grand chamberlain, and to the Empress by the grand mistress of her household.

It had been announced that the Emperor would go to the Gaieté on the evening of January 3, to see a melodrama called *La Fausse Adultère*, very much in vogue at the time. He was prevented by a terrible and unexpected calamity, the assassination of Monseigneur Sibour, Archbishop of Paris. The prelate had gone that day to the church of Saint Etienne-du-Mont, where a novena in honor of Sainte Geneviève was in progress. He had just made the round of the sanctuary, blessing the kneeling throng, when a man issuing from the crowd sprang upon and struck him with a knife. The assassin did not try to escape. Brandishing his knife he shouted: "Down with the goddesses!" People thought he was mad; they did not know that he was opposed to the dogma of the Immaculate Conception and was alluding in this way to the Blessed Virgin and her mother. His name was Verger and his age thirty. He was a suspended priest who thought he had grounds of complaint against the clergy and had determined to avenge himself. Although the Bishop of Meaux had recently written him: "We think you need to be treated in a private hospital," the doctors declared him responsible after an examination, and he was executed on the place de la Roquette, in presence of an immense crowd, during the night of January 29.

To superstitious people the murder of the Archbishop may have seemed a fatal omen for the new year and the stability of the dynasty. It was Mgr. Sibour who had intoned the *Te Deum* at the time of the reëstablishment of the Empire. It was he who had received the Emperor and the Empress at the door of Notre Dame on the day of their marriage and the day of their son's baptism. The ball which was to have been given at the Tuileries January 8 was countermanded, and on the 10th the obsequies of the Archbishop were celebrated with great pomp in the metropolitan church. Great and painful emotion was manifested, but the sad impression was soon dispelled. Four days later both the court and the city had resumed all their usual animation.

January 14, Prince Napoleon assembled in the Palais-Royal all general officers then in Paris who had taken part in the Crimean War. Among the fifty-two guests were Marshals Pélissier the Duke of Malakoff, Canrobert, and Bosquet, Admiral Hamelin, Generals Regnaud de Saint-Jean d'Angély, de Salles, Niel, and MacMahon. Prince Napoleon had begged his father, King Jerome, to preside at this military banquet, where nine veterans of the First Empire were present. The brother of Napoleon I. proposed this toast: "To the Emperor, the Empress, and the Prince Imperial, to whom I wish, for the good of our dear country which he is called to govern, the wisdom and skill of his august father."

Prince Napoleon afterwards raised his glass in honor of the commanders in chief of the army of the Crimea. He spoke as follows: "To Marshal Saint-Arnaud, the audacious chief who died after the Alma, having the tricolored banner of regenerated France as his shroud!

"To Marshal Canrobert, who was able to maintain the army amid circumstances so difficult, and to remit to his successor, as he said himself, troops inured to war and ready to undertake anything.

"To Marshal Pélissier, Duke of Malakoff, who immortalized himself by the taking of Sebastopol, and whose rare and persevering energy enabled him to overcome the obstacles by which he was surrounded on all sides."

The Prince afterwards paid a touching tribute to the brethren in arms who had met death as worthy sons of France, and thus concluded his speech: " The immense advantage of this war, I affirm it with pride, is that you have proved that France always has her grand army."

The Marshal Duke of Malakoff replied: " Monseigneur, it falls to me to thank Your Imperial Highness for assembling us around the brother of the Emperor Napoleon I., the most illustrious of the remaining representatives of his immortal epopee. . . . The eulogies you have given the army I had the honor to command are all the more precious because they happily remind us that Your Imperial Highness has shared its labors and valiantly contributed to its success."

The former King of Westphalia then spoke: " I thank Marshal Pélissier," said he, "for having associated my name to that of the grand army. I am glad to be able to respond by proposing a toast to our brave armies by land and sea, and in particular to our glorious army of the Crimea, which, with the swiftness of the eagle, has seized the first occasion to place itself worthily beside the old phalanxes of Marengo, Austerlitz, and Jena."

The winter of 1857 was very brilliant. The invitations to the grand balls at the Tuileries were very numerous. These were official festivities intended especially for military men and functionaries; uniform or a court dress was indispensable. On every step of the grand staircase stood one of the hundred-guards, majestic and motionless as a statue. At the moment when Their Majesties, followed by officers and ladies of their households, left the salon of the First Consul and entered the hall of Marshals, an usher announced: " The Emperor ! " and the orchestra began the air of Queen Hortense: *Partant pour la Syrie*. The sovereign wore the uniform of a general of division, white knee breeches and silk stockings. The Empress, in dazzling toilet, wore on head, arms, and neck the finest diamonds of the crown. Their Majesties always opened the ball by a quadrille of honor, in which age did not prevent great personages from figuring, and which was danced in the hall of the Marshals. Before withdrawing, the Emperor and Empress passed through this hall and the gallery of Peace, where dancing was likewise going on, stopping here and there before those to whom they wished to speak. Splendidly lighted, the château presented a magnificent appearance, but it was not well adapted to this kind of festivities; the apartments of the Empress not being open to the guests, there was no egress by way of the salon of the First Consul, the salon of Apollo, the throne-room, and the salon of Louis XIV., and it was not easy to make one's way to the gallery of Diana, where supper was taken standing. I remember what pains were taken by the chamberlains to avoid a crush at the entrance of this gallery. But these grand balls at the Tuileries were State ceremonies, more pompous than elegant. Two, much more select, were given on the 15th and the 22d of January.

The Emperor opened the session in the hall of Marshals, February 16. The speech from the throne was essentially pacific. The sovereign declared that as the best intelligence prevailed among all the great powers, it became a duty to labor in earnest for the development of the forces and riches of the nation. He said: "Although the moral amelioration and the material welfare of the greater number is the aim towards which civilization tends, yet we must not forget that it marches like an army. Its victories are never obtained without victims and sacrifices. These rapid means which facilitate communication, displace interests and throw into the background countries which do not yet possess them; these useful machines which multiply the labor of man set him aside in the first instance and for the moment leave many hands idle; these mines which circulate throughout the world a quantity of specie hitherto unknown, this increase of public wealth which increases consumption tenfold, tend to vary and to raise the value of all things; this inexhaustible source of riches which is called credit, begets wonders, and yet exaggerated speculation entails many individual ruins. Thence arises the necessity of coming to the aid of those who cannot keep up with the accelerated march of progress, and yet to do so without retarding progress. Some must be stimulated, others moderated; we must nourish the activity of this breathless, unquiet, unreasonable society which in France expects everything from government, and which, nevertheless, must be confronted with the limits of the possible and the calculations of reason."

This session was the last of the legislature. In his speech from the throne Napoleon III. thanked the deputies for the active assistance they had given him since 1852. He ended with words expressive of joy and confidence: " Strong in the concurrence of the great bodies of State and the devotion of the army, strong above all in the support of the people, who know that all my time is devoted to their interests, I anticipate a hopeful future for our country. France, without interfering with the rights of any one, has resumed her fitting rank in the world, and may now securely abandon herself to all that the genius of peace produces. May God not weary of protecting her, and then that may soon be said of her which was written of the Consulate by a statesman who was also an illustrious and national historian: 'Satisfaction was general and all who were free from the evil passions of parties rejoiced at the public power.'"

This homage rendered to M. Thiers was regarded as a signal of conciliation in matters of internal policy, and many even imagined that the minister of Louis Philippe would become that of Napoleon III. Parties continued to disarm, and the Emperor, at the summit of his desires, enjoyed a situation possibly unique in the world. What would it have cost him to maintain it? Simply to resist the impulse to adventures and always to preserve peace.

CHAPTER XVI

A BALL AT THE FOREIGN AFFAIRS

NAPOLEON III. passed from grave to gay. Monday, February 16, 1857, he had inaugurated the legislative session in the majestic apparel of sovereignty. The next day, Tuesday, February 17, hidden beneath the folds of a long domino, he was present at a fancy ball at the Ministry of Foreign Affairs.

France never amuses herself well except when victorious. For her, glory must walk hand in hand with pleasure. One may say that since her disasters she has not had one whole day of real gaiety. If all classes of Parisian society were full of animation and vivacity in 1857, it is because the country had nothing but successes at that time. Our misfortunes have made us serious. Masks and disguises would no longer be suitable in official society. For such diversions a young sovereign and a triumphant France would be required.

Nowadays the slightest acts and doings of fashionable people are recorded with the most minute details in the most important Parisian journals. The mania for publicity has assumed strange proportions.

It was otherwise at the beginning of the Second Empire. The rubric now designated under the new name of *mondanités* did not exist in the journals of Paris, and it was in the correspondence of Brussels newspapers, the *Indépendance Belge* and the *Nord* that one looked for the echoes of magnificent fêtes which, if they occurred to-day, would fill the columns of all the Parisian journals with descriptions.

After forty years, from 1857 to 1897, I remember the ball I am going to describe as if it had been given yesterday, so powerfully did the radiant images of the women who shone there impress my imagination.

I seem to perceive at the entrance of the salon, since occupied by a large picture representing the plenipotentiaries of the Congress of Paris, now replaced by a Gobelins tapestry after Rubens, the Count Walewski, Minister of Foreign Affairs, in the costume of a statesman of the old régime — the coat black velvet, ornamented with jet and a blue ribbon. Opposite the minister, and like him receiving the guests, appears the Countess Walewska, delightful as a Diana, the huntress of a Louis XV. ballet, a diamond crescent on her forehead, bow in hand, a tiger skin on her shoulders and a quiver filled with golden arrows.

The salons glitter with a thousand lights. All the greenhouses of Paris have been stripped to adorn them with flowers. The *coup d'œil* is fairylike. What a bevy of pretty women! Here is the Princess Mathilde, superb in blue damask; the Princess Joachim Murat as a marquise of the old court, in a robe of white damask ornamented with diamonds and roses. Princess Czartoryska, daughter of Queen Christina of Spain and the Duke de Rianzarès, as a citizeness of the times of Louis XVI., with a Necker bonnet; the quite young and charming Spanish ambassadress Maréchale Serrano (since Duchess de la Torre), in a Middle Age costume, high robe and a large cross on the breast; Madame Fleury, wife of the general, a grave and severe beauty, as a court lady of Marie Antoinette, in a flowered gown with immense paniers, hair dressed very high and powdered and surmounted with large plumes; Madame Taigny as a bat, in pearl gray; Mademoiselle Louise Magnan, daughter of the Marshal of France, master of the hounds, in a hunting habit of the time of Louis XV.; Lady Cowley, English ambassadress, in Queen Anne costume, Princess Callimaki in that of Maria de' Medicis; Baroness Seebach, daughter of Chancellor Nesselrode, wife of the minister of Saxony at Paris, as a Russian boyard of the time of Peter the Great, with a cloth-of-gold robe heavily furred and a profusion of jewels.

The majority of the ministers, generals, diplomats, and high functionaries are in black coats and knee breeches, with the Venetian mantle. A certain number of men are in domino. Some whose figure and appearance bear some resemblance to those of the

Emperor, flatter themselves as likely to be mistaken for him. Among the young men in costume I distinguish Count Olympe Aguado as a Wallachian; M. de Chassiron as a minion of the court of Henry III.; M. Albert de Vatimesnil in a Charles IX. dress, violet and gold doublet and a plumed toque; Count Armand (since minister of France at Lisbon) is very elegant in the uniform of a musketeer of the Louis XV. period; Vicomte de Bresson (since minister of France at Belgrade) has taken a Spanish costume in memory of his uncle, ambassador of Louis Philippe at Madrid.

One of the women most admired is the daughter of the Marquis du Hallay-Coëtquen, the young and superb Countess de Brigode (now the widow of her second husband Baron de Poilly). Her costume is most original and picturesque, that of an Indian equestrienne: corsage red morocco, covered with pearls and glass beads of different colors, skirts of gauze embroidered with foliage and flowers, mingled with gold and silver threads and fringed with feathers. This bizarre costume is completed by a panther's head and skin. Above the forehead of the amazon appears this head with green eyes the color of her own. On every side escape the long black tresses of the Countess, whose superb figure is deformed by the skin of the ferocious beast.

A woman has just entered the ballroom, and all eyes are presently concentrated on her. It is the Countess de Castiglione, the most fashionable of the reigning beauties. For a year society has been talking of her. Henry de Pène wrote in the *Nord*, in February, 1856 : " Decidedly, the queen of the season has been appointed. It is that incomparable beauty sent us by Italy, Madame the Countess de Castiglione. *The Italian woman in Paris*, such is the title of a symphony chanted by admiration from morning to night and from night to morning. Every one seeks to outvie his neighbor in praising her profile, her hair, her eyes; and, supreme consecration of her royalty, she already has enemies."

Virginia Oldoïni, Countess Vérasis de Castiglione, was born in Florence in 1840. She belongs to one of the best families in the city of the Medici. She lost her mother early, and her father, the Marquis Oldoïni, a mere embassy attaché when he became a widower, afterwards attained the highest grades of the diplomatic career. He was for a long time minister of Italy at Lisbon. Through her mother, Virginia Oldoïni is the granddaughter of the great Tuscan jurisconsult, Antonio Lamporecchi. It was in his palace on the banks of the Arno at Florence that her earliest years were spent. While yet a child her charms made her famous in Florentine society. By the time she was thirteen she had a box of her own at the Pergola and her private carriage at the Cascine. When barely fifteen she married a Piedmontese, Count Vérasis de Castiglione, who became equerry to King Victor Emmanuel. She has excited general enthusiasm in Turin, London, and

Paris. Count Henri d'Ideville has said of her in his *Journal d'un Diplomate:* "It is agreed that she is marvellously beautiful; but I would boldly affirm in addition that she surpasses many women by a superiority of intelligence and character which in no wise yields to that superiority of grace, elegance, and beauty, which each of them concedes to her." In the preface of this book an academician, M. Edouard Hervé, describes her as follows: "A woman whose beauty Greece would have divinized, and who would have been reserved as a model for a Phidias or a Praxiteles; an antique marble which has wandered into our profane century."

The Countess is not lavish of herself. She seldom appears in society. Whenever she does so it is an event. Behold her entering the salons of the Ministry of Foreign Affairs in the middle of the fête. She is dressed as the queen of hearts, a symbolic costume, for it is an allusion to the innumerable hearts which the Countess "draws after her," as Racine would have said. On her head glitters a crown formed of hearts. Her marvellous hair ripples around her forehead and falls in cascades on her neck. Her skirts and corsage are laced with chains composed of hearts. Her train is caught up on the hip. 'Tis a bewitching costume.

Who is this rag-picker whose extreme elegance causes a sensation? Oh the charming costume! Knee breeches of white satin; flesh-colored silk stockings; a vest also of white satin spangled with gold suns and hearts; a black velvet mask on the face; on the head a policeman's cap adorned with a string of diamonds; a basket of gilded osier on the back containing bouquets of gardenias and white camellias which the gallant rag-picker distributes to the ladies as he passes; in the right hand a silver hook, in the left a lighted lantern whose glass door bears in colors the blazon: "Hearts and suns." This is the lantern of Diogenes. The rag-picker sees a blue domino who is walking slowly. He recognizes the Emperor by his figure, and going up to him he says: "I am looking for a man; I have found him," and he extinguishes his lantern. This amiable rag-picker is a young diplomate, Count Amelot de Chaillou, whose career has since been brilliant, and who has been minister of France, first at Buenos Ayres, where he adopted the niece of a cacique who had been made a prisoner of war and whose tribe had been nearly destroyed, and afterwards at Brazil, where the Emperor Dom Pedro treated him as a friend.

The two persons of whom every one is chiefly thinking at the ball are those one does not see but whom each tries to discover under their sheltering dominos. Count Amelot de Chaillou has recognized the Emperor. But where is the Empress?

Two women in dominos are seated on a bench in the middle of the salon beside the ballroom which ends in the supper room. I approach these women. The sound of their voices is familiar to me and reveals their identity. One is the sovereign, the other

her lady of the palace, the beautiful Countess Gustave de Montebello, wife of the Emperor's aide-de-camp. I am dressed as a page of Marie Antoinette, and they are the functions of a page with which the Empress has the kindness to invest me. She charges me to seek out the persons with whom she wishes to speak, among others General Canrobert in domino, and an envoy of the Bey of Tunis wearing a very correct costume as an Arab chief. This was General Kherédine, who afterwards entered the service of the Sultan and became his Grand Vizier. Towards the close of the evening the two dominos disappeared without my having the indiscretion to follow them.

A little later, when the majority of the guests had gone into the supper room, I saw two mysterious women drawing near the table where people supped standing. One of them had discarded her domino and wore a delightful Bohemian costume. The mask which hid the lower part of her face did not altogether conceal her glowing beauty. Impossible to dream of a more graceful gait, a finer figure, eyes more sparkling. The Empress — for it was she — seeing that I recognized her, asked if I belonged to the Inquisition. I replied that the inquisitors made their neighbors tremble, while for my part I was trembling before her. Her Majesty deigned to reassure me by some kindly words, and asked by what means I came to recognize her. I said that it was by her fan, "a talisman," I added, "who knows; perhaps a sceptre; in any case, that of beauty."

CHAPTER XVII

THE GRAND DUKE CONSTANTINE AND THE KING
OF BAVARIA

IN the spring of 1857 Napoleon III. received a visit to which great importance was rightfully attached, for it was the prelude and the pledge of a definitive reconciliation between the French and the Russians. His guest was the Grand Duke Constantine, brother of Czar Alexander II. Born September 9, 1827, Constantine Nicolaievitch, grand admiral of Russia, a prince of lofty intelligence, was an ardent patriot. Having enthusiastically approved the orthodox zeal and the warlike policy of his father, the Emperor Nicholas, he was bent on carrying the war in the Crimea to extremities so long as hostilities were in progress. His arrival in Paris was the beginning of a new era.

The Grand Duke arrived at Toulon April 20, on the steam frigate *Olaff*, accompanied by the screw-steamer *Wiborg* and two frigates. The French squadron of evolution, commanded by Vice-Admiral Tréhouart, was ranged in two lines in the roadstead traversed by the Russian squadron. Sailors standing in the yards saluted the passage of the Grand Duke, who was also greeted by a volley of artillery from all the French vessels. As soon as the *Olaff* was moored to the new chain at the entry of the arsenal, Vice-Admirals Tréhouart and Dubourdieu went aboard the Russian frigate to pay their respects to the Grand Duke, who afterwards landed at the arsenal, where he reviewed the naval troops. The next day he visited all the vessels of the French squadron. April 23, he was present, with the officers of the French squadron, at a ball given in his honor by the maritime prefect. April 25, he visited the arsenal and went aboard the *Suffren*, a school ship of naval cannoneers, where all the school exercises and some firing with solid shot were performed in his presence. April 26, he heard Mass on board the *Wiborg*. On that day the officers of the French marine gave the officers of the Russian marine a dinner on board the *Bretagne*, the admiral's ship. The 27th, the Grand Duke went by post to Marseilles. Returning to Toulon the following day he embarked on the French despatch boat, the *Eclaireur*, placed at his disposal to witness the launching of a packet belonging to the Imperial Messageries.

The Grand Duke reached Paris at five o'clock on the last day of April. Prince Napoleon was awaiting him at the Gare de Lyon, which was draped with French and Russian colors. One of the halls had been arranged as a reception room, and its benches were occupied by a large number of ladies, the majority of whom belonged to high Russian society. The Grand Duke was welcomed by Marshal Magnan, the prefect of the Seine, the prefect of police, General Luders, Count Kisseleff the Russian ambassador, the minister of Würtemberg, and all the personnel of their legations. The double row was formed by a battalion of grenadiers of the guard and another of the line. The Grand Duke, accompanied by Prince Napoleon, entered a carriage drawn by four horses. The cortege, escorted by two squadrons of the regiment of guides, crossed the boulevards, the rue de la Paix, the rue de Rivoli, passed beneath the arch of the Carrousel, and arrived at the Tuileries between a double line formed by a battalion of gendarmerie of the guard. Awaiting the Grand Duke at the head of the staircase of honor, the Emperor received him most graciously and led him into the salon where the Empress was. In the evening the Prince dined at the table of Their Majesties with all the members of his suite. Count Kisseleff, Prince Tolstoy, secretary of the Russian embassy, and Colonel Albedinski, were also present at the dinner.

The Grand Duke visited the Louvre, May 2. In the museum of sovereigns he examined carefully the objects which had belonged to Charlemagne, Saint Louis, Anne of Brittany, Francis I., Henry II., Henry III., Henry IV. He seemed especially captivated by the camp bed of Napoleon, his little hat, and his gray overcoat. In the naval museum, which he visited last, he found occasion to display the extent of his naval acquirements. In the evening he was present at a ball at the Ministry of Marine, where he made the round of the salons with the Princess Mathilde on his arm.

The Grand Duke remained in Paris until the 14th of May. On the 6th he was entertained at the Hôtel de Ville by the municipal council, who offered him what was called a *restricted fête*, the Emperor having decided that the city should reserve all great fêtes for crowned heads, with the exception of those motived by some national ceremony. On the 11th he accompanied the imperial family to Fontainebleau, where they remained until the evening of the Grand Duke's departure from Paris.

The visit of the Grand Duke Constantine was immediately succeeded by that of Maximilian II., King of Bavaria. At that time the minister of France at Munich was the Baron de Méneval, son of the secretary of Napoleon I. The Baron, who soon afterwards renounced the diplomatic career in order to become a priest, had written to Count Walewski, January 28, 1857: " I am well aware, although Baron Von der Pfordten has not yet officially apprised me of it, that it is King Maximilian's greatest desire to spend some weeks in Paris during the coming month of May. A person whose position and close connection with the court of Bavaria are such as to make him cognizant of the King's sentiments has confided this desire to me, adding that His Majesty would probably not return to Munich without gratifying an old inclination to go and offer the Emperor the homage of his respectful sympathy."

May 12, Baron de Méneval said in another despatch: "Public attention and interest are directed toward the stay the King intends to make in Paris. Pride and sensitiveness, the two dominant passions of the German character, are, I must say, somewhat preoccupied with the reception awaiting the King at the Imperial court, as well as with the impression he may produce there. The public, and above all the Bavarian court, view with some apprehension the approach of King Maximilian to that dazzling scene where he will be confronted with the splendor and grandeur surrounding the throne and the person of our Emperor. For my own part, I am convinced that the result of this visit will be satisfactory, and that it will leave the best and most satisfactory impressions on the mind of the King. France, in fact, can but win increasing confidence and admiration in Europe, by offering to foreign sovereigns the noble and cordial hospitality for which they are so eager and so grateful."

Born September 28, 1802, Maximilian II. was the eldest son of King Louis II. He was the pupil of Schelling. In consequence of his father's abdication he ascended the throne March 21, 1848. Well versed himself in philosophical studies, he protected letters and the sciences. In 1842 he had married a Prussian Princess, Marie, daughter of William, uncle of Frederic William IV., King of Prussia. He was the brother of Otho, King of Greece.

Maximilian II. arrived at Lyons, at the Gare de Perrache, at half-past six in the evening of May 15. Twenty-one discharges of cannon were fired as he left the station. Troops of all arms formed a double line from the station to the Hotel de l'Europe where the King was to alight. Marshal Castellane, commander-in-chief of the army of Lyons, rode at the right side of his carriage. Generals Count Partouneaux and Luzy-Bouat succeeded each other at the left accordingly as the King passed in front of their respective divisions.

Marshal Castellane wrote in his journal: "The King of Bavaria is about five feet four inches in height. He is learned and obliging; he says amiable things. He is fond of the arts. He is the grandson of King Maximilian I., who, under the name of Prince Max, commanded the foreign regiment of the Deux-Ponts in the service of France under Louis XVI."

To receive the Bavarian sovereign Napoleon III. had sent to Lyons his aide-de-camp, General Baron de Béville, his equerry Count de Riencourt, and Count Charles Tascher de La Pagerie, first chamberlain of the Empress. Concerning the latter Marshal Castellane adds: "Count Charles de La Pagerie, son of the grand master of the Empress's household, is a man of forty-five; he was educated in Bavaria, where he has been a page. He is an excellent man."

On the 17th the King left Lyons for Paris. Just as he was about entering the train, the Marshal presented to him the generals, who, after he had passed in front of their brigades, had all gone to the station. The King was amiable to each of them, and said he should never forget the attentions paid him at Lyons.

We have said that the Grand Duke Constantine left Fontainebleau the 14th of May. The Emperor and Empress had remained there to await the King of Bavaria, who was expected on the 17th. There was a hunting party in the forest on the 16th, but Napoleon III. was not present. Having learned that the health of Senator Vieillard, one of his oldest friends, was causing great anxiety, he took the first train, accompanied only by General de Montebello, and went in a cab from the Lyons station to the house of the man whom he had loved from childhood. He profited also by this circumstance to bid another farewell to the Grand Duke Constantine, who was to go away that evening.

The King of Bavaria arrived at Fontainebleau at six o'clock in the evening. He was received at the station by Marshal Magnan, General Fleury, the prefect of Seine-and-Marne, and the general commanding the department. Several court carriages awaited the sovereign and his suite. A squadron of chasseurs of the guard formed the escort. In the court of the Cheval-Blanc, also called the court of the Adieux, a battalion of grenadiers of the guard formed a double line. A detachment of hundred-guards was drawn up on the steps of the horseshoe staircase. Followed by the officers of his household, the Emperor went to the foot of the stairs to receive the King. The Empress with all her ladies stood at the top. The presentations were made in the gallery of Francis I., and the dinner served in the gallery of Henry III., decorated with the frescoes of Primaticcio.

May 18. Napoleon III. and the King of Bavaria got into a small carriage which the Emperor himself drove, and visited the environs. On the same day some invited guests from Paris came to spend a week at the château. In the evening the actors of the Comédie-Française played the *Bataille de Dames*, by Scribe and Legouvé. Many invitations for this representation had been sent out to the principal functionaries and notabilities of the city, as well as to the officers of the garrison. The next morning the Emperor presided at a ministerial council. In the afternoon he went out for a drive with the King of Bavaria in a wagonette. The Dowager Grand Duchess of Baden, the Princess Marie, Duchess of Hamilton, and all the other guests, took a long stroll in the forest. In the evening, the Emperor offered to his royal guest a night fête, which was enchanting. At ten o'clock, thousands of Bengal lights illuminated the English garden and lighted up the entire architecture of the palace. The lake was furrowed by boats draped with flags and ornamented with colored lamps. Choruses from the Opéra, placed in the little pavilion in the middle of the lake, alternated with the band of the grenadiers of the guard. A display of fireworks composed by Ruggieri, the pieces of which were wafted just above the level of the water before the final bouquet, brought to a close an entertainment which had been favored by splendid weather.

May 24. The Emperor, the Empress, and the King of Bavaria heard Mass in the chapel of the château. Afterwards they started for Paris, where they were received at the Gare de Lyon by Prince Napoleon, who had returned the day before from Germany. The King dined in the apartments he occupied in the pavilion of Marsan.

May 27. The King received the diplomatic corps in his apartments at the Tuileries. In the evening the Emperor gave a grand dinner, after which the Bavarian sovereign went to the Opéra, where they were playing the *Trouvère*. On the 29th he visited the tomb of Napoleon, the church of Sainte Clotilde and the Sainte-Chapelle. In the evening he was present at a representation at the Gymnase.

May 31. Baron de Méneval wrote from Munich to Count Walewski: " The welcome which the King of Bavaria is now receiving in France, the attentions of which he is the recipient at the hands of the Emperor, touch both the heart and the vanity of his subjects very sensibly. I am perfectly convinced that his sojourn in Paris will greatly heighten the personal esteem and consideration in which he is

L

held by the Bavarians. The splendor which surrounds the Emperor, the admiration felt for him by his friends as well as by his enemies in Germany, the high idea generally entertained of his character and his judgment, do in fact give infinite value to the kindliness with which he receives, and seem to heighten the merit of the Prince who is now his guest. I meet no one who is not effusive to me concerning the magnificent and cordial welcome which the King is receiving in Paris. I know that he is himself profoundly affected by it, and that his letters to the Queen are filled with gratitude towards the Emperor. The effect produced upon him by this journey will, I think, be lasting, and I congratulate myself on having contributed to inspire him with the idea."

June 2, in honor of his guest, the Emperor reviewed eight regiments of cavalry and six mounted batteries on the grounds of the hippodrome at Longchamps. The Empress and the Dowager Grand Duchess of Baden appeared in an open calash in front of the troops. The following day, the King visited Versailles, dined at Paris with the Bavarian minister, Baron Wendland, and went to the Porte Saint-Martin.

June 4, the Emperor held another review at the hippodrome of Longchamps in presence of the King. The troops were infantry, engineers, and a regiment of the foot artillery of the guard. After the evolutions, the two sovereigns went over in front of the tribunes, where the Empress had just made her appearance. The King dined with Their Majesties at the château of Saint-Cloud, and chatted in the most gracious manner with all the courtiers. He charged the Marquise de Contades to remember him kindly to her father, Marshal Castellane, and told her and her sister, the Countess Hatzfeldt, wife of the Prussian minister, that he had been much pleased at Lyons, where he had bought some beautiful stuffs for the Queen. On the 8th of the month he left Paris to return to his dominions. On the 17th, Baron de Méneval addressed the following despatch to Count Walewski: "The King retains the profoundest and most grateful memory of his stay at Fontainebleau and at Paris. Although it is a custom at the Bavarian court that foreign ministers never obtain audience of the King except to present their credentials or cabinet communications, His Majesty has nevertheless chosen to depart from this etiquette, very rigorously observed in other cases, in order to express to me in person the gratitude and admiration inspired in him by the welcome of Their Imperial Majesties. The King sent for me to come to his cabinet this morning, and very kindly described to me, in the greatest detail, the different episodes of his sojourn in France. He spoke with genuine enthusiasm of the grandeur and splendor which environ the throne of the Emperor, of the nobility of his character, the dignity of his person, and the affability of his manners. His Majesty's praises of the kindliness and beauty of the Empress were inexhaustible.

"'Your Emperor,' he said to me, 'is not merely the greatest sovereign of Europe, he is also the best of men. I have had long and interesting conversations with him, and consequently I have had occasion to appreciate the kindness of his heart and the sureness of his judgment. I love him as much as I admire him, and I have the utmost confidence in the loftiness of his character and the nobility of his sentiments.'

"To receive me, the King had put on the insignia of the order of the Legion of Honor, a thing he has done for no one else, which he told me had been conferred by the Emperor in person."

At this period, the relations of France with all the Germanic states, without exception, were intimate. Napoleon by no means suspected that Germany, whose language he spoke so well, whose literature he admired so much, for which he had such a genuine sympathy, so real a predilection, and whose sovereigns showed him so great a deference, would one day, through a grievous and terrible misunderstanding, become so fatal to him and to France.

CHAPTER XVIII

PRINCE NAPOLEON IN GERMANY

IN 1857, Napoleon III. was endeavoring to conciliate Russia, Prussia, and the secondary states of Germany, which he wished to detach from Austria in anticipation of the day when he would have to fight against that power and make war in Italy. He sent Prince Napoleon as an official envoy to Berlin and Dresden at the very time when the Grand Duke Constantine and the King of Bavaria were receiving a brilliant and cordial welcome at the Court of the Tuileries.

From the time when he left France, Prince Napoleon maintained an irreproachable attitude. No more paradoxical tirades, no more audacious theories, no further trace of the demagogue or the tribune. The former member of the extreme left disappeared. Nothing remained but the great noble, the imperial highness, the son and grandson of kings. In every foreign court where he appeared during the reign of his cousin his success was complete.

Leaving Paris May 7, 1857, the Prince arrived the same day at Cologne. At Magdeburg he abandoned the strict incognito until then preserved. The reception given him in the latter city was splendid. General de Brandt and Major de Treskow, attached to his person during his stay in Prussia, were awaiting him there; the first had served with distinction in Spain in the armies of Napoleon I., and the second had made several campaigns in Algeria with the French troops.

The Prince arrived in Berlin May 8. He was received at the station by Prince George of Prussia, Princes August and William of Würtemberg, Prince William of Baden, Marquis de Moustier, minister of France, and the personnel of the legation. On his way to the king's palace he was received with respectful sympathy by the crowds encumbering the public thoroughfare. According to the programme, King Frederic William IV. was to come at seven o'clock in the evening from Charlottenberg to Berlin to await there the visit of his guest. But by a very flattering change in this arrangement, the sovereign, forestalling the cousin of Napoleon III., took him by surprise and remained with him for a quarter of an hour. This call was immediately returned, and the French Prince was presented by the King to the Queen and the princesses of the royal family.

At half-past eight in the evening Frederic William IV. appeared in his box at the opera with Prince Napoleon on his right, and presented him, in a way, to the select audience crowding the theatre. The next day, in honor of his guest, the sovereign reviewed the guard in Unter den Linden. He gave the Prince the left, that is to say, the side next the troops. The weather was fine. A prodigious crowd kept up a constant series of acclamations.

At four o'clock the King offered the Prince a military banquet to which all the generals and superior officers were invited. The service of honor was magnificent. The great officers of the crown fulfilled the duties of their charge, and the pupils of the military school, dressed in the traditional page's costume, waited on the princes and princesses. At dessert Frederic William IV. drank to the health *of the French Prince*, adding: "I desire that the illustrious family to which he belongs may long be the prosperity of France, and that this great nation may always remain the friend of Prussia." In the evening all the Court were present at a representation of *Ferdinand Cortez* at the opera.

On Sunday, May 10, Prince Napoleon attended Mass at the Catholic church, where the grand master of ceremonies awaited him. He afterwards received the diplomatic corps at the palace, and also Baron von Humboldt, to whom he showed the greatest deference. There was a gala dinner that night at the royal palace in Charlottenberg; the Prince wore the broad ribbon of the Black Eagle, which the King had sent him during the day. He would have liked to spend the evening in his own apartments; but it was hinted that this would be a disappointment to Berlin society, who had come in a body to the opera house, hoping to see him. He complied with a good grace and occupied the little royal box in company with the Prince of Prussia, the future Emperor William. The ballet of *Saltanella* was given.

May 11, Prince Napoleon went to visit Potsdam. The garrison, under command of Prince Frederic Charles, was drawn up in the grand court. The French Prince paid a respectful visit to the tomb of Frederic the Great. The man in charge of it had known the Prussian hero; it was he who had opened the vault for Napoleon I. in 1806, and now in 1857 he led thither the nephew of the victor of Jena, the vanquished of Waterloo. The Prince went subsequently to meditate at Sans-Souci, in the room where Frederic the Great breathed his last, and which has been religiously preserved in the condition it was in at that moment. At the New Castle, the Princess had him shown the study of the great man, his military maps, his books, all of them French, his autographs, and his verses annotated by Voltaire. On his return to Berlin, the whole population seemed to have turned out into the streets; the approaches to the railway station and the palace were thronged. The Prince, in full uniform, seated in an open carriage, passed through the crowd and was greeted with continuous acclamations. Old men who had witnessed the entry of Napoleon I. into Berlin were amazed at the resemblance existing between the uncle and the nephew. In the evening there was a ball at the mansion of the French legation, at which the King and all the royal family were present.

The future Emperor William showed the utmost attention to the cousin of Napoleon III. One might say he did him the honors of the Prussian army during the manœuvres, which lasted at least four hours, and seemed greatly flattered when, on May 13, the Prince sent him, in the name of the Emperor of the French, the broad ribbon of the Legion of Honor.

Marquis de Moustier wrote to Count Walewski: "The Prince of Prussia has received the grand cordon of the Legion of Honor with unmistakable marks of sincere satisfaction. Both he and the King wore the insignia at the dinner which he gave to His Imperial Highness, and when I was taking my leave he deigned to make some very enthusiastic remarks on the pleasure it had given him to be present at my ball and to receive me in his own house, and congratulating himself on the fortunate circumstances which had permitted him to deviate in that particular from the too rigid etiquette of the court."

Prince Napoleon left Berlin May 14, after having sent to Baron Humboldt the cross of a grand officer of the Legion of Honor. The Prince and the King parted with expressions of the utmost cordiality. In a despatch of May 15, addressed to Count Walewski, the Marquis de Moustier expressed himself as follows: "Prince Napoleon has left the most favorable impression here, and in all that he has done has given evidence of a tact, a moderation, and an acquaintance with the court of Prussia which might have disarmed the most persistent ill-will, could any such have been evinced in presence of the royal family. The *Gazette de la Croix* has not found a word to say, and, in an article which has made a sensation, it has paid tardy but surprising justice to the wisdom and skill of the Emperor's policy and to the high position he has achieved in Turkey. However, it insisted on proving that the visit of the Prince was wholly one of courtesy and had no political importance."

From Berlin Prince Napoleon went to Dresden, where the court of Saxony gave him as brilliant a reception as the court of Prussia. The Saxon sovereign at the time was King John, a very learned and enlightened monarch, the author of a fine translation into German of Dante's *Divine Comedy*, and the husband of the Princess Amelia of Bavaria. Prince Napoleon enjoyed himself greatly in Dresden. May 15, he visited the battlefield near the city with the Prince-royal, grand-nephew of the faithful ally of Napoleon I. He spent the evening with the Queen Dowager, the reigning Queen, and the Archduchess Sophia, mother of the Emperor of Austria. May 16, he went to Pilnitz to wish the King many happy returns of his birthday, and then went with him to Moritzburg, a hunting-seat three leagues from Dresden, built on a most picturesque site in the midst of the woods by the Elector Augustus, King of Poland. After a dinner served to the accompaniment of hunting-horns they went to a clearing in the forest to behold a curious spectacle: herds of stags, bucks, and wild boars coming freely from their haunts in the woods to take the food distributed to them daily at a given hour.

May 17, the Prince heard Mass in the Catholic church. The reigning family of Saxony is Catholic. The music in the king's chapel is admirable. During the day the Prince received the diplomatic corps and the Saxon Chevaliers of the Legion of Honor, all of whom had served in the armies of Napoleon I. In the evening he dined with Baron Forth Rouen, minister of France. May 18, he visited the battlefield of Lutzen, and supped in the evening at the French legation in company with Herr von Beust, who, after having been president of the ministerial council of Saxony, passed, some years later, into the service of Austria, where he became chancellor of the empire. May 19, the Prince quitted Dresden. On the 24th he was in Paris.

The reception given by the Germans to the nephew of Napoleon I. proved that an agreement might exist between them and the French. Germany experienced a feeling of mingled love and hatred toward the great Emperor. So colossal, so poetic, so marvellous a figure as that of the conqueror had profoundly impressed the German imagination. It is a German, Heinrich Heine, who is the author of the *Two Grenadiers*, probably the most beautiful of all the poems inspired by the Napoleonic epic. It was of Napoleon that Germany could say : —

    Tu domines notre âge ; ange ou démon, qu'importe?
    Ton aigle dans son vol haletant nous emporte.

L'œil même qui te fuit te retrouve partout.
Toujours dans nos tableaux tu jettes ta grande ombre.
Toujours Napoléon, éblouissant et sombre,
   Sur le seuil du siècle est debout.[1]

It was he who had been the protector of the Confederation of the Rhine; he who had set the royal crown on the heads of the electors of Bavaria, Würtemberg, and Saxony; he who had struck the most redoubtable blows at Germanic feudalism; he who, possibly without being aware of it, had been one of the chief promoters of German unity. Before fighting against Napoleon the Germans had served gloriously under his banners, and taken part in nearly all his victories. Hence they recalled the Napoleonic epopee with pride, and all who had formed part of his armies had eagerly claimed the medal of Saint Helena which Napoleon III. had instituted.

More than one family tie existed between the second Emperor and the German sovereigns. Prince Eugène de Beauharnais, brother of Queen Hortense, had married a daughter of the first King of Bavaria. The Dowager Grand Duchess of Baden was a Beauharnais, the adopted daughter of Napoleon I. Jerome Bonaparte, former King of Westphalia, was the widower of a daughter of the first King of Würtemberg.

Was a definitive reconciliation, a sincere union,

---

[1] Thou swayest our age; angel or demon, what matters it? — Thine eagle in its breathless flight bears us along. — The eye that shuns thee finds thee everywhere. — Ever thou dost cast thy great shadow in our pictures. — Ever Napoleon, splendid and gloomy, — Stands on the threshold of our century.

impossible between imperial France and Germany? We do not think so. What would have been required to bring about a result so desirable for the general interests of civilization? It would have been necessary that, loyal to the principle of nationalities, Napoleon III. should declare in a formal and categoric manner that he was irrevocably resolved not to dispute with Germany the possession of the Rhine provinces, countries especially German. He ought also to have given pledges to the secondary states. He was too much preoccupied with Prussia, where he was always deceived, and too little with Bavaria, Saxony, and the Grand Duchy of Hesse, whose statesmen would gratefully have accepted the encouragement and moral support of France in their resistance to the ambitious and encroaching policy of Prussia. Napoleon III. committed the great fault of neglecting these lesser states, which one day were to be so fatal to him, and which he might so easily have conciliated if he had convinced them of his desire to respect their territories, and, at need, to defend their rights. Unfortunately, instead of pursuing this policy, in which he would have gained the sympathies of Russia, he left his intentions under a cloud of suspicions and misunderstandings which his enemies turned to their own advantage, and which ended in making possible an improbable alliance between Prussia and those lesser states which she coveted.

In 1857, nobody dreamed of such a contingency.

After his return to France, Prince Napoleon talked at length to the Emperor concerning his journey to Berlin and Dresden. Both were equally well satisfied with it. Each was well acquainted with and fond of Germany, whose language they spoke as fluently as French, and where they had acquired part of their education. Both believed that the Rhine could flow peacefully between peoples whose mutual prosperity would be a pledge of concord and prosperity for the entire world.

This justice must be rendered Prince Napoleon, that he always remained opposed to the idea of a rupture between France and Germany. Perhaps, if he had been in Paris in 1870, the war would not have been declared. As to Napoleon III., if in 1857 he was dreaming of making war on Austria in order to render Italy free from the Alps to the Adriatic, it may be affirmed that a war against Prussia and the secondary German states never entered his thoughts. It was fatality which dragged him into it thirteen years later.

CHAPTER XIX

THE INTERNAL SITUATION

THE internal situation of France was almost the same in 1857 as at the beginning of the Second Empire. Although deprived of power, the old parties had retained their convictions and few new adhesions were effected, but the very great majority of the country remained faithful to Napoleon III. The alliance between the government and the clergy continued to be close. The Emperor took good care not to allow his Italian schemes to be suspected. Interests were secured, and, with the exception of certain more than usually perspicacious minds, no one anticipated the adventures and complications of the future.

All honest republicans disavowed the criminal plans of Mazzini and his adepts. Drawing back, and taking care not to foment troubles, they awaited events.

The legitimist party remained passive in the majesty of its principles. Count de Chambord had been guilty of the error of forbidding all legitimists to take the oath to the Empire, thus excluding them from political life, where they might have gained experience and qualified themselves for important parts. It is not easy to understand how a prince who had permitted his adherents to take the oath to Louis Philippe had forbidden them to take it to Napoleon III., closing thus all access to public functions or legislative duties, and converting them, as one might say, into stay-at-home emigrants. This unfortunate decision had annihilated the legitimist party, if not from the social, at least from the political, point of view.

Moreover, up to the time of the Italian War, Count de Chambord did not criticise the ideas of the Emperor, which would have been his own had he reigned. The Constitution of 1852 pleased him; he would willingly have appropriated it to the shadow of the white flag. He said that he had decided to maintain universal suffrage, and he did not think it unwise for France to subject itself to a press law more rigorous than that which had been, if not the cause, at least the pretext, of the Revolution of 1830.

Let us add that the abandonment of the projects of fusion between the elder and the younger branch of the Bourbons had divided the royalist party against itself and thrown it into confusion. The Duchess of Orleans had not thought herself authorized to pledge the future of her young son. Legitimists and Orleanists retained their political convictions and their distinctive tendencies.

It was chiefly among the former adherents of Louis Philippe that respect for parliamentarism had been preserved. As Duke Victor de Broglie expressed it, they regretted "those generous institutions which were the accomplishment and the pride of their happiest years."

The French Academy had become the rendezvous of a polished and literary opposition which had maintained, one may say, a purely academic character, and with which it would have been a mistake on the part of the government to concern itself. April 5, 1856, occurred the reception of the Duke de Broglie, replacing one of the best diplomatists of the July monarchy, Count de Sainte-Aulaire. The Duke had seized the occasion to make an eloquent eulogy of Louis Philippe. He said: "Honored during many years, I would not venture to say by his friendship, but by his kindness, summoned several times to his councils, preserving for his memory a useless, and at my age, an unmeritorious fidelity, I await with confidence the judgment which history will pass upon it; history will say whether the eighteen years of peace which he gave us were attained at the expense of the honor and interest of the country; whether his wisdom does not count for something in the prosperity whose fruits are replenishing our hands; whether the army formed by him has shown itself worthy of France; whether its sons have shown themselves worthy of that army."

March 26, 1857, took place the reception of Count de Falloux, replacing Count Molé, who justly praised that great minister of Louis Philippe. Napoleon III.

had the good taste not to take offence at the homage paid to his predecessor. When the Duke de Broglie, in his quality as a newly elected academician, went to pay his official visit at the Tuileries, the sovereign received him with his usual urbanity, and said: "I hope, Monsieur le Duc, that your grandson may speak of the second of December as you have spoken of the eighteenth Brumaire."

Unfortunately, the imperialist journals had less tact than the Emperor. M. de La Gorce has good reason to say: "Napoleon III. expressed himself better than his agents, better than his ministers; and especially better than his flatterers." The official and semi-official sheets lauded all acts of authority without reserve and without distinction, and uselessly attacked the old parties in their past and in their presumed tendencies.

The press, which had been called the fourth power of the State at the time when three powers were officially recognized in the State, had played only a secondary part since the régime of 1852. Ceasing to be faithful organs of parties, the journals could at most timidly collect and reproduce in covert words the enfeebled echoes of the opinion of which they essayed to be the representatives. Still, there were among them some which retained a real prestige, and the courteous and measured tone of their articles was no detriment to the talent of their editors.

Such was the general situation when, after five years, the government sprung from the *coup d'État* and the plebiscite made a new appeal to popular suffrage. The year 1857 brought the renewal of the Corps Législatif. The *Moniteur* of June 12 congratulated the outgoing Chamber on having neither transformed the tribune into a pedestal for interest or ambition, nor deliberated amidst political passions, nor improvised those amendments which formerly disturbed all the economy of the laws. The balloting was to begin June 21-22. The government had an easy triumph almost everywhere. The *Revue des Deux Mondes* wrote in its yearly summary for 1857: "Tired of its long struggles, satisfied with the repose it has been enjoying for five years, proud of the situation created for it abroad by the Eastern War terminated by an honorable peace, the nation easily allows itself to be carried along by the current of the Empire." The prefects exercised a decisive action over the docile masses, and the governmental candidates had almost no competitors. The legitimists did not put in an appearance, Count de Chambord having forbidden them to swear allegiance to the Emperor. The Orleanists felt that their hour had not come, and there was no chance for the republicans outside of the great cities. In the provinces but four candidates opposed by the government were entered on the lists: MM. Curé, Hénon, Plichon, and Brame, and of these the two latter were independents and not hostile. At Paris five republicans were nominated, MM. Carnot and Goudchaux at the first turn, and at the second General

Cavaignac, M. Émile Ollivier, and M. Alfred Darimon. Such was the germ of an opposition destined to grow incessantly and in a few years to become formidable.

July 16, just as the elections by ballot were completed at Paris, it was learned that Béranger was dead. The Empress, who had just sent to inquire about him, refrained from appearing at a theatrical representation that evening at which she had been announced to be present. The Emperor decided that the cost of the obsequies of *the national poet* should be defrayed by his civil list. They were celebrated at the church of Saint Elizabeth amidst a great array of troops and policemen. The organ played the air of the *Souvenirs du Peuple:* —

> "They will talk of his glory
> Long underneath the thatch.
> The humble roof in fifty years
> Will know no other story."

The electoral agitation had no consequences. "To-day," said the *Moniteur,* "when the contest is ended, and a majority of more than five millions of votes has plainly expressed the sentiments of the country, an end should be put to discussions which henceforth can have no other aim than to disturb the public mind in vain." The press held its peace and everything fell back into accustomed channels.

Algeria was pacified like France. After an expedition skilfully conducted by Marshal Randon, Kabylia had surrendered and the Arabs obeyed Napoleon with the same docility as the French. The imperialists were never tired of saying that the Empire was immovable.

CHAPTER XX

THE QUESTION OF THE PRINCIPALITIES

IN matters of external policy, the ideas of concord and universal pacification which seemed in the ascendency in the Congress of Paris, no longer took the upper hand in the relations between the powers. The diplomatic chess-board had been completely upset. An absolutely unexpected system of alliances produced itself. The new grouping of the powers was the antipodes of what it had been during the Crimean War. Europe, to the great surprise of the professional diplomatists, was suddenly divided into two camps: on one side, England, Austria, and Turkey; on the other, France, Russia, Prussia, and Sardinia. It was the question of the Danubian Principalities.

M. Louis Thouvenel, in a work equally curious and substantial, for which the unpublished papers of his illustrious father have supplied the elements, has retraced all the details and phases of the discussion with rare precision. This work is entitled: *Three Years of the Oriental Question, 1856-1859*. The author has very well understood the importance of this affair of the Principalities by which Napoleon III.

allowed the entire programme of his foreign policy to be inferred, and which may be called the prologue of the Italian War. M. Louis Thouvenel has said with much justice: "No one has ever made sufficiently plain to what degree the question of the Danubian Principalities tended to engender and to nourish bitterness between the cabinets of Paris and Vienna. For us the war of 1859 began as early as 1857. In politics as in love, there are no worse enemies than the betrayed friends of yesterday."

During the Congress of Paris, the French plenipotentiaries had proposed the reunion of the two principalities of Moldavia and Wallachia into one under the authority of a foreign prince and under the suzerainty of the Porte. This combination having raised the most lively objections on the part of Turkey and Austria, there had been an unwillingness to endanger the impatiently expected work of general peace; hence the solution of a question which gave rise to such serious disputes had been adjourned, and the only decision arrived at had been that a European commission should go to the Principalities to gather the wishes of the populations, wishes expressed by the local assemblies, known as *Divans ad hoc* on account of the special purposes for which they were to be convened.

In such a combination Napoleon saw his two favorite ideas brought into vigorous prominence, the principle of nationalities, and the right of peoples to dispose of their destiny. One might say he showed his hand in supporting this thesis, and introduced in the Balkans the programme which was to be that of his policy in Italy. Austria saw this plainly and opposed the union of the Principalities with a bitterness even greater than that of Turkey, although that power recognized in the system extolled by Napoleon III. a serious attack on the integrity of the Ottoman Empire and the signal for the enfranchisement of her Christian subjects.

At the Congress of Paris, Lord Clarendon had seemed to favor the idea of a union under a foreign prince. But, since then, England, under the influence of Lord Stratford de Redcliffe, her ambassador at Constantinople, had completely modified her view, and now antagonized violently, in union with Austria and Turkey, the combination to which she had at first given her approval.

The Grand-Vizier, Ali Pasha, said to M. Thouvenel, in July, 1856: "The former capitulations assure to the Wallachians and Moldavians princes selected from among their own nobles. We pledged ourselves *ab antiquo* to this condition only. The Wallachians and Moldavians cannot modify it without our consent. They become factions if they talk of a foreign prince. As to Europe, it has no more right to constrain us than it would have to oblige Austria, while leaving her the suzerainty of Hungary, to receive at Pesth a viceroy of her selection." The thesis of the Grand-Vizier, it must be owned, was in conformity with international stipulations and the

English doctrine, which then defended, as a dogma, the integrity of the Ottoman Empire. Advantageously to combat the theory of Turkey, Austria, and England, it was necessary to invoke boldly the right of peoples to decide their destinies for themselves. In diplomacy this was a real revolution.

When Napoleon III. proclaimed this novel principle, he was secretly blamed by nearly all French diplomatists, even by his ambassador at Constantinople, M. Thouvenel. The latter addressed at this time to his friend, M. Benedetti, director of political affairs in the Ministry of Foreign Affairs, private letters full of sharp criticisms on the external policy of the government. He wrote, November 10, 1856: "Are you very sure that those fallacious journals did not deceive us in announcing that on September 8, 1855, Sebastopol would fall under the combined efforts of France and England? . . . Oh! the great nobles of Moscow are wrong to jest over the tears of the too sensitive Morny. They ought rather to gather them up like pearls! However, to go from one thing to another, here I am in alliance with M. de Boutenieff (minister of Russia at Constantinople), and, moreover, I am beaten on equal terms with him, which is full of delightful promises for the future. At bottom, I have no desire to laugh. All that is as grave in reality as it is pitiful in appearance."

M. Thouvenel saw things under a gloomy aspect and augured no good from the campaign he was conducting, in spite of himself, at Constantinople against the former allies of France. He wrote again to M. Benedetti: "I have a scent which has never yet deceived me, and I wrote from Athens, officially, in 1850, that the question of the Holy Places would lead to war. That of the Principalities will end like the Egyptian affair in 1840, which is, God be thanked, quite enough."

He who, two years later, was to be the ardent partisan of the national Italian cause, did not in 1850 show himself favorable to the national Roumanian cause, and seemed not to share in any degree the humanitarian and advanced ideas of his sovereign. "Success for us is most doubtful," he wrote, "and to my thinking, we are doing ourselves a great deal of harm in order to hang the recognition of the Roumanians as a pendant to that of the Hellenes in the museum of our political illusions. I am profoundly distressed by the manner in which our foreign affairs are conducted, and in our history a severe chapter will follow that describing the last war." (Letter to the Duke de Gramont, May 26, 1857.)

In the end, M. Thouvenel learned to recognize that, in the mind of the Emperor, the Roumanian question was the prelude to the Italian question, and he then comprehended what had at the time seemed to him inexplicable. "I am somewhat more interested in ourselves than in the Roumanians," he wrote to M. Benedetti, "and it seems to me that we should get ourselves out of an intricate and dangerous scrape by notifying these gentlemen in advance as to what they may expect from us. I am reasoning, you understand, on the hypothesis that our policy is without reserves, and that *we are not anxious to regulate on the Po* the questions raised on the Danube. If there is an under side to the cards, I say nothing further."

There was, in fact, an under side to the cards, and M. Benedetti did not leave the ambassador in ignorance that the policy adopted by the Ministry of Foreign Affairs was the personal policy of the Emperor. M. Thouvenel replied: "I thank you for letting me into the *secret* of your tenacity on the subject of the union of the principalities. Of course, nothing remains but to let things go on."

However, things were singularly complicated at Constantinople, and the strife between the Porte, Austria, and England on one side, and France, Russia, and Prussia on the other, had assumed an acute form. It was especially bitter against the two ambassadors of the nations said to be united by the *entente cordiale*. June 18, 1857, Lord Stratford, wishing to celebrate an anniversary painful to French hearts, gave a grand dinner at Pera to which he invited the Prussian *chargé d'affaires*. It was the morrow of Waterloo over again.

The more strongly the national aspirations of the Roumanians affirmed themselves, the more obstinately was the English ambassador, in agreement with Turkey and Austria, bent on annihilating them *per fas et nefas*. The European commission, in which France was represented by Baron Talleyrand-Périgord, expressed the real wishes of the two principalities in vain. As the latter wrote, it was evident that in both Moldavia and Wallachia the union was the deepest wish of all honest hearts. On his entrance at Yassy, the French commissioner was received with enthusiasm. The shouts of "Long live France!" "Long live the Emperor!" "Long live the union!" were unanimous. But English, Austrian, and Ottoman diplomacy considered the principle of nationalities as null.

Prince Vogorides, whom the Sultan had appointed kaimakam, or lieutenant-governor, at Yassy, drew up the electoral lists for the Moldavian Divan with so evident a partiality and employed such fraudulent manœuvres that the majority of the electors refused to take part in the voting. "Vogorides has thrown off the mask," wrote M. Thouvenel. "He proceeds by blows, fraud, and violence, in a way to make even experts in such matters envious. I am rather in the way of the odious humbug he is making ready for us." The commissioners of France, Russia, Prussia, and Sardinia, in the Principalities formally protested against such elections. Austria, the Porte, and England wished to have them accepted as valid, because their validity would have been the triumph of the anti-unionists.

The resulting scandal made Napoleon III. indignant. In May, 1857, he said to Mehemet Djemil Bey, the Turkish ambassador at Paris: "We cannot take it ill that others should not be of our opinion; but we have the right to demand that they should treat us loyally, and that has not been done in the Principalities. I should be sorry if we had to quarrel over this question."

The Emperor, who was affirming his favorite principle of nationalities for the first time, was absolutely determined that his initial attempt should be a masterstroke. He took the unalterable resolution to obtain the annulment of the Moldavian elections at any cost, and no longer confiding in his diplomatists, he suddenly decided to go to Osborne and plead in person the cause of Roumanian nationality with the Queen. August 5, before embarking for Osborne, he telegraphed to his ambassador at the court of the Sultan to demand the absolute quashing of the Moldavian elections, and, if this satisfaction were not immediately obtained, formally to rupture the diplomatic relations between France and Turkey. That is what occurred.

August 6, at noon, the *Ajaccio* anchored before the palace of the French embassy. M. Thouvenel was on the terrace with all the members of his legation. At the twenty-first of those discharges of cannon "which," said he, "ought to excite remorse in the soul of Lord Stratford," he saluted for the last time the national colors, " with the patriotic emotion, but with the tranquillity of conscience which consoles the commander of a vessel forced to haul down his flag." Several friends of France were there, Madame Condouriotis, wife of the minister of Greece, Prince Lobanoff, Prince Stourdza, the Marquis de Souza, minister of Spain, and M. Testa, minister of Sweden. At the solemn moment when the tricolored flag was lowered, the crew of the *Ajaccio*, standing on the bridge and on the yards of the vessel, shouted, "Long live the Emperor!"

Some minutes after the salvo the ambassador went aboard the *Ajaccio*, and in three quarters of an hour arrived at Dolma-Baghtche, the residence of Abd-ul-Medjid. "Sire," said he, "for the last hour there has been no ambassador of France at Constantinople; but, as a private individual honored by the kindness of Your Majesty, I wished to take leave of you."

Abd-ul-Medjid: " How grieved I am that such an event, the rupture with a power which has done so much for my empire and for me, should happen under my reign!"

M. Thouvenel: "I do not wish to prolong a scene which troubles Your Majesty's heart as well as my own. Hence I withdraw; but, in this painful moment, I am supported by the consciousness of having fulfilled to the very utmost my duties towards the Emperor and towards Your Majesty."

The ambassador saluted. The Sultan followed him to the head of the staircase, and, so long as he was in sight, remained in the attitude of "a statue of despair."

M. Thouvenel wrote to Napoleon III.: "I ask the Emperor's permission to express to him the sorrow I experienced at having to lower his flag before the ingratitude and disloyalty of our adversaries, within two paces of the cemetery where repose thirty thousand of our brave soldiers." Such was the situation when Napoleon III. arrived at Osborne.

CHAPTER XXI

THE OSBORNE INTERVIEW

Wednesday, August 5, 1857. The Emperor and the Empress leave Saint-Cloud to go to Osborne, in the Isle of Wight, to pay a visit to the Queen of England. They arrive at Rouen at three o'clock, to the sound of cannon. The national guard and the troops are under arms. At five o'clock Their Majesties make their entry at Havre, where a gigantic triumphal arch has been erected. The houses are hung with flags and garlands of foliage and flowers. Young girls dressed in white offer a bouquet to the Empress; all the communes of the district are present with their mayors and their clergy at their head. Their Majesties drive through the city in an open carriage, preceded by the young men of Havre on horseback and escorted by a detachment of hundred-guards. On the arrival of the imperial cortège on the Place de la Bourse, where the American vessels are moored, the sailors on the yards make the air ring with hurrahs. The Emperor and the Empress then go aboard the imperial yacht, *La Reine Hortense,* where they dine. At nine o'clock the yacht, escorted by the despatch-boats

Ariane, Pelican, and *Corse,* quits the port to salvos of artillery and huzzas. The city is entirely illuminated and fireworks are set off.

Thursday, August 6. Their Majesties arrive at Osborne at nine o'clock in the morning of a superb day. Prince Albert and Prince Alfred have come to meet them on one of Queen Victoria's boats.

The Queen is delighted to do the honors of the Isle of Wight, "the island gem of England," to her guests. There the Queen is surrounded by universal veneration. Every time she comes, the principal tower of each castle, the little tower, the gable, and even the dove-cot of each cottage, are crowned with the national flag. Osborne House is the seaside residence which she prefers. The park and gardens are singularly beautiful. Avenues planted with large trees slope gently towards the shore. Portsmouth and Spithead are visible in the distance. The castle, built in modern style, with its two towers of unequal height, that of the signals, 107 feet, and that of the clock, 190; with its two magnificent terraces adorned with fountains falling into basins of bronze and marble; with its clumps of rare flowers grouped at the balusters, — presents a most agreeable aspect. It is peopled with statues, some after the antique, others the work of contemporary artists. The Italian sculptor Marochetti has executed several marbles for Osborne, among others, busts of Queen Victoria, Prince Albert, the Prince of Wales, the Princess Royal, and King Victor Emmanuel. The reception-rooms are on the ground floor and open upon the terraces.

After breakfast, the Emperor took a walk with Prince Albert, during which they talked at length on politics.

Friday, August 7. The Emperor and the Empress, with the Queen, Prince Albert, and the princes and the princesses, went aboard the royal yacht *Victoria and Albert*, for a sail which lasted two hours. In the evening there was a grand dinner at the castle.

Saturday, August 8. The Duke of Cambridge, Lord Palmerston, and Lord Clarendon arrived at Osborne, whither the Emperor had summoned his Minister of Foreign Affairs, Count Walewski, and his ambassador, Count de Persigny.

Sunday, August 9. The Queen is enchanted with the Emperor and the Empress. She writes to King Leopold that "nothing could be more amiable, kind, pleasant, or *ungênant* than both Majesties were. Albert," she says, "who is seldom much pleased with ladies or princesses, is very fond of her, and her great ally." The Queen adds that M. de Persigny's devotion to the Emperor, and his courage and uprightness in all affairs, are pleasant to see.

On both sides very amicable sentiments were expressed. The Emperor did not insist upon the immediate adoption of his favorite project, the union of the Danubian Principalities under the government of a foreign prince. General Fleury, who was present at the Osborne interview, has justly remarked: "It was to perform an act of conciliation without pledging the future too far; since this combination was to be carried into effect some years later under the authority of Prince Charles of Hohenzollern, now King of Roumania." Hence the fundamental question, that of the union of the two principalities, was adjourned as falling under the exclusive jurisdiction of the European Conference. But, since the will of the inhabitants was one of the elements of the question, Napoleon III. considered it just that this will should be enabled to express itself freely and not be falsified by a pretended election. He obtained a pledge that the English government would support at the Ottoman court the demand made by France, Russia, Prussia, and Sardinia for the annulling of the Moldavian elections. For the moment this was the essential point. The action of Lord Stratford de Redcliffe being disavowed, Napoleon III. declared himself satisfied.

Monday, August 10. The Emperor and the Empress embarked at Osborne for Havre. The farewells of the royal and imperial families were marked by the greatest cordiality. Two days later, the Queen wrote to King Leopold: "The visit we have just received has been satisfactory and agreeable in every way. Politically, it has been a blessing from Heaven, as Lord Clarendon says, for the unfortunate difficulties of the Principalities have been smoothed over and arranged in a satisfactory manner. The interview was tranquil and agreeable. Good Osborne in no way changed its unpretending privacy and simplicity. The Emperor talked frankly with Albert, and Albert did the same with him, which is a great advantage, and Palmerston said to me, the last day: 'The Prince can say many things which we cannot.' That is very natural.

"The Emperor, to whom I conveyed your message, has begged me to say a thousand kind things to you, and he added: 'The King is not merely very amiable. He has a great deal of good sense.'"

Lord Clarendon wrote to the Queen: "The importance of this visit cannot be overestimated, because the Emperor is France, and better still, France under its best aspect, because he permits himself to yield to generous impulses and to appreciate the truth. His alliance with England has therefore been renewed and strengthened at Osborne."

This is the letter which the Emperor addressed from the Tuileries to Queen Victoria, August 15, 1857: —

"MADAME AND DEAREST SISTER: — We left Osborne so touched by the kindly welcome of Your Majesty and Prince Albert, so penetrated by admiration for the spectacle of all the virtues which the royal family of England affords, that it is difficult for me to find expressions which will adequately express the loyal and affectionate sentiments we experience towards Your Majesty.

"It is so sweet to think that aside from political

interests Your Majesty and your family feel some affection for us, that in the first rank of my preoccupations I place the desire always to be worthy of this august friendship. I think that when one has spent some days with you in the intimacy of private life, he goes away a better man; so too, when one has learned to appreciate the varied knowledge and the lofty judgment of the Prince, one comes away wiser and more capable of doing good.

"Deign, I pray you, Madame, to say to him who so nobly shares your destiny, that I have the highest esteem and the sincerest friendship for him; and that is to say how greatly I count upon his own.

"As to Your Majesty's children, they are all gifted with such good and charming qualities that one loves them at sight, and that it becomes very natural to wish them all the happiness they merit.

"Adieu, Madame. God grant that two years may not elapse before we have the happiness of seeing you again, for the hope of doing so is the sole consolation for a painful separation.

"I beg Your Majesty to receive kindly the expression of the sentiments of high esteem and entire devotion with which I am of Your Majesty the good brother and friend,

"NAPOLEON."

The Queen, greatly touched by this affectionate letter, was particularly pleased by the Emperor's praise of Prince Albert. She said in her reply: —

"I cannot dispute the favorable opinion which

Your Majesty has formed of my beloved husband, because I know that he deserves it, since he has no ambition but to do good and to make himself useful when he can. In a position so isolated as ours, we can find no greater consolation and no more sure support than the sympathy and counsel of him or her who is called to share our lot in life, and the dear Empress, with her generous instincts, is your angel guardian, as the Prince is my true friend."

In French political circles the compromises that had been effected on the subject of the Danubian Principalities produced a good result. M. Benedetti, director of political affairs in the foreign office, wrote, August 14, to M. Thouvenel, ambassador of France at Constantinople: "You know what has been done at Osborne. To my notion, it is a complete success. We have been dignified and firm; we have not withdrawn a syllable of our claims, which we were the first to formulate, and England has undertaken to make them prevail at Constantinople, dragging along with her those good Austrians, who will come out of the struggle wonderfully lessened in public estimation. Look at Lord Stratford, *obliged* to make the Porte accept what he had *obliged* him to refuse. This is an unprecedented incident in the life of your colleague; better still, it is the most formal disavowal of his entire conduct. I envy you the spectacle which your two colleagues of England and Austria must resign themselves to giving you in presence of that public of Constantinople which will hardly believe its eyes."

The annulling of the Moldavian elections was declared by the Sultan, and the representatives of the four powers, France, Russia, Prussia, and Sardinia, who had broken off diplomatic relations with the Porte, resumed them. M. Thouvenel wrote: "There has been a first-class tragi-comedy. However, we are victors; we have *all* that we could ask."

There was no longer any cloud on the relations between France and England. The brightest days of the *entente cordiale* seemed to have returned. Shortly after the Emperor's return to France, Queen Victoria, with her husband and six of her children, made an excursion to the Channel Islands. On her way back from Jersey she landed at Cherbourg, August 19, without having given any notice to the city authorities. This unexpected appearance of the English sovereign on French soil was a new proof of the union existing between the two countries. The Queen was received at Cherbourg with the most respectful cordiality. She met there General Herbillon, the victor of Traktir, who thanked her for having conferred on him the order of the Bath. "I wear it with great pride," said he. The Queen was delighted to see the Crimean medal, on which her image is engraved, on the breasts of French soldiers and sailors. The next day she visited in detail the arsenals, the harbor, the gigantic works in progress, and drove through the environs of the city before returning to her vessel, highly satisfied with all that she had seen. August 21, she wrote to the Emperor:

"We have made an interesting and agreeable visit at Cherbourg. The works are magnificent and of colossal grandeur; the roadstead is admirable. The authorities were most attentive to us, and wherever we were recognized (for we wished things to be as private as possible), the people showed us the greatest affection. We made a little improvised excursion into the interior in a wagonette, with post-horses, which amused us very much. The country is superb. It is agreeable, in these days of a civilization which tends to bring all things to a common level, to find a simple, primitive population, still truly rustic, and regions still unspoiled by contact with railroads. Normandy is very beautiful. For us it was full of interesting souvenirs, for it was the cradle of England."

This *peaceful invasion of Normandy*, as the Queen herself called it, was a sign of the times. It proved how greatly the ancient jealousies had lost their force. The personal relations between Napoleon III. and Queen Victoria were excellent. Nevertheless the Emperor, in spite of the cordial welcome he had received at Osborne, was obliged to recognize that his schemes concerning Italy and his desire to change the map of Europe would not obtain the assent of the British government, and Prince Albert had very frankly told him what importance England attached to the maintenance of the treaties of 1815. It was towards Russia that Napoleon III. was to turn his eyes, in the hope of profiting by the bitterness felt by that power against Austria. But he took good care not to unveil his projects prematurely, and used every means to make it believed that a close union existed between himself and the English. One would have thought that he aimed at nothing but the perpetual maintenance of the peace of Europe.

CHAPTER XXII

THE OPENING OF THE NEW LOUVRE

AUGUST 14, 1857, took place one of the most memorable ceremonies of the reign of Napoleon III., the opening of the new Louvre. Nothing is more beautiful than those peaceful victories which cost neither blood nor tears, and which have as much splendor and often more durability than the others. To complete the Louvre in such a way that, united to the Tuileries, it would form a single edifice with that palace, had been, since the days of Francis I. and Catherine de' Medici, the dream of all French sovereigns, and notably that of Henry IV., Louis XIV., and the first Napoleon. But all had recoiled before the magnitude of the task to be accomplished, and their resolution had been arrested in the formative period. The Provisional Government of 1848 had been but four days in existence when it decreed, as the victor of Austerlitz had done, that the Louvre should be finished. The Legislative Assembly made a law of this decree, which Napoleon III. had the honor of putting into execution.

Monuments are always symbols of the régimes under which they were raised. For a colossal work like the completion of the Louvre a strong and firm government, prepared for large expenditures without having to be subject to control or criticism, was required. Napoleon III., "that sluggish man who is always in a hurry," as some one said of him, wished the work to go on quickly, and he was obeyed. He had expressed the desire that the reunion of the Louvre to the Tuileries should be accomplished within five years, and the desire was fulfilled exactly. The first stone of the works was laid July 25, 1852. August 14, 1857, the Louvre and the Tuileries formed but one palace.

In his work entitled, *France artistique et monumentale*, M. Havrard has thus summed up this gigantic performance: "A building on the rue de Rivoli joining that of Percier and Fontaine; two wings more than one hundred and sixty metres in length, united by two shorter wings, one to this building on the north, the other to the gallery beside the water, and forming interior courts; eight grand pavilions, two on the rue de Rivoli, six on the Place du Carrousel; everywhere on the pavilions, porticos, terraces, up to the roofs, the sculptor's work completing that of the architects; that part of the old Louvre which overlooked the Tuileries altered, and in the central pavilion an abundance of ornaments replacing the severity of Le Mercier: for this enormous task five years had been sufficient." The works, directed in the first place by the architect Visconti, and after his death in 1853 by the architect Lefuel, were pushed ahead with prodigious activity. The decoration contained more than fifteen hundred details of sculpture; one hundred and fifty statuaries labored incessantly. The most distinguished sculptors, Duret, Barye, Bosio, Cavelier, Dumont, Lequesne, Guillaume, Simart, etc., lent their most zealous rivalry to the work. During the year 1857, the Louvre had employed not less than three hundred and thirteen thousand two hundred and seventy-two days' work of artisans laboring on the spot, not to mention the lockmakers, carpenters, joiners, who worked at home, the quarrymen who dug out the materials, and the drivers who carted them over the roads. Only French iron and marble had been employed. The architect Duban had harmonized the work of the statuaries and the ornamenters. The completion of the work had opened two new ways of transit, one for pedestrians under the Sully pavilion, the other for carriages under the Richelieu pavilion. The entire work had cost thirty-six million francs.

The inauguration of the new edifice was surrounded with exceptional pomp. August 14, 1857, at two o'clock in the afternoon, the Emperor and the Empress, accompanied by the princes and princesses of the imperial family, as well as by the ladies and officers on duty, set out from the château of the Tuileries, crossed the Place du Carrousel after passing under the arch of triumph, and entered the Louvre by the Denon pavilion. Received on alighting from the carriage by M. Achille Fould, Minister of State, and by the great officers of the crown, they crossed a gallery intended for the museum of sculpture, ascended the staircase of the Mollien pavilion, and entered processionally into the hall where the ceremony was to take place. Here a throne had been erected, and opposite to it, to right and left of the passage by which it was approached, benches had been placed for the artists, employees, and workmen who had labored in the construction of the edifice. The Minister of State came forward in front of the imperial platform and made a speech which ended as follows: "Neither the war nor so many other difficulties which we have had to encounter have interrupted this work, the dream of so many kings, and which would be sufficient for the glory of an epoch of peace and prosperity. Your Majesty, whose presence has often excited the ardor of our workers, has desired to see them assembled before you after the completion of their task. All throng gladly around Your Majesty. All are conscious of having done their duty, and are proud of having had a share in this truly national work." After this discourse the crosses and medals were distributed. M. Lefuel, chief of the Louvre works, received the officer's cross of the Legion of Honor, and the statuary Bosio that of a chevalier. Each of the artists, contractors, and workmen whose names were called mounted the platform and received his recompense from the Emperor's hand. When the distribution was over, the sovereign indicated that he intended to speak. The spectators rose to their feet, and, amidst profound silence, Napoleon III. delivered the following address: —

"Gentlemen, I rejoice with you over the completion of the Louvre. I congratulate myself especially on the causes which have rendered it possible. These are, in fact, the order, the restored tranquillity, and the prosperity which have permitted me to finish this national work. I call it so because all succeeding governments have clung to the honor of completing the dwelling begun by Francis I. and embellished by Henry IV. In the Middle Ages, the king inhabited a fortress bristling with means of defence. The progress of civilization presently replaced the crenelles and the weapons of war by the results of science, letters, and the arts. Hence the history of monuments has its philosophy like the history of deeds. Just as it is remarkable that under the first Revolution the Committee of Public Safety should unwittingly have continued the work of Louis XI., Richelieu, and Louis XIV. by striking the final blow at the feudal system and pursuing that of unity and centralization, so there is a great lesson in beholding the idea of Henry IV., of Louis XIII., Louis XIV., Louis XV., and of Napoleon concerning the Louvre adopted by the ephemeral power of 1848. . . . The completion of the Louvre, to which I thank you for having contributed with so much zeal and ability, is not the caprice of a moment, but the realization of a plan conceived for the glory and sustained by the interest of the country during more than three hundred years."

Their Majesties withdrew amidst the acclamations of the crowded assembly, and returned to the Tuileries through the square court of the Louvre, the wicket of the Colonnade, the rue de Rivoli, the Richelieu pavilion, and the triumphal arch of the Carrousel.

At seven o'clock in the evening the Minister of State presided at a banquet given in the hall of the inauguration to four hundred and seventy guests, among whom workmen were in the majority. One of the guests was a woman, the widow of a stone-cutter, who, deprived of all resources by the death of her husband, had taken his place in the stone-yards. On the Minister's right sat M. Maret, a contractor, and on his left M. Riffaut, a working stonecutter and dresser. At dessert he proposed this toast: "To the Emperor! To the prosperity, the glory, the duration of his reign, so fruitful of great things! To him was reserved the completion of this long-suspended work. With so many other monuments, it will transmit his name to the recognition and the admiration of posterity. To the health of the Emperor!"

The yards had been closed all day, but the workmen had been paid as if they had worked. Napoleon III. was happy. He had just wished himself many happy returns of his fête.

CHAPTER XXIII

BIARRITZ

AUGUST 17, the Emperor departed with the Empress and the Prince Imperial for Biarritz, where he was to remain but a short time, and where he proposed to leave his wife while he went to the camp of Châlons, and afterwards to Stuttgart. Like the Empress, Napoleon III. had taken a violent fancy to this picturesque beach. After seeing the King of Würtemberg, who had gone there incognito, he left it with regret to inaugurate on the 23d his new estate in the Landes. Desiring to favor agriculture and to give an effectual proof of his affection for the rural populations, the Emperor had chosen two of the most desolate regions of France in order to become a cultivator there himself. These were Sologne and the Landes. The enthusiastic shouts which greeted his coming showed him that his idea had been comprehended. The domain he had just acquired in the Landes contained some fifteen thousand acres of marsh and heather. His Majesty had selected the points where the greatest efforts and the most experiments must be made.

In that part of it which was situated in the canton

of Sabres, there was already a small wooden farmhouse, not unlike a Swiss chalet, and comprising, besides the master's lodging, a stable, a cattle-shed, and a granary for fodder. At the station of Bouheyre, the Emperor accepted a breakfast offered him by the prefect of the Landes, M. Cornuau. Among the crowd of peasants in blue bonnets were noticeable the *échassiers*, those nomads of the Landes who run through the heather or spring across the marshes on stilts, and whose gigantic strides enable them to keep pace with the most rapid riders.

At Sabres the Emperor stopped before a mass of iron which represented the barren land and the impress of the imperial foot, with this inscription: "Napoleon III. is the first sovereign who has placed his foot on this arid land with the noble intention of fertilizing and regenerating it." At the village of Bouheyre the Emperor passed under triumphal arches formed of fir-branches and rose-heather. Preceded by a mounted guard of honor organized by the young men of the region, he stopped before a column bearing this inscription: "To Napoleon III., regenerator of the Landes, the grateful ironworkers."

To fertilize uncultivated lands had been one of the dreams of the prisoner of Ham which it delighted the Emperor to realize. Pleased with what he had seen in the Landes, he reached Paris on August 24, and left it again the next day for the camp of Châlons, that one of his creations which he valued most.

The Empress remained at Biarritz for several

weeks. For this place she did what the Duchess of Berry had done for Dieppe. It was she who made it the fashion. One might almost say that she invented it.

Biarritz, which is now a city of eight thousand souls, and one of the most famous seaside resorts for fashionable people in all the world, was nothing, fifty years ago, but a fishing-village, an obscure hamlet whose name no one ever mentioned. The Empress Eugénie was allured by the picturesque aspect of this beautiful beach covered with fine sand, and by the strangely shaped rocks which emerge at varying intervals: the *Coustelette*, the *Frégate*, the *Roche-Ronde*, the *Roche-Plate*, the *Rocher de la Vierge;* by those poetic and mysterious grottoes, the grotto *des Écrits*, the *Chambre d'Amour*. The latter has its legend: the shepherd Ousa and his betrothed, Edera, were walking at nightfall on the shore, exchanging words of love, and deaf to the murmur of the rising tide. Surprised by the water they took refuge in an excavation perfidiously offered them by the steep cliff, where they were found next day enveloped in seaweed and each other's arms.

The azure sea, the dark-foliaged pines, the yellow rocks, form a mass of color well calculated to charm an artist. The main beach, about a kilometre in length as far as Cape Saint Martin, where there is a lighthouse, and which is cut in two by a little promontory; the second, that of the Basques, where the waves, meeting no obstacle, attain extraordinary violence; the mountains on the horizon, the Rhune, the Haya, the Jalzquivel, — combine to form a panorama as original as grandiose. A dweller there has said, " Between the superb ocean and the verdant landscape, Biarritz shines like a diamond inserted in a sheet of emerald."

For the Empress the great charm of Biarritz was possibly its nearness to Spain. Faithful to her first country, she loved to find herself among persons whom she had known from childhood. No language seemed to her finer or more sonorous than her mother-tongue. Many Spaniards came to greet her at Biarritz, where she enjoyed all that is pleasant in the life of a private individual while retaining all the prestige of sovereignty. September 17, 1857, she made an excursion on Spanish soil to Saint-Sebastian, which was especially enjoyable.

Situated on an islet of the gulf of Gascony which is connected with the continent by a wooden bridge, Saint-Sebastian, a fortified town, is the seat of the general captaincy of Guipuzcoa.

To account for the pleasure the Empress experienced in being formally received in a Spanish town, one must remember the sentiments she always cherished for Spain and for Queen Isabella, of whom her mother, the Countess de Montijo, had been the *camarera mayor*. The ambassador of Spain at Paris, the Duke de Mandas, has recently communicated to me two curious letters which bring out plainly those sentiments of the Empress. Her marriage to Napoleon III. had been agreed on when she wrote as follows to her sovereign: "Madame, Your Majesty will allow me to allude to what my mother has the honor to lay more fully at your feet, and to restrict myself to rendering to Your Majesty, on this occasion which overwhelms me with so much honor, the loyal tribute of my emotions. Aggrandized by the designs of Divine Providence which I accept without knowing them, all my inclinations accord with my duties in urging me to renew here the sincere profession of the sentiments of respect, loyalty, and love towards your august person in which, for my happiness, I was brought up.

"I am confident, Madame, that Your Majesty, well persuaded of what I have just expressed, will deign to consider the event which leads me to the throne as a fortunate one. I am above all confident that Your Majesty, satisfied with my personal sentiments, will be convinced, as I earnestly pray, that in the high and dangerous position I am to occupy, I shall have no thought but that of contributing to the utmost of my power to draw still closer the ties which unite two great nations and two great monarchs to whose service I shall be perpetually devoted by love and duty.

"May Your Majesty deign to receive with kindliness this declaration so cordially made!

"May God preserve the precious life of Your Majesty for as many years as may be necessary for the Spanish monarchy!

"At the feet of Your Royal Majesty,
"EUGÉNIE DE GUZMAN, COUNTESS DE TEBA.
"PARIS, Jan. 20, 1853."

The following is a translation of Queen Isabella's reply:—

"COUNTESS DE TEBA,—It is with the utmost satisfaction that I received your letter of the 20th. The singular destiny devolved upon you by Divine Providence, and the sentiments of love and devotion for me personally which you manifest at such supreme moments, fill me with satisfaction and gratitude for your noble loyalty.

"You may rely on my entire consent to a union so glorious for you, and be assured of the wishes I make for your happiness and that of the Emperor in desiring that, both guided by the hand of the Almighty, you will conduct that great nation to the highest degree of prosperity and well-being.

"In the difficult and dangerous path which you must hereafter follow, always take confidence in the Supreme Being for your guide, and the duty of sacrificing everything for the Emperor and for France.

"Such are the sentiments of the Queen and the counsels of your affectionate
"ISABELLA."

Since her accession to the throne, the Empress Eugénie had neglected no means of maintaining the most cordial relations between Paris and Madrid, and she certainly never suspected that a day would come when the affairs of Spain would be the indirect cause which would bring about the fall of the Napoleonic dynasty. Remote from such presentiments, she looked once more upon her native soil with transports of delight.

September 17, 1857, Her Majesty, accompanied by her two ladies of the palace, the Countess de Montebello and the Viscountess de la Poëze, as well as by the Marchioness de Contades, embarked at Biarritz with her sister, the Duchess of Alba, on the steamboat *Coligny*. She arrived at Saint-Sebastian as night was falling. The city was illuminated. The air rang with shouts. The band of the Almanza regiment played the national airs. Her Majesty's first visit was paid to the church of Santa Maria, where the Royal March was played on the organ. Next she went to the town hall, which occupies one entire side of the Plaza Nueva, a fine square surrounded by porticos and houses with iron balconies constructed on a uniform plan. All the authorities paid her their respects; she was served with ices, and when she made her appearance on the balcony of the hall, all the people hailed her with enthusiastic applause. She returned to the port preceded by a band and a torchlight procession. The *Coligny* was illuminated by Bengal lights, which cast reflections on the immense crowds on the jetty. The bridge of the vessel was converted into an elegant dining-room. The sail back to Biarritz was charming. After dinner a piano was brought to the bridge and dancing went on under the moon and stars. The sea was as clear and tranquil as a lake.

On the same day — September 17, 1857 — the Emperor, in the camp of Châlons, was receiving the visit of the Duke of Cambridge, cousin of Queen Victoria.

CHAPTER XXIV

THE CAMP OF CHÂLONS

NAPOLEON III. left Paris August 29, 1857, for the camp of Châlons. Accompanied by Generals Espinasse, de Failly, de Montebello, Fleury, his aides-de-camp, and Prince Joachim Murat, he arrived there towards seven o'clock in the evening. The entire imperial guard was assembled, comprising an effective force of twenty-two thousand men and five thousand horses. The Emperor assumed command immediately on his arrival, General Regnaud de Saint-Jean d'Angély, commander-in-chief of the guard, fulfilling merely those of major-general.

The camp of Châlons was a recent creation of Napoleon III. It dated from 1856, the time when General Fleury and Colonel de Castelnau had been sent to reconnoitre the ground, stake out the barracks, and designate the site of the imperial and general quarters. This manœuvring ground, an immense quadrilateral where one hundred thousand men can manœuvre at ease, is the largest in the entire world.

A pavilion had been erected for Their Majesties; to left and right of it were two small barracks intended for the ladies of the palace; to the right of these there was a vast salon, and to the left a dining-room which could seat a hundred guests. The tents of the officers of the Emperor's household were to right and left in an alley behind the imperial pavilion and leading to the stables; the latter were situated in the middle of a pine-grove, and were easily capable of housing a hundred saddle-horses. Opposite these stables was the quarter of the squadron of hundred-guards, with barracks and mess for officers and soldiers. All this ensemble of wooden buildings were painted alike. In no European camp were there better organized imperial or royal quarters.

Napoleon III. was never happier than when in the midst of his troops, and especially of his guard. There he felt himself truly Emperor, *imperator*. He had always had a passion for military matters and believed in his own talents as a tactician and his aptitudes as a commander-in-chief. Having suffered greatly on account of his absence from the Crimean battlefields, he counted on taking his revenge. While conducting the manœuvres of his troops at Châlons he promised himself to lead them soon to victory. He loved the soldiers and was loved by them. He knew how to talk to them in a suitable way. They found him gentle, kindly, and benevolent. General Fleury says: "Greatly inclined to encourage inventions, he was constantly planning possible improvements in the hygiene and nourishment of the soldiers. Not satisfied with questioning the colonels as to the results obtained, whether with regard to a new style of shoes or a change of habiliments, the Emperor collected the opinions of the soldiers of the guard, whom he questioned one by one. His solicitude was constant and fatherly, and his generosity unbounded. How many officers of every rank owe to him the comfort of their families! How many unfortunates were succored in those audiences which were always granted!"

Napoleon III. felt at ease in a camp. As his body was long and his legs short, he looked particularly well on horseback and was an excellent rider. The uniform became him and he made a grand appearance in face of the troops.

On his arrival the Emperor addressed the following order of the day to the troops: "Soldiers! I have assembled you here under my command because it is useful that the army should imbibe the same spirit, the same discipline, the same instruction in the common life of camps. Now the guard, as a select corps, should be the first to maintain by constant efforts the rank given it by its former traditions and its recent services on the field of battle. The Romans, says Montesquieu, considered peace as an exercise and war as an application; and, in fact, the successes obtained by young armies, are, in general, only the application of serious studies made during peace."

The order of the day terminated by these counsels, given to the chiefs and to the soldiers: "I recommend to the one a paternal severity, to the others a necessary obedience; to all good will and to all a rigorous observance of dress; because dress is respect for the uniform, and the uniform is the emblem of that noble art of abnegation and devotion of which you ought always to be proud. Never forget that every characteristic sign of the army, beginning with the flag, represents a moral idea, and that your duty is to honor it. This camp, therefore, will not be an idle spectacle afforded to public curiosity, but a serious school which we shall be able to render profitable by sustained labors, and of which the results will be evident if the country ever has need of you."

The camp of Châlons wore a holiday aspect. The presence of a sovereign then in full prestige was an honor and encouragement to troops that were gay, in good health, and proud of themselves. The richness and variety of the uniforms; the recollection of the recent exploits of the guard in the Crimea; the enthusiasm excited by military things in all classes of French society; the fine appearance of the troops, their perfect discipline, their excellent bands; the dinners in the imperial quarters, where all the generals, superior officers, and the eldest in each grade were invited in turn to the sovereign's table; the affability of the Emperor, who, after the morning and night repast of from sixty to eighty covers, chatted familiarly with his guests, the immense proportions of an unrivalled manœuvring ground, — all contributed to give to the inauguration of the camp of Châlons an exceptional attraction and charm.

Napoleon III. displayed great activity. He mounted a horse daily, was present at all the partial exercises, visited the environs so rich in historic souvenirs, and in every village through which he passed left behind him proofs of his munificence. A crowd of peasants, coming from ten to fifteen leagues distance, remained whole days in front of the imperial quarters and went away content after they had seen the Emperor. All the exercises were performed with perfect regularity. The camp presented an admirable ensemble. The guard manifested that precision, that coolness in the manœuvres, which it was its duty to present as an example to the entire army.

Religious ceremonies blended with those that were military. September 5, the Cardinal-Archbishop of Rheims came to visit the sovereign and remained all day at the camp. On the 13th, Mass was celebrated on an altar in the open air, in the midst of the troops, by Mgr. Honoré, coadjutor of the Bishop of Châlons. At the elevation the clarions sounded, the drums beat a salute. Nothing could be more grandiose than this homage to the God of armies.

September 17, the Emperor received at the camp two illustrious guests, Englishmen who had taken a glorious part in the Crimean War, the Duke of Cambridge, cousin of Queen Victoria, and Lord Cardigan, the hero of the famous charge of Balaclava. The Duke of Cambridge was accompanied by three aides-de-camp,—Lord Burghersh, Colonel Clifton, and Colonel Maude. To do honor to the cousin of Her

Britannic Majesty, the Emperor sent General Fleury and two platoons of the hundred-guards to meet them at the Mourmelon station and act as their escort to the imperial quarters. A double line of cavalry extended all along the way. During the day, Napoleon III. and the Duke of Cambridge went together through the camp. The prince, whose valor was known, was the object of very enthusiastic demonstrations on the part of the troops. They remembered the Alma and Inkermann and Balaclava. They saw again with pleasure the red uniforms of their former companions in arms. The following day, the Duke of Cambridge and Lord Cardigan were present at manœuvres which, like those of the previous day, were commanded by the Emperor in person.

On Sunday, the 20th, Mass was celebrated in a more than usually solemn manner. It was said by the Emperor's first almoner, Mgr. Menjaud. The troops, in full uniform ranged around the altar, the cavalry on horseback, the artillery with its batteries harnessed, presented a magnificent appearance. After Mass, all the imperial guard filed past the sovereign and the English prince amidst a considerable concourse of visitors from the neighboring towns, and even from Paris. On the 21st the Emperor and the Duke of Cambridge bivouacked with the guard at Suippe. The next day the Duke took leave of the sovereign, who went with him to the Mourmelon station. During five days the cousin of Queen Victoria had been loaded with attentions and courtesies. He had witnessed grand manœuvres, experiments in shooting, superb dinners, performances on an improvised stage. He had been fêted, petted, greeted with applause. The Emperor would not have received a sovereign better.

Napoleon III. had a very special reason for giving the English prince so brilliant a welcome. On leaving the camp of Châlons he was going to Stuttgart to meet the Emperor of Russia, an interview which could not fail to disquiet England. In lavishing attentions on the Queen's cousin he was striving to prove that a Russian alliance would not destroy the English one.

The Emperor left for Stuttgart September 23, after having remained a month at the Camp of Châlons. He was to stop on the road at Lunéville, Strasburg, and Baden.

CHAPTER XXV

STRASBURG AND BADEN

THE capital of Würtemberg was a fortunately selected spot for an interview between the Emperor of the French and the Czar. Alexander II. took a keen interest in the sovereigns of the secondary states of Germany, whom he considered as friends and clients. The Emperor Nicholas, his father, was the son of a princess of Würtemberg, and this family tie had established and maintained amicable relations between Stuttgart and St. Petersburg. On the other hand, it was to Napoleon I. that Duke Frederic of Würtemberg owed the royal crown and an increase of his dominions after the battle of Austerlitz. Jerome Bonaparte, former King of Westphalia, who had married the daughter of King Frederic, was the brother-in-law of the son and successor of that monarch, King William.

One might say that the Stuttgart interview had been arranged for at least a year. In going to this city Napoleon III. returned the visit paid him by the King of Würtemberg in 1856. King William had left the Tuileries enchanted with his reception, and he congratulated himself on being able to do the honors of his own capital to the Emperor in return. Let us add that the Princess Mathilde had gone to Stuttgart in 1856, on the occasion of her uncle's feast-day. Her beauty, grace, and wit had produced the best impression there, and her visit, which was meant to be short, was prolonged by express invitation of the sovereign. Nor let us forget that one of the best friends of Napoleon III., the Queen of Holland, was the daughter of the King of Würtemberg, who felt a great affection for her, and saw her often. All these influences and souvenirs combined to assure the Emperor the most sympathetic and cordial reception from Würtemberg and its sovereign. All Germany, with the possible exception of the German states of Austria, looked favorably on a journey which from Strasburg to Stuttgart was simply a series of ovations.

In the morning of September 24, 1857, Napoleon reviewed a cavalry division at Lunéville. At three o'clock he arrived at Strasburg, accompanied by two of his aides-de-camp, General Fleury and General de Failly, as well as by one of his orderlies, Prince Joachim Murat. He was received at the station by the authorities, the deputies of the department, and Vicomte de Serre, Minister of France at Carlsruhe. The railway station had been brilliantly illuminated. A vast platform was occupied by the ladies of the city, who rained flowers upon the sovereign as he passed. A triumphal arch surmounted by the imperial eagle, and covered with emblems, had been erected at the entry of the street leading from the station. Private homes and public buildings were hung with flags, and adorned with garlands surrounding the Emperor's escutcheon. After passing through the reception-room, Napoleon III. found the mayors of all the communes assembled in the court of the departure platform, and was received by them with acclamations. No province of the empire was more devoted to him than Alsace. He spoke to several of the city magistrates, and charged them to tell the constituencies they represented how deeply he felt the marks of confidence and sympathy which they had given him under all circumstances.

On leaving the station the Emperor mounted a horse and went with his escort to the house of the prefecture, where apartments had been made ready for him. Halting on the Place Kléber, he reviewed the troops of the division, who saluted him with enthusiastic cheers. He received the authorities at the prefecture, where the Grand Duke of Baden arrived at five o'clock.

The Grand Duke of the period was Frederic William Louis, born in 1826, and married in 1856 to a daughter of the Prince of Prussia, the future Emperor William. The latter had not failed to tell his son-in-law how pleased he had been with his reception at the Tuileries at the end of 1856. In 1855 the Grand Duke had likewise been the guest of Napoleon III., and had felicitated himself greatly on the

P

attentions paid him. And finally, the Dowager Grand Duchess of Baden, Stéphanie de Beauharnais, who had remained in the Grand Duchy after the death of her husband, the Grand Duke Charles Louis Frederic, in 1818, was doing her utmost to establish lasting relations of good neighborhood and friendship between France and Germany.

The Vicomte de Serre, minister of France at Carlsruhe, wrote September 15, 1857: "In case the Emperor should pass through Badenese territory, the Grand Duke would prize inestimably the opportunity of testifying to His Majesty the sentiments of respectful friendship and profound gratitude with which he was imbued two years ago by the kind and friendly reception accorded to himself at the imperial court. On this hypothesis, the Grand Duke would especially hope that, if the Emperor should rest at Manheim or at Baden, he would not refuse to alight either at the palace of Manheim or the castle of Baden, and the wishes of His Royal Highness would meet entire fulfilment if, in passing through Carlsruhe, the Emperor would deign to stop and accept there the hospitality which he would be so happy to offer him."

Arriving at Strasburg, the Grand Duke complimented the Emperor and received his promise to breakfast with him the next day at Baden. In the evening, Napoleon III. dined at the prefecture with the prefects of the upper and lower Rhine, the bishops of Strasburg and Mulhouse, the generals, mayors, and deputies. He afterwards went to the theatre. In the hall, as well as in the approaches to it, he was greeted with acclamations. Private houses, the steeple of the cathedral, and the public buildings were illuminated.

At this period the inhabitants of Strasburg and those of the Grand Duchy of Baden were on excellent terms. The two shores of the Rhine did not look askance at each other across the stream. The fashionable society of Paris had adopted Baden as one of its favorite meeting-grounds. This vogue of Baden, already existing under the reign of Louis Philippe, had increased under that of Napoleon III. Nothing more brilliant in the sporting world or that of fashion existed than the races and the season at Baden. Parisians of distinction, members of the Jockey Club, society women, artists, literary men, thronged thither. Alsatians and Baden people were incessantly crossing the bridge of Kehl, and bore each other no grudge. These, from the top of the terrace of the cathedral of Strasburg, beheld without jealousy the verdant fields of the grand duchy. Those saw without anxiety the French pontoniers performing their evolutions on the Rhine, that flood which has so often streamed with blood. Old quarrels and old rancors seemed to be appeased. Napoleon III., who in his childhood and youth had inhabited the château of Arenenberg, in Switzerland, on the frontier of the Grand Duchy of Baden, had often come to Constance and had many friends in

Baden. His accession to the throne had given pleasure in this country where he was beloved.

The Emperor quitted Strasburg at eight o'clock in the morning of September 25, for Stuttgart. On the German bank of the Rhine a considerable crowd had collected to meet him. The city of Kehl was draped with Badenese and French flags. Arriving at Baden at ten o'clock, Napoleon III. was received at the station by the Grand Duke, the Grand Duchess Stéphanie, and the Prince of Prussia. Accompanied by them, he went in an open carriage to the castle, where he dined with the grand ducal family and the future Emperor William. As he was leaving the palace, the Grand Duke called his attention to a company of guards which had preserved the flag it had under the First Empire, when the Badenese were companions in arms of the French.

The Emperor left Baden at half-past one. All along the road to Stuttgart he received evidences of the cordial sympathy of the Germanic peoples. At Rastadt, a federal fortress, built not long before in defiance of France, the inhabitants came to meet him with acclamations. The soldiers had adorned their caps and shakos with green branches as if for a holiday. The regimental bands played *La Reine Hortense*. Salutes were fired by the artillery on the ramparts. At Rastadt Napoleon III. was complimented by Their Grand-ducal Highnesses William and Maximilian, by the governor of the fortress, and by the War Minister of the Grand Duchy of Baden.

The Grand Duke and the Prince of Prussia went with him as far as Carlsruhe, where he met with the same enthusiasm on the part of the people, and the Grand Duchess Stéphanie insisted on accompanying him to Bruchsal, the railway junction of the grand duchy and Würtemberg.

CHAPTER XXVI

THE STUTTGART INTERVIEW

WILLIAM I., King of Würtemberg, was entering his seventy-seventh year at the time when Napoleon III. became his guest. He had reigned since October 20, 1816, and, not merely in his own dominion but throughout all Germany, he enjoyed a special consideration due not less to his great age and his quality as dean of European sovereigns than to his character and lofty wisdom. The liberal policy he had adopted throughout his reign rendered him justly popular.

Many family ties existed between the court of Russia and that of Stuttgart. The Emperor Paul, father of the Emperors Alexander I. and Nicholas, married a princess of Würtemberg, that charming woman who, when she came to France with her husband, then hereditary Grand Duke, under the title of Countess du Nord, had so great a success at the court of Louis XVI. and Marie Antoinette.

The first wife of William of Würtemberg was a widow of the Emperor Paul; the Prince Royal of Würtemberg married a daughter of the Emperor Nicholas; the Grand Duchess Hélène, daughter of

Paul of Würtemberg, the King's brother, was the widow of the Grand Duke Michael, son of the Emperor Paul. Hence Alexander found himself at home in Stuttgart, where he exercised a legitimate influence, and where he was respected, loved, and honored.

Stuttgart, with its one hundred and forty thousand inhabitants, its palaces and modern buildings, its picturesque situation, its verdant ring of wooded hills and vine-clad slopes, is one of the prettiest cities in Germany. It was a well-selected environment for the interview of the two Emperors.

Thursday, September 24, 1857. The Czar arrives at Stuttgart without the Empress, and installs himself at the villa of his brother-in-law, the Prince Royal, a charming residence some two miles from the city.

Friday, September 25. At the station of Bruchsal, Napoleon III. finds the Marquis de Ferrière, minister of France, with all the personnel of the legation, and General Baur, who had been sent to meet him by the King. At half-past four he arrives at Stuttgart. The King and the princes of the royal family receive him at the station and conduct him to the palace, where the Emperor Alexander II. comes to pay him a call.

Napoleon III. dines with the King and Queen, and then goes to the villa of the Prince Royal in company with Their Majesties and the princes and princesses, to spend the remainder of the evening. The great avenue conducting thither is brilliantly illuminated. All those holding positions at court, all the ministers, and the diplomatic corps are assembled. The presentations are made for France by the Marquis and Marquise de Ferrière; for Russia by its minister at Stuttgart, Count de Beckendorf. The Czar has brought with him his Minister of Foreign Affairs, Prince Gortchakoff; the minister of his household, Count Adlerberg I.; his aide-de-camp, General Count Adlerberg II.; his ambassador at Paris, General Count Kisseleff; his equerry, Count Tolstoï. With Napoleon III. are his Minister of Foreign Affairs, Count Walewski; his new ambassador at St. Petersburg, Count de Rayneval; two of his aides-de-camp, General Count de Failly and General Fleury; and one of his orderly officers, Prince Joachim Murat. The most cordial and animated conversation goes on during the evening. At eleven o'clock the Emperor of the French returns to the palace of Stuttgart with Their Majesties of Würtemberg, while the Emperor of Russia remains at the villa of his brother-in-law, the Prince Royal.

Saturday, September 26. During the morning Napoleon III. goes to return the Czar's call at the villa of the Prince Royal. At eleven o'clock he is joined there by the King of Würtemberg, who takes him to see the place where he keeps his breeding stud of three hundred blooded horses. The two dine together afterwards in a fine residence which the Würtemberg monarch had erected near this establishment, justly celebrated in Germany; and, after an excursion in the picturesque valley of the Necker,

ALEXANDER II
Emperor of Russia

they return to the palace of Stuttgart. The Emperor of the French occupies himself with his Minister of Foreign Affairs, and then calls upon the Queen of Würtemberg, the Queen of Holland, and the Grand Duchess Hélène. At half-past four, without other escort than General Baur, the king's aide-de-camp, he walks in the city like a private individual, but is the object of respectful curiosity. At six he dines with the royal family in the castle of Walhelma, a beautiful construction in the Moorish style, on the model of the Alhambra, situated in the valley of the Necker, beside Stuttgart, in the midst of delightful gardens. Here Napoleon III. hears some good news; the Empress of Russia has just arrived at Stuttgart. As the Empress Eugénie had not come there, Alexander II. had at first decided that the Czarina would not come either, and she had remained in the neighborhood. But the Czar has been so well satisfied with his first relations with Napoleon III. that he has changed his mind and sent word to the Empress to come immediately to Stuttgart. She arrives there in the evening of the 26th with Queen Amélie of Greece, daughter of the Grand Duke Paul Frederic Auguste of Oldenburg, and wife of King Otho. The Empress of Russia, Marie Alexandrovna, born in 1824, was the daughter of Louis II., Grand Duke of Hesse. She had married the Grand Duke Alexander, afterwards emperor under the title of Alexander II., in 1841.

On learning that the Czarina had arrived at Stuttgart, the Emperor of the French immediately left the castle of Walhelma and hastened to the villa of the Prince Royal to pay his respects. He afterwards returned to Walhelma, where he finished the evening with Their Majesties of Würtemberg.

Two emperors, an empress, a king and three queens —not counting imperial or royal highnesses — were then assembled at Stuttgart. Napoleon III. was at his ease amidst this brilliant pleiad. A witness of the interview, General Fleury, describes him as being as calm as usual, making gallant headway against the seductions deployed against him, not insensible to the attentions by which he is overwhelmed, but nevertheless not intoxicated by them. "It was the peculiarity of the Emperor," adds the general, "never to seem surprised by his amazing fortune. He seemed like a sovereign returned from exile and continuing the reign he had begun."

Sunday, September 27. This was the anniversary of the King's birth. After assisting at Mass in the Catholic church, amidst a crowd which saluted him with acclamations, Napoleon III. went to offer his congratulations and good wishes to King William. The King afterwards conducted the two Emperors, the Empress of Russia, the Queens of Würtemberg, Holland, and Greece, the princes and princesses, to Cannstadt to witness the people's feast, an agricultural ceremony instituted by himself at the beginning of his reign, and yearly celebrated on his birthday. The ladies were in full dress, the men in uniform. Surrounded by his family, his court, and the diplomatic body, the venerable sovereign, the Nestor of Europe, the crowned patriarch, distributed, in presence of his guests, the agricultural prizes to the peasants gathered there from all the provinces of the kingdom.

At five o'clock there was a grand dinner in the palace of Stuttgart, and afterwards a gala representation at the royal theatre. When the King, with the emperors, queens, princes, and princesses, made his entry into the grand box in front of the stage, the theatre rang with applause. The hall glittered with lights and jewels. It was a magnificent sight.

Monday, September 28. The Czar breakfasts with the Emperor Napoleon at the villa of the Prince Royal. The Prince, to give them an opportunity of speaking freely, has invited them alone, excluding even his father. The day is an anniversary. It is forty years to a day since Napoleon I. and Alexander I. met each other at Erfurt.

After breakfast, the Prince Royal leaves his two august guests alone with each other in his study. According to the confidences imparted by the Prince Royal to M. Gustave Rothan, secretary of the legation of France at Stuttgart at the time of the interview, this is what passed between the two sovereigns on September 28, 1857.

The interview lasted more than an hour. The ice was broken at the last minute. "After cool beginnings," writes M. Rothan in the *Revue des Deux Mondes* of December 31, 1888, "they separated with brows unruffled, almost radiant, reasons of state having prevailed over prejudices. The Emperors had ratified the protocol agreed on by their ministers. They had promised not to undertake anything without mutual consultation, and to support each other loyally by the action of their diplomacy whether in the East, if complications should arise there, or in Italy, if a quarrel were to break out between France and Austria. In the latter eventuality, Russia assured us, in the first place, her sympathetic neutrality, and, if fighting occurred, she promised, without actually pledging herself, the concentration of one hundred and fifty thousand men on the frontiers of Galicia; they had gone so far as to foresee an eventual alliance."

Alexander II. left Stuttgart that day. Napoleon III. did not go until the next one. In parting, the two Emperors seemed well satisfied with each other, and it was said among their followers that the interview had been a success.

Tuesday, September 29. Napoleon III. quitted Stuttgart at half-past eight in the morning, after warmly thanking the King. Between two lines formed respectively by the cavalry of the royal guard and a troop of the line, he went to the railway station, hung as before by the French and Würtemberg flags. As he was about to enter the train, he was saluted by the princes and principal dignitaries of the court. The Prince Royal wore the broad ribbon of the Legion of Honor which the Emperor had sent him. One might have thought himself back at the Tilsit interview and the days of the Confederation of the Rhine.

CHAPTER XXVII

THE RESULTS OF THE INTERVIEW

THE Stuttgart interview had caused the Austrian government the keenest and most justifiable anxiety. The Emperor Francis Joseph sought to reassure himself by likewise obtaining an interview with the Emperor Alexander II. The Czar had left Stuttgart September 28, 1857. October 1 he had an interview with the Austrian monarch at Weimar. He was accompanied by his Minister of Foreign Affairs, Prince Gortchakoff, but Francis Joseph had taken care not to bring his own Minister of Foreign Affairs, Count de Buol, whose attitude during the Crimean War and at the Congress of Paris had deeply offended the Russian government.

Francis Joseph arrived at Weimar October 1. Alexander II., wearing the uniform of the Austrian hussars, awaited him at the head of the staircase of the grand-ducal castle. The two sovereigns embraced. They had a long conversation without witnesses, and in the evening were present at a representation of Wagner's *Tannhäuser*, directed by Liszt. The next morning at seven o'clock the Emperor of Austria left Weimar for Dresden. The Czar departed an hour later.

That same day the Vicomte des Méloizes, minister of France at Weimar, wrote to Count Walewski: "Austria desired the interview, Russia accepted it; and the Grand Duke facilitated it by placing his palace at the disposal of the two Emperors. As to the meeting itself, although a certain intimacy prevailed, I am assured, between the sovereigns in their two or three conversations, they do not seem, if one may judge from their looks, to have produced a very real reconciliation. During all the time that I was able to observe them at the palace, there was no communication whatever between them, and the way in which they quitted Weimar, at an hour's interval, although they were taking the same road, seems to indicate that their interview did not create a desire to remain longer together. The grand marshal tells me that when the two sovereigns met for the first time, the Emperor Alexander wore an expression of sorrowful gravity which was remarked by every one. . . . It was noticed that at dinner and at the theatre the countenance of the Emperor of Austria, marked by a certain air of embarrassment, which is perhaps habitual, never lost its gravity. The Emperor Alexander, on the contrary, appeared very gay. The two sovereigns embraced each other twice in taking leave. These adieux, I am told, were very effusive. This time, as throughout the whole day, the advances came from the Austrian Emperor."

In fine, the interview of Weimar, far from attenuating the impression produced by that of Stuttgart, had no result but that of bringing its importance into full relief. Curious details on this subject are found in a despatch which the Vicomte de Serre, minister of France at Carlsruhe, addressed to Count Walewski October 4, 1857. The Grand Duchess Hélène of Russia, who had just arrived at Baden, had a long conversation with the French minister. "Madame the Grand Duchess," wrote the Vicomte de Serre, "has assured me that she considers the interview of Stuttgart a most fortunate event for both empires, and especially for Russia. It pleased her to behold in it the point of departure of a close alliance whose consolidation and progress she desires all the more ardently since she has always regarded it, even under the reign of the late Emperor Nicholas, as imperiously demanded by the interests of both nations. If she may be believed, the time is past for suspecting France, wrongly considered as the focus of revolutions merely because she is and ought to be the centre of civilization. The prejudices which formerly alienated from France the instinctive sympathies of Russia became extinct with the late Emperor, or, at most, exist only in the thin-sown ranks of sundry faultfinders of the old aristocracy, always ready to take sides against the governmental policy, be it what it may. Setting aside this imperceptible and powerless minority, Russia would be unanimous in desiring the closest union with France as the sole means of opening to her the paths of civilization and progress. She would comprehend at present that in applying her forces to defend the narrow principles of legitimacy and public order, she had, in fact, merely served the interests of Germany and Austria. The last war, and still more the very different attitude of the several powers since the restoration of peace, had shown her at the same time on which side lay real strength united to loyalty, where she ought to place her friendship and where seek her alliances. Tired of being exploited for the benefit of central Europe and worn-out theories of government, she would hereafter base her alliances, not on the affinities of abstract principles, but, like England, on the practical agreement of positive interests."

Was not the Grand Duchess Hélène here predicting the alliance which the Emperor Nicholas II. and M. Félix Faure recently proclaimed on board the *Pothuau?*

The Grand Duchess assured the Vicomte de Serre that the Emperor, her nephew, had received impressions at the Stuttgart interview which linked him more closely than ever to the Emperor of the French and to France. Her Imperial Highness regretted only that the reunion of the two sovereigns had been of such short duration, for, she added, the more the Emperors saw of each other, the better they seemed to understand and mutually appreciate each other's lofty qualities. Even the Empress of Russia, who did not at first favor the interview at Stuttgart,

Q

as the Grand Duchess was not careful to conceal, had been obliged by the express invitation of the Czar to go there; but, once in presence of Napoleon III., she had been unable to resist the attraction felt by all under an irresistible influence.

The Vicomte de Serre concluded his despatch as follows: "As to the interview at Weimar, Her Imperial Highness merely alluded to it in a rather scornful way as an event without the slightest political importance. Not very favorable to Austria in general, she seemed to me almost to regret that the Emperor Alexander should have lent himself to a superficial reconciliation with the Emperor Francis Joseph. For that matter, in this particular Madame the Grand Duchess simply reproduced the expressions used by all Russians without exception. Those most conversant with the policy of their government are never weary of saying that the interview of Weimar, several times solicited by the Emperor of Austria, had only been conceded by the Czar because he was tired of refusing. . . . M. de Fonta, minister of Russia at Frankfort, tells me that Prince Gortchakoff has authorized and even asked him to declare that though Russia desires to live in peace with her neighbors, and consequently with Austria, she has yet no intention of re-establishing with that power the intimate relations which have been destroyed forever."

And now let us see how the Stuttgart interview was regarded at St. Petersburg. In the absence of

Count de Morny, M. Baudin, *chargé d'affaires* of France, wrote to Count Walewski, October 16, 1857: —

"Prince Gortchakoff said to me: 'Nothing could be more satisfactory than the impression which my sovereign and myself brought back from Stuttgart and from our conversations with the Emperor Napoleon and Count Walewski. It is a great thing, this reconciliation between our two emperors, this perfect conformity of views which has been established between them and their governments on all the questions they attempted to examine, this resolution which they have taken mutually to agree on all that may hereafter arise, small and great. It is chiefly in the future that the interview of Stuttgart will produce its fruits.'"

Prince Gortchakoff repeated to the *chargé d'affaires* of France that the Emperor Alexander was wholly satisfied with the personal relations into which he had just entered with the Emperor Napoleon; said that the Empress of Russia had not appreciated less her acquaintance with His Imperial Majesty, and added that she had expressed great regret at not having been able to meet at Stuttgart the Empress of the French. As to Prince Gortchakoff himself, he showed that he was personally flattered and grateful for the welcome he had received from Napoleon III., and he praised exceedingly — these are his own words — "that elevation of character, that great political sense, those views at once wide and practical, that perfect candor and clearness," which he had been privileged to know.

M. Baudin terminated his despatch as follows: "Such is the impression which the Russian Minister of Foreign Affairs seems to have brought back with him from Stuttgart. That of the Russian public, which is beginning to return to St. Petersburg, naturally cannot be so well founded. It is generally good. At the same time, society in this country, which seldom goes very deeply into things, feels its self-love somewhat wounded by the relatively secondary part which the Emperor of Russia played at Stuttgart, and by the deference he showed towards the Emperor of the French, 'that sovereign of yesterday,' as certain people say here, in calling on him first, and by the indifference with which his journey was received by the German press and people, the latter thronging about Napoleon III. as he passed, and the former making a thousand commentaries with which they did not honor the Emperor Alexander. They are at the same time pleased to see that Russia has such a friend and displeased at the great place he has taken and which the interview of Stuttgart has rendered so manifest. They know what to think of the military power of imperial France, and the Russian travellers who visit Paris in such great numbers daily make known its splendor and its internal prosperity. They are thoroughly aware of its preponderance in external politics, but they do not quite like to own up to it. The Stuttgart interview has brought it into undeniable prominence, and that explains the mixed character of the sentiment awakened here in certain minds by the circumstances of this interview, and which they try at least to conceal from me under an appearance of admiration and deference for the Emperor of the French."

On the whole, Napoleon III. had just obtained a great success. He had not signed a treaty of alliance offensive and defensive at Stuttgart, but he brought back a protocol of general agreement and the assurance of a sympathetic neutrality in case of war against Austria. That sufficed him. As M. Rothan has remarked, he did not like to bind himself; he preferred to keep an open door and leave things to the fatal arrangement of circumstances.

M. Benedetti wrote to M. Thouvenel, October 15, 1857: "The interview of Stuttgart has fulfilled all its promises. After having talked of everything, the two Emperors and their ministers separated with promises of mutual esteem and confidence in the full and complete acceptation of those terms. It was a question of the Principalities, you understand. At bottom, Russia does not desire the reunion, and we are going to move very gently in the direction of the *administrative reunion* solely; one fact certain is the personal success of our Emperor in Germany. You know that the Empress of Russia was not at all inclined to go to Stuttgart, and that she feigned indisposition. But the Emperor Alexander was so charmed with his first conversation with the Emperor

Napoleon that he cut short these hesitations by summoning the Empress immediately to Stuttgart, and they say that Her Majesty now shares her husband's sentiments towards our sovereign. Nor has he met with less success among the people. His journey was like an ovation. Coming after the Osborne interview, all this creates an incomparable situation for us."

Had Napoleon III. remained faithful to the pact of Stuttgart he would always have retained this situation. So long as he was the friend of Alexander II., he had nothing to fear from the English or the Germans. It was by Russia's favor, and in spite of England, that he could give back to France her natural frontiers on the southeast, and protect the Christians of Syria. With the support of the cabinet of St. Petersburg everything succeeded with him; without it, the earth failed under his feet. What would it have cost him to avert all his misfortunes? Simply, non-intervention in the affairs of Poland, and readiness to maintain against all assaults the true alliance, the only one which could have secured glory and safety to imperial France.

CHAPTER XXVIII

THE BEGINNING OF 1858

DURING the first years of the Second Empire, the opera of *Le Prophète*, that work whose striking situations, imagined by Scribe, had inspired Meyerbeer with appropriate music, was often played. In the fourth act, John of Leyden appears under a canopy in the Cathedral of Munster, amidst shouts, the blare of trumpets, and clouds of incense, and at that very moment three Anabaptists, dressed in black, menace him with their poniards. This scene made the Emperor thoughtful. Like the Prophet, amidst his triumphs he had incessant conspiracies to dread. His Anabaptists were the Italian bravos who had sworn his death.

The victor of December 2d had disarmed French hatreds. Those of his subjects who blamed his policy the most had abandoned the idea of killing him. In spite of the irritating souvenirs of the *coup d'État*, the unjust deportations, the draconian and illegal severities of the mixed commissions, the workmen had forgiven Napoleon III., knowing that he concerned himself with their welfare, and when they saw him going unescorted into the most populous quarters of Paris, they praised his courage. But the foreign assassins, the adepts of Mazzini, remained implacable. These, like the Old Man of the Mountain, had a band of murderers in their pay whose fixed idea it was to assassinate the Emperor. London was the headquarters where they organized plots intended to break out in France, The police of Paris were in perpetual alarm. In 1857, three emissaries from London had been arrested for plotting against the Emperor's life, and tried in August by the Seine Court of Assizes. They were Italians, Tibaldi, Bartoloni, and Grilli, the first of whom was sentenced to transportation, and the others to ten years' imprisonment. The trial proved that these three individuals had been hired by the Mazzinian sect, which had erected murder into a system. At the beginning of 1858 those immediately surrounding the sovereign knew that this sect was more active than ever, and that a catastrophe was probably impending. But Napoleon III., being a fatalist, and inaccessible to fear, refused to make any change in his usual habits, and would not take any kind of precautions against the murderers, of whose actions he was notified. When he went out of the Tuileries he did not communicate to the secret police detailed to protect his life the route he intended to follow. He said one day, as Marshal Magnan was expostulating with him on his temerity: "I object to remonstrances. I do not intend to put myself in leading-strings, but to remain free to act as I please. Do not forget what I say, Marshal."

The public was not aware of the ceaseless anxieties which disturbed the Emperor's friends. The year 1858 had opened very well. The season at Paris promised to be very brilliant. At home, the Empire encountered no serious opposition. Abroad, it maintained the most harmonious relations with all the powers. The interview of Stuttgart had been a triumph for Napoleon III., acclaimed in Germany no less than in France. The imperial institutions seemed more solid than ever. The edifice, soon to be menaced by a thunderbolt, seemed immovable and indestructible.

I was at Brussels early in 1858. Count Walewski had sent me there with the ratification of a postal treaty concluded between France and Belgium. I was staying at the house of my cousin, General Plotinckz, commanding superior of the civic guard, and was expecting to remain some days longer with him, when the minister of France, M. Adolphe Barrot, a diplomat of great merit, and brother of the famous orator, sent me word to come immediately to the legation. On my arrival he told me that he would entrust me with a very important despatch, and that I was to start that evening for Paris by the seven o'clock train. He added that when I arrived, during the night, I must go directly to the Ministry of Foreign Affairs and have the chief of the cabinet awakened. This was M. Frederic de Billing, in whose own hands I must place the despatch confided to me, and of which I did not know the contents. I punctually executed my orders. M. de Billing was sleeping at the Ministry, in the room which, forty years later, now serves me as an office. I excused myself for awaking him by alleging the instructions I had received in Belgium. He thanked me, turned his head on his pillow, and went to sleep again.

I have since learned the contents of the despatch, which was not opened until the next morning. It announced the existence of a plot against the Emperor's life. An Italian named Pieri had arrived from England at Brussels, January 7, where he bought the shell of a fulminating bomb. A clockmaker who got wind of the sale went to the office of the French legation, where he urgently requested an interview with the minister himself. On being received by M. Adolphe Barrot, he said to him: "I am not one of the Emperor's partisans; all my sympathies are with the Orleans princes, but I wish to prevent a crime." He then described the suspected man and gave most precise details concerning his movements in Brussels. M. Adolphe Barrot hastily wrote a despatch — the one I conveyed to Paris — containing the declarations of the clockmaker. We shall see later on that, but for M. Barrot's vigilance, both the Emperor and Empress would probably have succumbed.

The man thus denounced to the Paris police was an Italian named Pieri, a native of Lucca, and fifty years of age. Condemned for theft in Tuscany, he had presented himself in France as a political refugee in 1833. Ten years later he enlisted in the foreign legion. Afterwards he served in Tuscany, where he became a major, but was dismissed in 1849. On returning to France he was recognized as a dangerous man and expelled in 1852, in spite of his protestations of humble respect for the person of Napoleon III. There was a peace officer named M. Hébert in Paris in 1858 who remembered Pieri very well. The police made very energetic efforts to lay hands on the latter, but up to January 14 had completely failed. They were aware of his plan, but they did not know that he merely took a secondary part in the conspiracy of which Orsini was the organizer and leader.

A native of the Roman States and aged thirty-nine years, Felix Orsini had associated himself from early youth with the enterprises of the most heated demagogues. In 1845 the supreme tribunal of Rome had condemned him to the galleys for life for conspiring against the pontifical government. The following year, thanks to the amnesty accorded by Pius IX., he recovered his liberty, but without evincing any signs of repentance. Two years afterwards he became a member of the Roman Convention, and then extraordinary commissioner to Ancona and Ascoli. There he was guilty of many abuses of power and of great exactions, yet without enriching himself personally. When the temporal power of the Pope was re-established he wandered into England, Switzerland, Piedmont, and Lombardy, travelling with false passports, now calling himself Celsi and again Herwag. Under the latter name he was accused in 1855 of having arranged a plot against the life of the Emperor of Austria. Incarcerated in the citadel of Mantua, through the complicity of a woman he succeeded in making his escape and took refuge in London, where he gave public readings which gained him a livelihood.

After having made one of Mazzini's adepts and instruments, Orsini resolved to form a band of his own and become a chief conspirator. He met Pieri in Birmingham in 1857, and planned with him an attempt on the life of the Emperor. The two put themselves in communication with a French political refugee named Simon Bernard, a regular customer of the Swiss café in Bow Street, London, which was the usual rendezvous of the most dangerous of the emigrants. Together with Pieri and Bernard, Orsini employed himself in the fabrication of bombs, and in order to the perpetration of the crime added to his circle two obscure acolytes, a Neapolitan named Gomez, aged twenty-nine, — who had served in the foreign legion in 1853 and 1855 and had been condemned for abuse of confidence at Marseilles, whom Orsini attached to himself as a domestic, — and a young man of twenty-five, born in Belluno, who was called Charles de Rudio. He belonged to a noble Venetian family which owed its decline to dissoluteness rather than to poverty. His father and mother had been compromised in political troubles, and, after leading a wandering life he himself had at last settled in Nottingham, England, as a teacher of languages.

Provided with a false passport under the name of Thomas Allsop, Orsini left England November 28, 1857, stopped for some days in Brussels, and went from there to Paris December 12, taking good care to include the bombs in his luggage. At Brussels he commissioned a man named Zeghers to bring a horse which he had just bought to him at Paris, and entrusted to his care ten half-cylinders in iron which he said were to be used as gas-fixtures. Zeghers presented these at the custom-house of Valenciennes, where they were regarded as of so little importance that no duty was collected on them. He did not suspect that these half-cylinders were to be used in the making of fulminating bombs, and on reaching the Parisian hotel where Orsini had put up, he left them in plain sight along with the brushes he had used in grooming the horse. On Orsini's arrival he made haste to conceal objects which might have attracted attention.

Installed since December 15 in a furnished apartment on the ground floor of No. 10 rue Mont-Thabor, the leader of the conspiracy had given himself out for an Englishman and provided himself with visiting cards engraved with the name of Thomas Allsop. January 8 he was rejoined by two of his accomplices, Pieri and Gomez. Simon Bernard was to remain in England. In Paris Orsini was now awaiting the arrival of Charles de Rudio, whom he had not met, and whom Bernard was to send him. The latter gave a sum of money and a passport under the name of Silva to Rudio, who left London January 9, with instructions to go at once on reaching Paris to rue Mont-Thabor, No. 10, to the house of Mr. Allsop, and give him a pair of gold spectacles, the sign agreed on for his recognition. Things happened in this manner, and the four conspirators were together. The police were looking for Pieri only, and had not discovered him. As to the three others, their names were not known nor their presence in Paris suspected.

At this moment the public was chiefly occupied with the funeral of Mademoiselle Rachel, who died at Cannes, January 3, and was buried at Paris, January 11. An immense crowd assisted at the obsequies of the woman whose talent was a national glory. In the evening there was no performance at the Théâtre-Français where she had had so many triumphs. But there was soon no further thought for the actress; other poniards than those of Melpomene occupied attention, and the public was looking at a tragedy in the street, in front of a theatre, which was more terrible than those of Racine and Corneille.

Orsini, a dilettante of crime, made ready for the attempt with the calmness and the bearing of a gentleman. He used to ride in the Bois de Boulogne, seeking opportunities to see the Emperor, following him everywhere, and saying of him: " He has no fear." As was remarked by the imperial prosecutor in his charge, this was neither the expression of regret nor remorse, but of hope. Orsini said to himself: "He suspects nothing, I shall have him, I am sure of reaching him."

CHAPTER XXIX

THE ATTEMPT OF JANUARY 14

THERE is never any performance at the Opéra on Thursday. By exception one was given on Thursday, January 14, 1858, as a benefit for the retiring baritone, Massol. And it was known that the Emperor and the Empress were to be present at a representation announced to be very brilliant. The weather was superb and the night starry. The streets and the approaches to rue Le Peletier were thronged.

At eight o'clock Orsini, Pieri, de Rudio, and Gomez left their lodging, No. 10 rue Mont-Thabor. The parts had been assigned between the four accomplices. The two largest bombs were given to Gomez and de Rudio, Orsini kept two smaller ones, Pieri had taken a fifth similar in size to those of Orsini. It had been agreed that Gomez should throw the first one, Rudio the second, then Orsini, and Pieri the last. It was also agreed that on reaching rue Le Peletier they would take positions on the pavement in front of the principal entrance of the peristyle, between the houses and the crowd of spectators, on a line with No. 21.

Orsini shall go on with the story: "I noticed on

the way that Pieri was lagging behind, and I even said to de Rudio that he made me feel as if he wanted to desert. On arriving at rue Le Peletier he had passed in front of us. We rested two minutes at the corner of the street and the boulevard. We had scarcely entered rue Le Peletier than I met Pieri coming towards us in company with a gentleman whom I did not know. He winked at me in passing, but I did not understand that he wanted to tell me he had been arrested."

Pieri had in fact just been arrested in rue Le Peletier, near rue Rossini, by officer Hébert, who had his description. He was taken to the guard-house, where he was found to be carrying a fulminating bomb and a five-barrelled revolver loaded and primed.

The Emperor and the Empress had not yet arrived. The reigning Duke of Saxe-Coburg-Gotha, who was to witness the play from the imperial box, was awaiting Their Majesties at the foot of the stairs, chatting meanwhile with General Fleury. During the day the Duke had gone out in a carriage with Napoleon III. In crossing the Pont-Neuf, in front of the statue of Henry IV., the Emperor, thinking of the plots which menaced his life, said to the German Prince, "The only thing I dread is a poniard such as Ravaillac's. In any other case the criminal always hopes to save himself by flight, and that thought paralyzes his strength." At the foot of the Opéra staircase General Fleury was bragging to the Duke about the new organization of the surveillance service, and adding that there was nothing more to be feared but plots similar to that of the Hippodrome, where the Opéra-Comique would not be repeated.

It is half-past eight. The imperial procession comes into rue Le Peletier, headed by a carriage containing the officers of the household; then comes the escort formed by a platoon of lancers of the guard; and finally the two-horse carriage containing the Emperor and Empress, and on the front seat an aide-de-camp, General Roguet. Arriving opposite the principal entrance of the theatre, the imperial carriage is driven more slowly so as to enter the reserved passage at the extremity of the peristyle; at this moment three explosions are heard at an interval of a few seconds, the first in front of the imperial carriage and in the last rank of the lancers, the second nearer and a little to the left of the carriage, the third beneath it. Gomez had just thrown the first bomb. Then Orsini had said to de Rudio: "Throw yours!" Rudio had in fact thrown it and at once hidden himself in a cabaret, where he heard the third explosion, produced by one of Orsini's bombs. The first one had extinguished all the gas-jets illumining the front of the theatre merely by the commotion it produced. The glass in the peristyle and in the windows of adjoining houses all flew into splinters. The immense awning which protects the entrance in summer was perforated in spite of its extreme solidity. Struck by seventy-six projectiles, the imperial carriage is literally riddled. One of the horses dies at once, the other is badly hurt. The three footmen and the driver are wounded. Several discharges have entered the carriage. General Roguet has received a violent contusion over the ear which results in his losing a great deal of blood. The Emperor's hat is pierced by a projectile. The robe of the Empress is bloodied, and one hundred and fifty-six persons have been hurt. Among the victims are twenty-one women, eleven children, thirteen lancers, eleven guards of Paris, thirty-one agents or officers of the police prefecture. There is a general commotion, an indescribable tumult, a scene of alarm and horror. The Emperor and Empress do not leave the carriage until after the last explosion. Preserving their coolness, they seem to have no anxiety except to care for those who are wounded. Just as some one is singing the fragment of *William Tell* which opened the evening's performance, they enter the hall. An immense acclamation greets them. They bow their thanks to the public, and as soon as they have taken seats in their box the representation proceeds.

After the morceaux from *William Tell* came the first act of *Mary Stuart*. I have lately had the honor (October, 1897) of chatting with Madame Ristori, now the widow of Marquis Capranica del Grillo, and surrounded by all respect. In describing the representation of January 14, 1858, she said: "When I reached the passage where Mary Stuart, addressing Mortimer, exclaims: 'The arm of the assassin! That is my sole, my real terror,' the Emperor, seated beside the Empress, calm and impassible, gave me a glance that I shall never forget." The all-powerful sovereign, master of France, adulated by Europe, felt that he also had but one fear, the assassins. He too, looking the tragedienne in the face, had a touch of tragedy.

The representation, which was to finish by the *Bal masqué de Gustave* — Gustavus III. of Sweden assassinated in a theatre, — went on without any change in the programme. Their Majesties remained until it was over. At midnight, when they left the Opéra, a great many houses on the boulevard had been spontaneously illuminated, and as they drove by a considerable crowd greeted them with cheers. Among the persons who had come to the Tuileries to congratulate them on having escaped death as by a miracle, Their Majesties found the English ambassador, the president of the Senate, members of the diplomatic corps, senators, and deputies. The Emperor maintained his imperturbable tranquillity, but his face bore the traces of profound sadness.

And now let us see what had become of the murderers. The police had begun the most active investigations immediately after the outrage. Pieri, as we have said already, had been arrested before the explosion of the bombs. How did they contrive to seize Gomez, Rudio, and Orsini?

All the houses on rue Le Peletier, opposite the Opéra, were searched. One of them was the Broggi restaurant. There the police agents noticed a young man, apparently a foreigner, who was weeping and seemed in great trouble. He was asked for his name and address, and replied that he was called Swiney, and that for the last month he had been in the service of a Mr. Allsop, an Englishman, who resided No. 10 rue Mont-Thabor. Shortly after this, a five-barrelled revolver, loaded and primed, was found under a dresser in the restaurant Broggi, where it had been deposited by the so-called Swiney, who was no other than Gomez, and who ended by owning up to the fact. If he had not lost his head he would not have indicated the residence of Orsini, and the police would have been at a loss to seize the arch-conspirator.

After launching his first bomb, Orsini had been one of those wounded by it, and this not only prevented him from throwing the second, but made those around him suppose that he was a victim and not a murderer. He went into the Vautherin pharmacy, No. 34 rue Laffitte, between rue Rossini and rue de Provence, to have his wounds attended to, and on leaving it, a compassionate person named Decailly led him by the arm to a carriage-stand on the corner of rue Laffitte and rue de Provence. A cab took him to his apartment in rue Mont-Thabor. There he believed himself in safety and had just gone to bed when the police entered. He said at first that his name was Allsop, and that he was an Englishman and a brewer. But as soon as he comprehended that the information given by Gomez had ruined him, he avowed that he was Felix Orsini, aged thirty-nine, and a native of Moldola in the Roman States.

As to Rudio, after launching his bomb he had taken refuge in a cabaret. The confusion enabled him to escape, and he quietly returned to the Hôtel de France, No. 132 Montmartre, where he lodged, and where he thought he was safe. Unluckily for him, his address was given by Pieri, as that of Orsini had been by Gomez. The two murderers, both equally agitated, had supplied the information which the police would have been unable to extort. As soon as he was arrested, Pieri had said that he lodged with another person at the Hôtel de France et de Champagne. The agents went with all haste to this hotel, where, in a double-bedded chamber, they found a young man who at first called himself Da Silva, but ended by avowing that he was Charles de Rudio, aged twenty-five, and born at Belluno, in Venetia.

Thus it was that within a few hours, thanks to an extraordinary chance and to information furnished by the guilty men themselves, the police were enabled to lay hands on the four authors of the crime.

M. Chaix d'Est-Ange will say in his speech as public prosecutor: "The buckler which shields the Emperor and Empress is visible to everybody. If Orsini had not been wounded, the fourth bomb would have been thrown, and if Pieri, who was nearest to the cortège, had not been arrested a few minutes before it approached, who could depict the misfortune we should have had to deplore? Yes, it was necessary that by a miracle Pieri should be recognized by possibly the only man who remembered him, and that, by a second miracle, Orsini, after launching his first bomb, should be wounded, not dangerously, but sufficiently so to be marked on the forehead and blinded by a veil of blood which Providence cast over his eyes in order to prevent the greatest of crimes."

At present, may it not be asked whether, from the point of view of the interests of his dynasty, it would not have been better for Napoleon III. to die at a moment when his reign had as yet been characterized only by success? Alas! although so short, human life is yet often too long, even for men whose existence seems the most necessary to their country. If Louis XVI. had died in 1783, after signing the glorious treaty of Versailles which consecrated the independence of the United States; Napoleon in 1811, when the birth of a son crowned the summit of his desires; Charles X. in 1830, on the morrow of the taking of Algiers; Louis Philippe in 1846, after the great success of the Spanish marriages; Napoleon III. in 1858, assassinated like Cæsar at the zenith of his fortunes, — Providence, in giving these sovereigns a timely death, would have spared them the catastrophes which wrecked both them and their dynasties. But on the morrow of the Orsini attempt, nobody made such reflections as these, and on every side thanks were returned to God who had preserved the life of the Emperor.

CHAPTER XXX

AFTER THE OUTRAGE

THE morning after the crime the Emperor and Empress went out in an open carriage and drove without an escort through the boulevards, where they were greeted very warmly. Subsequently they visited, at the Gros-Caillou hospital, those of the wounded who had formed part of their escort on the previous evening.

January 16, they received at the Tuileries the members of the diplomatic corps, of the Senate, the Legislature, the Council of State, and the Municipal Council. The president of the Senate, M. Troplong, spoke as follows: "The revolutionary spirit, driven from France, has chosen its domicile abroad and made itself cosmopolitan. It is from these exterior citadels, raised against Europe in the midst of Europe itself, that fanatical assassins are sent with orders to cast fire and sword upon the prince who bears the buckler of European order on his powerful arm; odious conspirators whose policy consists in assassination, and who attack even feeble women, not knowing that among them there are those whose courage rises even to heroism. But, since these implacable revolutionists have communized their furies of destruction, why do not governments and peoples lend each other a joint support for their legitimate defence? The law of nations authorizes it; equity and mutual interests make it a duty."

The famous jurisconsult, president of the Senate, ended his speech in an almost lyric tone: " Yes, Sire, God, who says by the mouth of the prophet, ' Withdraw from me, ye men of blood!' will not permit that crime should interrupt too soon the mission of restoration and progress which He has imposed upon you. Long live the Emperor!"

Count de Morny, president of the Corps Législatif, spoke next. The following passage was the most noticeable in his address: " We cannot disguise from you, Sire, that the populations we have recently visited are disturbed concerning the effects of your clemency, which is too much in accordance with the goodness of your heart; and when they see such abominable attempts prepared abroad, they wonder why neighboring and friendly powers are unable to destroy these laboratories of assassination, and how the sacred laws of hospitality can be applied to ferocious beasts."

In making his brief acknowledgments to the great bodies of State, the Emperor declared that, although he was determined to take such measures as should be deemed necessary, he would not depart from those paths of prudence and moderation which he had previously followed.

The sympathies of Europe came prominently into view. Count de Persigny, ambassador of France in England, wrote from London to Count Walewski, January 16: "I was at Badminton, at the house of the Duke and Duchess of Beaufort, when tidings of the frightful outrage reached me. Going to London, I found the whole city profoundly affected. As in Paris, public opinion everywhere manifests energetic indignation against that infamous sect of assassins who up to now seem to have found an inviolable asylum in English laws. . . . At the first news of the attempted crime, Lord Palmerston and Lord Clarendon wrote to me, the latter in the name of the Queen, and there arrive momentarily at the embassy new testimonies of sympathy for the Emperor. As to that band of scoundrels who direct these frightful crimes from here, I think that after such an event it will not be difficult for me to obtain some measures respecting them from the English government."

January 18, Napoleon III. opened the session of 1858 at the Tuileries, in the hall of the Marshals. His discourse, one of the most eloquent he ever delivered, produced a very deep impression. He said: "Let us not forget that the progress of every new power is for a long time a struggle. Whatever one may say, the danger does not lie in the excessive prerogatives of power, but rather in the absence of repressive laws. . . . I eagerly welcome, without pausing at their antecedents, all those who recognize the national will. As to provocators of disturbances and organizers of conspiracies, let them know that their time is over."

The close of the imperial speech was received with genuine enthusiasm. "I thank Heaven," said Napoleon III., "for the visible protection with which it has sheltered us, the Empress and myself, and I deplore that so many victims should have been made in order to attack the life of a single man. However, these plots carry with them more than one useful lesson: the first is that the parties which have recourse to assassination prove by desperate efforts their weakness and their impotence; the second is that an assassination, even though successful, has never aided the cause of those who armed the assassins. Neither the party that struck down Cæsar, nor that which aimed at Henry IV., reaped profit from their murder. God sometimes permits the death of the just, but He never permits the triumph of the cause of crime. Hence these attempts can disturb neither my security in the present nor my faith in the future. If I live, the Empire lives with me; and if I fall, the Empire would be still further consolidated by my death, for the indignation of the people and the army would be an additional support for the throne of my son. Let us look forward to the future then with confidence; let our daily labors for the welfare and the greatness of the country be undisturbed by anxious preoccupations. God protect France!"

The Assembly rose as one man and cheered him with the utmost enthusiasm.

Count de Persigny continued to hope that the English government would take the necessary measures. He wrote to Count Walewski, January 18: "Yesterday, during the day, Lord Palmerston called on me twice without finding me at home. I went to his house, and, in his absence, Lady Palmerston was eager to tell me that she hoped the trial would disclose the complicity of other refugees in England, and that I need not doubt the sentiments of Lord Palmerston as to all that ought to be done.

"I am unwilling to close this despatch without telling you how greatly people have been struck by the courage and coolness of the Emperor and Empress under these terrible circumstances. Still, they knew what might be expected from the character of the Emperor; but the Empress has appeared under a wholly new light and has gained universal admiration."

January 20, the *Moniteur* published the following paragraph: "Amidst the general reprobation excited by the outrage of January 14, it has made us indignant to see a Belgian journal, the *Drapeau*, in its issue of January 17, highly approve the assassination of the Emperor. We await the decision of the Belgian government."

Meantime, the dispositions of the English government continued favorable. In a despatch of January 21, M. de Persigny says: "I must not forget to tell you of the prodigious effect produced by the Emperor's speech. Mr. Disraeli told me yesterday that the last part of it seemed to him the most magnificent piece of written eloquence in any known language. But, apart from this merit, the speech has so admirably replied to the attacks made here against our government, that it will floor the mischievous English press for a long time to come."

January 25 the marriage of the Princess Royal with Prince Frederic of Prussia (the future Emperor Frederic III.) was celebrated in London. In Paris, the English ambassador and Lady Cowley gave a grand ball at the embassy in honor of the event. At this ball, as everywhere else, Napoleon III. never lost his imperturbable calm and his impassible attitude. He exhibited neither preoccupation nor anxiety. But, at bottom, he was conscious of being greatly menaced, and he cherished no illusions as to the bitterness of the assassins. What confronted one in the attempt of January 14 was neither an isolated fact nor the crime of a madman or a fool; what had occurred was merely an episode of an incessantly renewed conspiracy. The court retained all its brilliancy, all its animation; but a vague terror reigned there. Every time her husband left the Tuileries, the Empress wondered whether he would return alive. Most precise details, coming not merely from England but from Belgium, Switzerland, and Piedmont, described the sect of assassins as irrevocably bent upon continuing its system of murders.

We cite, among other warnings, this telegraphic despatch addressed to Count Walewski by Prince de La Tour d'Auvergne, Minister of France at Turin: "Count Cavour is informed by a report of the Sardinian police that in one of the outings which the Emperor will take, whether in a carriage or on horseback, several individuals dressed as workmen, among whom there will be some children, are to approach the Emperor as if to present petitions. When His Majesty stops, they will fling at him five egg-shaped objects which, being enveloped in a very delicate covering, are capable of exploding at the slightest shock. These projectiles will be filled with an adhesive material which will stick to garments like glue and produce fumes and an odor which may produce sudden death by asphyxia. This information has been sent from London to Count Cavour."

January 27, the Emperor issues a decree dividing the troops of the line stationed in the interior of France into five great military commands confided to the marshals of France. This decree is generally considered a proof of the mysterious perils which menace the sovereign. He looks at the situation himself as if he were about to be assassinated, and speaks of the regency and the Emperor *minor*.

February 1, M. Achille Fould, Minister of State, bears an imperial message to the Senate. These words occur in it: "Messieurs the senators, the senatus-consult of July 17, 1856, leaves an uncertainty which I think it useful to terminate from to-day. In effect, it does not confer the regency on the Empress, or, in her absence, on the French princes, except the Emperor has not otherwise disposed by public or secret act. I believe I shall satisfy the wishes of the public as well as obey a sentiment of lofty confidence in the Empress by designating her as regent. Moved by the same sentiments, I designate in her absence, as her successors in the regency, the French princes according to the hereditary order of the crown. I have appointed a privy council which, with the addition of the two French princes (Prince Jerome and his son Prince Napoleon), will become the council of the regency by the mere fact of the accession of the Emperor minor, unless, at that moment, I have appointed some one else by a public act. This privy council, composed of men possessing my confidence, will be consulted on great affairs of State, and prepare itself, by studying the duties and necessities of the government, for the important part which the future may hold in reserve for it."

After reading the message, M. Fould acquaints the senators with the existence of letters patent expressed in the following terms: " Wishing to terminate from to-day the uncertainties resulting from the senatus-consult of July 17, 1856, and to give our beloved spouse the Empress Eugénie a mark of the high confidence we have in her, we have resolved to confer and do by these presents confer upon her the title of regent, to bear that title and exercise its functions from the day of the accession of the Emperor minor, all in conformity with the arrangements of the senatus-consult concerning the regency."

The letters patent of February 1 are followed by a decree of the same day which appoints a privy council obliged to assemble under the presidency of the Emperor. Cardinal Morlot, the Marshal Duke of Malakoff, M. Achille Fould, M. Troplong, Count de Morny, M. Baroche, and Count de Persigny are appointed members of this council. February 7, General Espinasse is appointed Minister of the Interior and of Public Safety. Before describing his ministry, we are about to relate the mission of General della Rocca and the trial of Orsini and his three accomplices.

CHAPTER XXXI

GENERAL DELLA ROCCA

GREAT anxiety prevailed in Turin, especially in official circles. What did Napoleon III. think of the situation? Would he hold all Italians responsible for the crime of some of them? Would he open his eyes to the revolutionary centre existing in Piedmont, to the proceedings of political refugees who were always getting up disturbances there, to articles like those in Mazzini's journal, *Italia e Popolo*, which extolled assassination? Italian national aspirations had declared enemies in the Emperor's circle and even among his counsellors. Would they not try to exploit Orsini's attempt against the policy of Count Cavour? The entire plan of this minister rested upon the armed concurrence of France. Apart from such a combination he saw not the slightest chance of wresting Milan and Venice from Austria. If Napoleon III. were to change his tactics, if, conformably with the views of several of his ministers, he adopted the Austrian alliance, all the scaffolding so laboriously erected by M. de Cavour would tumble down. The moment was critical.

At this time Victor Emmanuel conceived the idea

of sending his chief aide-de-camp, General della Rocca, to Paris to congratulate the Emperor on his escape from assassination, and to induce him to persevere in his Italian sympathies.

At first sight, the task did not seem an easy one. The adversaries of Piedmont criticised his conduct severely. The Pope's nuncio in France, Mgr. Sacconi, exclaimed: "Behold the fruit of the agitations stirred up by M. Cavour." Baron Hübner, ambassador of Austria, said that the time had come to form a close alliance between the court of the Tuileries and that of Vienna. It was claimed that Piedmont was an arsenal, a laboratory of conspiracies. Attention was called to the fact that five days before the outrage, Mazzini had published at Genoa a manifesto full of hatred, wrath, and sinister predictions. It was added that on the morrow of the crime a Piedmontese journal, the *Ragione*, had excused murder. These incidents were envenomed, and a rumor that the days of Count Cavour were counted got into circulation.

The envoy of King Victor Emmanuel had to contend against great prejudices, and, though a soldier of distinction, to apply himself to diplomacy. General della Rocca, who died in 1897 at the age of ninety, the latest survivor of the generals of the Italian army, was born June 20, 1807. He possessed his sovereign's entire confidence and was not a new acquaintance to Napoleon III. Twice already he had been extremely well received at the Tuileries. He was there at the close of 1855, with Victor Emmanuel, then so petted by the Emperor.

In his work, *Ricordi storici e anedottici del generale Della Rocca*, the general has given some curious details concerning this sojourn of the King at Paris. Victor Emmanuel had been a widower for two years. Napoleon III. wanted him to marry a Hohenzollern princess, a daughter of Prince Antony of Hohenzollern-Sigmaringen, who had just sold his insignificant principality of Sigmaringen to the head of his family, the King of Prussia. This princess was a relative of the Emperor, since her mother was a daughter of the Grand Duchess Stephanie of Baden, who was a Beauharnais. In a remarkable essay on the work of General della Rocca, Count Joseph Grabinski has noted that at this time Napoleon III. was far from suspecting that a son of Prince Antony of Hohenzollern would afterwards provoke the Franco-Prussian War and be the cause of the fall of the Second Empire.

General della Rocca went again to Paris in 1856, and was present at the baptism of the Prince Imperial. When he once more appeared at the Tuileries, January 24, 1858, bearing an autograph letter from the King to the Emperor, he was excited and disturbed. He had just learned that Napoleon III. had said: "Piedmont is an asylum of revolutionists and assassins. Orsini stayed there several times, and Mazzini constantly goes there without the police paying the slightest attention to him." Accompanied by Marquis de Villamarina, minister of Sardinia at Paris, and by Count Charles de Robilant, artillery captain and orderly officer of His Sardinian Majesty (the same who was Minister of Foreign Affairs from 1885 to 1887), he presented himself at the Tuileries and remitted Victor Emmanuel's letter without comment.

January 26, a ball was given at the court of Turin. The next day Prince de La Tour d'Auvergne, minister of France, wrote to Count Walewski in a private letter: "I was able to see M. Cavour again last evening at the court ball, and to tell him once more how useful I thought it would be if he should adopt some serious measure concerning the press, or, at any rate, the *Italia e Popolo*. I reminded him of the constant good-will of the Emperor with regard to Piedmont, and the obligations imposed by it, under existing circumstances, on the government of Victor Emmanuel. I called his attention to the fact that while in Switzerland, Belgium, and even in England a disposition to do something was manifest, it would be truly unaccountable if our friendly advances should receive a less favorable reception at Turin, or if, under any pretext of legality, there should be any hesitation about suppressing the official organ of assassination, the *Italia e Popolo*, or prosecuting the *Unione* and the *Diritto*, which had glorified in a way the outrage of the 14th. Count Cavour, as in our former conversation, intrenched himself behind the necessity of a law and the difficulty of his personal position."

In the same letter, Prince de La Tour d'Auvergne added these really curious remarks: "I should think it indispensable, in case there is question of insisting with Count Cavour in order to obtain a more obvious proof of his good-will, that Your Excellency should explain yourself clearly to Marquis de Villamarina. The plan of the defenders of the existing state of things and its continuance is, in fact, at this moment, to insinuate that I am *an agent who goes beyond the desires and intentions of his government.* They have recourse to a thousand petty manœuvres of this sort which plainly prove, it seems to me, that they are at bay, and to which, for my part, I attach no manner of importance."

It soon became evident that Napoleon III. did not dream of renouncing his Italian sympathies. February 3, on occasion of the foreign princes who had come to congratulate him, he reviewed several corps of his guard and of the army of Paris in the court of the Tuileries and Place du Carrousel. Beside him were three princes of Prussia, Frederic Charles, Adalbert and Albert, Prince Francis of Lichtenstein, the Prince of Hesse, and the Prince of Paskiewitch. He was accompanied by five marshals of France, Vaillant, Magnan, Pélissier, Canrobert, Bosquet, and by General della Rocca. Behind him came a brilliant staff in which a large number of foreign officers were noticeable. Prince Napoleon, on horseback beside the Emperor, wore the broad ribbon of the Black Eagle of Prussia. The Empress and the Prince

Imperial were present at this review, the first since the outrage. "The Emperor," says General della Rocca, "rode at the head of his staff. At a certain moment, turning to the side where the group of extraordinary ambassadors was, he saw me and by a gesture invited me to approach him. He kept me beside him nearly all the time, calling my attention to one regiment and another in such a way that the spectators might have believed that the review was given in honor of the representative of King Victor Emmanuel."

So then, at a time when the relations between Paris and Turin seemed very tenuous, and when more than one diplomatist fancied that Napoleon III., irritated against the revolutionary agitations of Piedmont, would turn towards Austria, the taciturn and mysterious sovereign was clinging more fondly than ever to his dream of uniting with Victor Emmanuel against that power. At a period when the policy of the Sardinian government was exciting lively apprehensions in official circles, the Emperor, while seeming to judge the cabinet of Turin severely, showed himself most courteous and attentive to the first aide-de-camp of the King and secretly approved the tendencies of Count Cavour.

General della Rocca says again: "Early in February, an invitation to dinner was sent to me and Count Robilant from the Tuileries, and, at the same time, a letter from the minister of the Emperor's household, saying that I would be received in private audience by the Emperor the same evening. An hour after the official dinner, during which the Emperor wore the broad ribbon of the *Annonciade*, and at which the Marquis de Villamarina and I occupied the places of honor, the Emperor invited me into his cabinet."

Face to face with the general, the Emperor began by saying that the King's letter seemed to him affectionate, and that in reply he meant to write to him at length. He then talked about the *Ragione* newspaper which, having been tried as guilty of apologizing for assassination, had just been acquitted, and added that the Piedmontese code was insufficient to prevent the excesses of the press. Then he said that Piedmont had not much to expect from England, while all its interests counselled a close union with France. He affirmed, moreover, that he was very sure of his army, and that it was ready to march with the greatest zeal into any country which was pointed out to it as a refuge of assassins.

"During this first private audience with the Emperor," adds General della Rocca, "the Emperor was as courteous to me personally as he was severe with respect to my government. In dismissing me, he invited me to come and see him at the Tuileries whenever I desired between nine and ten o'clock in the morning."

On learning by means of a letter from General della Rocca the details of the private interview of February 5, Victor Emmanuel was at first disquieted, but he soon became reassured. Several men devoted to the Italian cause were among the Emperor's close confidants, notably M. Mocquart and Doctor Conneau, who were much more conversant than his ministers with his projects. An ardent Milanese patriot, Count Arese, was probably his best friend. Nevertheless, the emotion produced by fear of the Emperor's displeasure was such that Count Arese himself did not venture to come to Paris, dreading to find him irritated against Piedmont. Doctor Conneau wrote to him, January 29: "I told the Empress that you asked me to present your respects. At first she thought that you had arrived in Paris, and was greatly delighted. When I told her what prevented your coming, she exclaimed: 'But there are Italians and Italians. Happily the bad ones are few. I love the good Arese greatly. Tell him I hope he will come here to spend some days next spring. I cannot show him a houseful of children, but I will show him a sample which will not displease him.' I give you the words as she spoke them so as not to weaken their importance."

Honest and patriotic Italians were doing their utmost to repudiate all connection with a handful of assassins who excited almost universal reprobation. The wife of the Sardinian minister at Paris remitted to the Empress a bouquet made at Genoa, and sent to the sovereign by Piedmont, together with some verses by the poet Proti. When he had another audience, General della Rocca found the Emperor quite friendly to the Piedmontese government. "A letter which the King had written me," says the general, "was to be read by me to the Emperor of my own motion, so to say, giving myself meanwhile the appearance of hesitating and almost refusing to acquaint him with its contents. I was to pretend to be acting on my own responsibility and to be going beyond my instructions." This little comedy succeeded.

At the end of his letter, Victor Emmanuel thus expressed himself: "According to what I have just said to you, my dear La Rocca, the Emperor ought to be well persuaded of my good intentions, and to see that things had been done even before he demanded them. If he wishes me to resort to violent measures here, let him know that I would lose all my influence. . . . If the words you have sent me are literally those of the Emperor, tell him, in the best words you can find, that a faithful ally is not treated in this way, that I have never permitted violence from any one, that I always pursue the path of stainless honor, and that, for this honor, I answer only to God and my people; that we have held our heads high for eight hundred and fifty years and that nobody will make me lower mine, and, with all that, I yet desire nothing but to be his friend."

After listening to the last phrase, Napoleon III. exclaimed: "That is what is called having courage. Your king is a brave man, I like his answer. He shows himself under these circumstances to be just what I supposed him in 1855. It pleases me to see

once more that Victor Emmanuel is somebody. . . .
I am sure we shall understand each other. Write
to him at once; tranquillize him concerning my
intentions; express my regret for having pained
him. . . . I love Italy, and I will never be Austria's
ally against her. My antecedents ought to reassure
you. And if I had occupied in 1849 the place I
occupy at present, I should certainly have gone to
the assistance of Charles Albert."

Prince de La Tour d'Auvergne wrote to Count
Walewski: "Turin, February 16, 1858. I had the
honor to see the King yesterday morning. His
Majesty told me he had just received a perfectly satisfactory letter from General della Rocca, and that
the assurances of friendship and good-will which the
Emperor had charged the general to convey to him
had completely effaced the impression which General
della Rocca's first report had caused.

"Turin, February 19. The Chamber of Deputies
resumed its public sessions yesterday. The government availed itself of the occasion to propose the
project of a law modifying the composition of juries,
and establishing in a more precise manner in what
the apology for assassination consists. They say the
law will pass by a sufficiently strong majority. The
extreme right and the extreme left will be the only
parties to make a lively opposition. As to the left
centre, it seems most eager to seize this occasion to
manifest its sympathies with France."

On the whole, General della Rocca had completely

VICTOR EMMANUEL
King of Sardinia

succeeded in his mission. He deserved the eulogies of his sovereign, who said to him in a cordial letter: "I embrace and thank you with all my heart. You have rendered me a great service, and got out of the scrape wonderfully well, better than a diplomatist."

February 20, the general was received for the last time in private audience by the Emperor, who let him clearly understand, and even authorized him to say to the King, in a confidential but positive way, that in case of war by Piedmont against Austria, he would come with his faithful army to fight beside his faithful ally, Victor Emmanuel. "Say also to M. Cavour," added Napoleon III., "that he ought to put himself in direct correspondence with me, and that we should certainly understand each other."

The general terminates as follows the account of his final audience: "So then I had been a skilled diplomatist without knowing it, and I still rejoice at it, more on account of the results obtained than on my own. Respect for truth obliges me to say that the good star which has guided me in the serious circumstances of my life so arranged that at the very time of my sojourn in Paris, and when Napoleon III. was showing himself more friendly towards us, he received through M. Piétri, prefect of police, a letter which Orsini had written him from his prison, in which the conspirator repeated to the Emperor what I had been obliged to tell him, namely, that the Italians had taken the firm resolution not to endure Austrian domination any longer. This letter must have affected the Emperor deeply, and reminded him of his early years, when he and his brother had likewise conspired for the deliverance of Italy. Ripe reflection made him see that an alliance with Piedmont might be advantageous to France and to his dynasty, and he unhesitatingly resolved to act in our favor."

The war with Italy was decided on.

CHAPTER XXXII

THE ORSINI TRIAL

FEBRUARY 25, the assizes court of the Seine assembled under the jurisdiction of first president Delangle to try Orsini and his three accomplices. The act of accusation, drawn up and read by Attorney General Chaix d'Est-Ange, produced very little impression; it merely stated facts already known. Then followed the interrogatories. Gomez, whose only concern was to save his own head, stammered out some humble explanations, and declared his repentance. "I was M. Orsini's servant," said he, "and I obeyed his orders."

Rudio alleged as his excuses the fear with which his accomplices inspired him and his extreme poverty. "At London," said he, " in 1856, I had been offended because I was suspected of being an informer of the French government, so I was obliged to go to extremes; I sacrificed myself to vanity so as not to be called a traitor." As he owned up to the money he had received from Orsini, President Delangle said to him: "So you belong to an honorable family which has held a considerable rank. You voluntarily quitted the cadet school at Milan, you shirked labor, you threw yourself into revolutionary movements, and gradually you have become an assassin, a mercenary assassin for three hundred and thirty francs which have been given you, and twelve shillings a week which have been promised to your wife."

Pieri got off a series of unlikely lies and theatrical declamations, which produced no effect whatever.

The only striking interrogatory was that of Orsini. "It was in the course of last year," said he, "that Pieri and I began talking of the plan put into execution on January 14. We were convinced that the surest way to make a revolution in Italy was to produce one in France, and that the surest way to do that was to kill the Emperor." He then went into the most precise details concerning the preparations for and the execution of the attempt. "I loaded the bombs myself in my room on rue Mont-Thabor. I had to dry the powder myself, watch and thermometer in hand, before the fire; if a spark had fallen on it, I should have been blown up, with all in the house." After the accused had coolly described all the scenes of the crime, this dialogue took place between President Delangle and him: —

The President. — What co-operation did you count upon in Paris in case your abominable attempt had succeeded?

Orsini. — I said to myself: When something happens at Paris, that will probably destroy the system pursued in France in reference to Italy, and doubtless bring about an insurrection in my country.

The President. — And was it in hope of an insurrection in Italy, and to restore to her the liberty of 1849, that you became an assassin in France?

Orsini. — I wished to give Italy independence; for no liberty is possible without independence. I have written in this sense to M. Cavour. He has not answered me.

The President. — You wished, I repeat, to give Italy the liberty she had in 1849, the liberty of the triumvirs with murder and robbery. And you did not recoil before the frightful disasters your crime would have entailed. Sit down.

The witnesses were then heard, but they disclosed no new facts.

The second and last hearing took place February 26. The Attorney General, M. Chaix d'Est-Ange, made a long charge which ended as follows: " France and the world have been miraculously saved. Providence has protected the Emperor, the Emperor whose courage and confidence had not disarmed the arms of the murderers! On the very scene of the outrage, amidst the carnage, when the victims were stretched upon the pavement, a universal cry proceeded from the crowd. Presently that grand acclamation came nearer; it is sounding still, and the bell of the *Te Deums* is yet ringing in our ears. There was no one who did not comprehend that the world was saved.

"I mistake, and I ask pardon for my words. No, the efforts of the assassins would have been powerless. Providence protects the Emperor, and had they cast him under their feet, they would not have slain with him the order and the institutions he has founded. Institutions remain.

"Mourning France would have risen as one man in the name of the heir of the throne. The Emperor may perish; his name and his race will survive!"

After a recess of twenty minutes, M. Jules Favre, Orsini's advocate, began his plea as follows: "Gentlemen of the jury. Would that I might for an instant banish from my mind the painful emotions which besiege it, in order to render a public and sincere token of admiration to the eminent orator you have just listened to. He has long given lustre to our order, where his place remains empty, where the memory of his person will remain loved and glorious. He must necessarily add brilliancy to the functions he has accepted, and which must borrow new authority from the prestige of his words."

After this eulogy of his former confrère, now Attorney General of the Empire, the republican advocate sought to represent the outrage as a purely political crime: "The true day of justice," said he, "is that on which the accused appears before you; it is there that he brings his last word, his last explanations, his justification and his defence. Listen, then, to the accused, and say whether his words are those of boasting or of weakness."

Great was the surprise of the audience when Jules Favre added: "Hold, he has left his last testament, his prayer, in a writing addressed to the Emperor from his prison, a writing which I am about to read to you, *after obtaining permission to do so from him to whom it was addressed.* It is thus expressed:—

"'To Napoleon III., Emperor of the French:—

"'The evidence I have given against myself is sufficient to send me to death, and I shall submit to it without asking pardon, as much because I will never humble myself before him who has killed the nascent liberty of my unhappy country, as because, in my situation, death is a benefit.

"'Near the close of my career, I nevertheless wish to make another effort in aid of Italy, whose independence has made me, up to this day, brave all dangers and anticipate all sacrifices. It is the object of all my affections, and it is this final thought which I wish to embody in the words I address to Your Majesty.

"'To maintain the existing equilibrium of Europe, either Italy must be made independent, or the chains in which Austria holds her must be tightened. Do I ask that the blood of Frenchmen shall be shed for Italians to accomplish this deliverance? No, I do not go so far as that. Italy demands that France shall not intervene against her; she demands that France shall not permit Germany to support Austria in the struggles soon to break out. Now, this is precisely what Your Majesty can do if so disposed. On your will depends the welfare or the misfortunes of my country, the life or death of a nation to which Europe owes in great part her civilization.

"'Such is the prayer which I dare address to Your Majesty from my dungeon, not despairing lest my feeble voice should not be heard. I adjure Your Majesty to restore to my country the independence which her children lost in 1849 by the fault of Frenchmen themselves.

"'Let Your Majesty remember that Italians, among them my father, gladly shed their blood for Napoleon the Great, wherever he chose to lead them; remember that they were faithful to him up to his fall; and that so long as Italy is not independent, the tranquillity of Europe as well as that of Your Majesty is only a chimera. Let not Your Majesty repel the last cry of a patriot on the steps of the scaffold; deliver my country, and the benedictions of twenty-five millions of citizens will follow you in posterity.

"'From the prison of Mazas.

"'Signed: Felix Orsini.

"''February 11, 1858.'"

As an orator, Jules Favre was a bit of a tragedian. There was something strange and lugubrious in his eloquence. In listening to his sombre, grave, pathetic voice, one felt a presentiment that his name would be blended with the agonizing hours of our history. When it expressed sinister ideas, as in the Orsini trial, this powerful voice, broken by a sort of hiccough which resembled a sob or a death rattle, made one shudder. One seemed to see the scaffold already rising for the accused, of whom the orator was trying to make a martyr. After reading what he called his client's last will, "Orsini," said he, "has bowed before God, comprehending that His decrees condemned his enterprise. To-day he is about to die. From the border of his grave he addresses him against whom he feels no hatred, him who may be the saviour of his country, and says to him: 'Prince, you glory in having sprung from the entrails of the people, from universal suffrage; well, then, resume the ideas of your glorious predecessor; Prince, heed not the flatterers, be great and magnanimous, and you will be invulnerable.'"

The defence terminated in these words, which transformed it into a sort of funeral oration: "You have no need, gentlemen of the jury, of the adjurations of the Attorney General; you will do your duty without feebleness or passion. But God who is above us, God before whom the accused and their judges will appear, God who will judge us all, God who will measure the extent of our faults, God will pronounce on this man also, and will perhaps grant him a pardon which earthly judges would have believed impossible."

Three advocates, Nogent Saint-Laurens, Nicolet,

and Mathieu, afterwards pleaded, the first for Pieri, the second for Gomez, the third for Rudio. Sentence was then pronounced. Orsini, Pieri, and Rudio were condemned to the penalty of parricides, Gomez to compulsory labor for life.

It has been said that Napoleon III. would have much preferred to spare the lives of all the prisoners, but was prevented by his ministers. For Rudio alone the death penalty was changed to compulsory labor for life. It has also been claimed that the Emperor saw Orsini mysteriously in his prison; but we have found it impossible to verify the exactness of this assertion, which is also improbable. What seems certain is that the prefect of police, M. Piétri, had an interview with the condemned, in which he revealed to him the intentions of Napoleon III. with regard to Italy, and the folly there would have been in causing the disappearance of the only man who had the power and the will to liberate her.

March 9, four days before ascending the scaffold, Orsini, then in the Roquette prison, vestibule of the guillotine, addressed the Emperor in a second letter still more solemn than the first. He said in it: "The sentiments of Your Majesty towards Italy are no slight consolation for me at the moment of death. Soon I shall be no more. Before rendering my last vital breath I declare that assassination, no matter under what pretext it may veil itself, does not enter into my principles, even though, by a fatal aberration of mind, I organized the attempt of January 14. But assassination was never my system, and I have contended against it, at the peril of my life, by my writings and by my political life. Let my compatriots, instead of relying upon assassination as a means, learn from the mouth of a patriot about to die that their abnegation, their devotion, their union, their virtue alone, can assure the deliverance of Italy, render her free, independent, and worthy of the glory of their sires. I am going to die calmly, and I desire that no stain shall sully my memory. As to the victims of January 14, I offer them my blood in sacrifice, and I beg that Italians, once become independent, may some day indemnify those who have suffered. Your Majesty will permit me, in closing, to beg the grace of life, not for myself, but for those of my accomplices who have been condemned to death."

The execution of Orsini and of Pieri took place March 13, at seven o'clock in the morning. An hour and a half earlier, the condemned had been notified that their appeal for mercy had been rejected by the Court of Cassation. They were assisted in their last moments by two chaplains, Abbé Hugon and Abbé Rottelet. M. Maxime du Camp, who witnessed the proceedings, described them as follows to Marquis de Laborde: Orsini retained his air of haughty elegance. Pieri appeared rather as a man of the people. Both had to undergo the penalty of parricides, and as such they were led to the place of punishment in their shirts, with bare feet, and heads covered with black veils. When Pieri's shoes were taken off, "If I had known," said he, "I would have washed my feet." The scaffold was erected on Roquette Place. The two Italians climbed its steps with firmness. The crowd, so often jeering and ignoble at such spectacles, was this time thoughtful and silent; it seemed to be wondering whether great events would not soon be the consequence of this execution. Before laying his head under the knife of the guillotine, Orsini cried in a strong and vibrating voice: "Long live Italy!" They were his last words.

CHAPTER XXXIII

GENERAL ESPINASSE

THE appointment of a military man as Minister of the Interior and the presentation of a draconian law such as that of general safety, prove the trouble and consternation caused by the Orsini outrage in official circles. Since the explosion of the infernal machine under the Consulate and that of Fieschi under the reign of Louis Philippe, no such panic had been seen. One would have said the ground was trembling under the Emperor's tread, and that a black veil, covered with blood, had suddenly overspread the prosperity of his reign. His court, so joyous and brilliant, felt paralyzed, and sought by a rigorous policy to ward against the dangers which seemed to threaten it.

February 7, 1858, General Espinasse was appointed Minister of the Interior as successor to M. Billault, and to this title was added that of "Minister of General Safety." This appellation was sufficient to indicate the part assigned him.

General Espinasse was forty-two years old. Born April 2, 1815, at Saissac in the department of the Aude, he entered the military school of Saint-Cyr in

1833. After gaining his first promotions in Algeria, he commanded in 1849 the 42d of the line at the time of the siege of Rome. General de Saint-Arnaud, under whom he made in 1851 the campaign of Kabylia, summoned him to Paris to take part in the *coup d'État*, and it was he who occupied the Palais Bourbon in the night of December 1-2. General of brigade in 1852, aide-de-camp of the Emperor, commander in 1854 of a brigade of the army of the Orient, he merited by his bravery and his military talents in the Crimea the rank of general of division. He notably distinguished himself at the battle of Traktir and the assault of the Malakoff. He was one of the youngest and most brilliant of French generals.

The court desired the new Minister of the Interior to have a hand of iron, but was not careful about the velvet glove. The Emperor wrote him in a private letter: "The body social is gnawed by a sort of vermin of which it is necessary to get rid at any cost. There are also prefects who must be displaced in spite of their protectors. For this I rely upon your zeal. Do not seek by an inordinate moderation to reassure those who have been alarmed by your accession to the ministry. They must fear you, otherwise your appointment would have no excuse for being."

On his side, the Minister General formulated his programme as follows in a letter addressed to his sovereign: "If between 1848 and 1851 all social institutions had not incurred unequalled peril, you would be simply an ambitious vulgarian who had exploited to his own advantage certain evanescent troubles. If the country has seen and proclaimed in you its saviour, it is because that peril was immense and of such a character that six years are altogether too short a time in which to dispel it. France knows it, and France desires what she desired in 1851. . . . A universal cry has gone up towards you, a cry which it is only just to translate by these words: 'Guarantee to us once more the order of which you have made yourself the exponent and arbiter; since the same danger threatens us, be what you already have been to avert it from our heads.'"

In his circular to the prefects, General Espinasse declared that France, tranquil and glorious, had relied too far on the soothing of anarchical passions, that the Emperor's generosity had nourished this hope by multiplying pardons and amnesties; but that in the end an execrable outrage had opened all eyes and revealed the savage resentments, the culpable attempts still cherished by the revolutionary party. The conclusion arrived at by the general was that it was necessary to give France by an attentive surveillance the guarantees which she required, and the circular terminated by the old formula of the *coup d'État:* "It is time that the good should be reassured and the wicked made to tremble."

It was not merely in the interior that the situation was growing gloomy. The relations between France and England had begun to be disturbed. At the end of January the *Moniteur* had inserted several addresses signed by colonels on behalf of their regiments, to protest against the Orsini outrage. Most of these addresses were irreproachable. The signers confined themselves to assuring Napoleon III. of their loyalty, and to declaring that if he had fallen under the blows of assassins the entire army would have risen as one man to defend the throne of Napoleon IV. But, in addition to this correct language, there were in some of them insults and violent threats against England which the *Moniteur* published without reflecting on their consequences. That of the 39*th of the line*, Colonel Hardy, contained this phrase: "In our manly hearts, indignation against the perverse, succeeding to our gratitude towards God, inclines us to demand an account from the land of impunity where lies the den of the monsters who shelter themselves beneath its laws. Give the order, Sire, and we will pursue them into their safe hiding places."

The 5*th regiment of mounted chasseurs*, Colonel Cassaignoles: "For the second time, the life of Your Majesty, so dear to the army, so precious, so indispensable to the peace and welfare of all Europe, has been imperilled by foreign hands. Odious assassins, miserable instruments directed by the enemies of society! ... Those enemies are beyond our reach; but, if our arms are paralyzed, Your Majesty's will and that of France could destroy these lairs of abominable conspirators."

The 22*d of the line*, Colonel Mattat: "We would not express our entire mind if we omitted to say we think it monstrous that demagogues of the worst kind can find anywhere in the world a refuge where they are permitted peacefully to regulate the assassination of sovereigns and the overthrow of peoples. In France as elsewhere, the law cannot remain powerless. To conceal nothing, in short, it seems impossible to consider as friends governments capable of giving asylum to bandits to whom the proclamation of regicide is permitted with impunity, and who end by hurling defiance at honesty and civilization by massacres like that of the rue Le Peletier."

These addresses exasperated British pride and susceptibility to such a point that for an instant a rupture seemed imminent between France and England.

At the same time, the law of general security produced a very lively sensation. It had been presented to the Corps Législatif on February 1. Its eight articles resulted in a provision conferring on government a vague and formidable right to proscribe its enemies without a trial, either by expelling them from its territory, or by interning them in France or Algeria. Here is the list of those for whom administrative good pleasure was to take the place of all judicial guarantees: all men who in May and June, 1848, in June, 1849, or in December, 1851, had been either condemned, interned, expelled, or transported as a measure of security; all who should have been condemned for outrages against the Emperor or the imperial family, for conspiracy tending to disturb the State by civil war, for the illegal employment of armed force, for devastation and public pillage, for fabrication of false passports; all who had been guilty of less well defined offences; rebellion, even unarmed, providing it were by bands, provocation to disobedience to military men, the making or even the simple keeping of arms and munitions of war, any sort of participation in insurrectionary movements. Moreover, the law created several new offences, notably that of manœuvres at home or abroad with intent to trouble public peace, and that of holding up the Emperor's government to hatred or contempt.

In the liberal party there was a movement of unanimous reprobation against such a project. It was characterized as *a law of suspects*. M. Alfred Darimon, in a note requested from him by Prince Napoleon with intent to place it before the eyes of the Emperor, wrote as follows towards the end of March: "On the morrow of the outrage, astonished Europe is told that the Empire is undermined at its foundations, that it is surrounded by conspiracies, that it is menaced by secret societies, that if recourse is not had to measures which permit the government to do what it pleases with a certain category of citizens, all is up with it. In other words, it has just been proclaimed that seven years of a glorious policy have been useless, that all must be begun over again, even the *coup d'État*. Parties were dead, they are resuscitated; they came to the Empire, they are repelled."

To strike Frenchmen in order to punish a crime

committed exclusively by Italians for an Italian object, seemed neither just nor logical. The Corps Législatif, in spite of its habitual docility, showed a significant aversion against the project. The government sought to allay scruples by publishing in the *Moniteur* of February 13 a note stating that the new measures were a part of an aggregate plan long ago resolved upon, that the appointment of General Espinasse to the Ministry of the Interior in no way modified the imperial policy, and that the law of general security would, moreover, be applied with moderation.

The committee elected by the Corps Législatif to examine the projected law, selected Count de Morny to draw up its report. The latter, always skilful in evading difficulties, declared in his report that those who did not conspire had nothing to fear from a law aimed neither at legitimists, Orleanists, nor even at moderate republicans. The government would respect all their memories, all their hopes, and would hold none responsible but demagogues and the instigators of conspiracies. M. de Morny added that the new state of things would be transitory, and that the intervention of high functionaries would prevent all contempt or intemperate severity.

The debates opened, February 18, before an audience much larger than usual. M. Émile Ollivier delivered a superb speech against the proposed law. "I wish," said he, "to show myself, not a man of party, but an honest man; I have but one object, that of paying homage to justice." The eloquent orator thus closed a discourse which produced a great impression: "The law ought to be rejected, not through a spirit of paltry opposition, but through wisdom, even through devotion to the sovereign, and to point out the true path which should inaugurate the policy of the future."

After two days' discussion the project was adopted. There were but twenty-four deputies who voted against it. In the Senate the law encountered but one opposing voice. "But that voice," M. Darimon has said in his remarkable work entitled, *Histoire de douze ans*, "that voice was worth a thousand: it was that of General de MacMahon. The sessions of the Senate, not being public, the general's discourse was known only to a very small number of persons. Foreign journals tried to introduce it into France, but they were intercepted at the frontier. If this speech had become widely known, it would have produced considerable effect on public opinion."

In virtue of the new law, four hundred persons were arrested and three hundred of them transported to Algeria. "This execution accomplished," says M. de La Gorce in his *Histoire du Second Empire*, "the government, whether through a recovery of *sang-froid*, through moderation or repentance, refused to push any further so unexpected and inopportune a repetition of the *coup d'État*." March 25, the *Moniteur* announced that the end proposed had been attained, and that even those who found themselves under the stroke of governmental severity had nothing to fear if they did not render themselves guilty of new deeds. The law of general security remained like a sword of Damocles, but it almost never fell.

Napoleon III. was hesitating between two paths: that which led to reaction, and that whose end was the coronation of the imperial edifice by liberty. The rigorous policy and the policy of pacification each had partisans among the advisers of the sovereign. General Espinasse represented the former, which was opposed by Prince Napoleon. Wishing to justify his programme, the general minister addressed a note to the Emperor which, after the 4th of September, was found among the papers of the Tuileries. "Of two things one," said he in this note; "either Your Majesty wishes to modify your system, give the lie to your antecedents, cease, as I think, to respond to the wishes and most imperative needs of the country, and then, I admit, I neither am nor can be the man for such a mission; or else Your Majesty wishes, with good reason, to persevere in the principles of vigilant authority which are and should remain the bases of your government, while relaxing, in due measure, that which an exceptional position has necessarily stretched too tightly; and in that case the reins can be properly loosened only by a man who is capable of shortening them vigorously in case of necessity. To remove that man is to furnish new food to public anxiety, to justify it by an appearance of versatility and weakness, without in the least contenting those who, at bottom, aim at overthrowing imperial institutions."

Here the general posed as a necessary man, and offered his resignation in case his ideas were not accepted by the Emperor. This resignation was accepted, and General Espinasse, made a senator, was replaced June 15 as Minister of the Interior by M. Delangle, who did not add to this title that of Minister of General Safety. At the same time a new ministry, that of Algeria and the Colonies, was created in favor of Prince Napoleon, who was thus called to a place in the council. The exceptional policy brought into play by the crime of January 14 was suspended, and an initial orientation towards the liberal Empire of 1870 might already be divined.

CHAPTER XXXIV

COUNT DE PERSIGNY

ONE of the consequences of the attempt of January 14 was to stir up complications between France and England, which for several weeks assumed a very serious character and subjected the alliance of the two nations to a very rude trial.

The ambassador of Napoleon III. near Queen Victoria, since May 7, 1855, was Count de Persigny. Born at Saint-Germain-Lespinasse, in the department of the Loire, January 11, 1808, he had just completed his fiftieth year. His career, like that of his sovereign, had been filled with troubles and vicissitudes. The son of an officer of the First Empire who perished at the battle of Salamanca, he had come out first from the military school of Saumur in 1826, but left the military service in 1833. Under the reign of Louis Philippe he wrote in the legitimist journals before embracing Bonapartism, of which he was one of the most ardent apostles and principal precursors. He contributed greatly to the organization of the Strasburg conspiracy. The indictment represented him as "a man of brains and resolution, active, intelligent, possessing more fully than any one else the secret of the springs on which the plot rested." Arrested with Prince Napoleon, he succeeded in escaping and took refuge in England. Having also taken part in the Boulogne expedition, he was condemned to twenty years of detention. Imprisoned at first at Doullens, he obtained permission to be transferred to the military hospital of Versailles. Towards the end of Louis Philippe's reign, he was simply interned within the enclosure of that city, where he enjoyed entire freedom of action. A deputy to the Legislative Assembly in 1849, he was one of those who aided the Prince-President most in gaining supreme power. He had been in the struggle; he was at the triumph. Napoleon III., one of whose good qualities was the sentiment of gratitude, overwhelmed him with honors. He appointed him Minister of the Interior and senator in 1852, ambassador at London in 1855, grand cross of the Legion of Honor in 1856, member of the Privy Council in 1858. He married him, May 27, 1852, to a charming young girl of nineteen, the offspring of the marriage of the General Prince de Moskowa, eldest son of the illustrious marshal, with the only daughter of the famous banker, Jacques Laffite.

Possessing a wonderful acquaintance with the language, manners, and institutions of England, Count de Persigny had none but friends in the upper classes of English society. A convinced partisan of the alliance, in equal favor with Whigs and Tories, much appreciated by the Queen and her ministers, he greatly enjoyed himself in London, where his reputation as the friend and confidant of the Emperor assured him exceptional force and authority as a diplomatist.

We have said before that, on the morrow of the crime of January 14, the ambassador of France could but congratulate himself on the attitude of the English ministry. But things soon changed. The beginning of complications was a despatch addressed by Count Walewski to Count de Persigny, January 20, 1858, and deposited February 8 by Lord Palmerston on the table of the House of Commons. In this despatch the Emperor's Minister of Foreign Affairs commenced by recalling the fact that the new attempt, like its predecessors, had been conceived in England; it was there that the authors of the conspiracy had leisurely prepared their means of action, studied and fabricated the instruments of destruction of which they had just made use, and from there that they had started to put their plan into execution. No nation respected more highly than France the right of asylum. But, is hospitality due to assassins? "Can English legislation," added Count Walewski, "continue to shelter men who put themselves outside of the common law and under the ban of humanity?" He concluded as follows: "The government of Her Britannic Majesty can aid us to avert the danger by giving us a guarantee of security which no State could possibly refuse to a neighboring State, and which we are authorized to expect from an ally. Fully confiding, moreover, in the good judgment of the English cabinet, we abstain from any suggestion as to the measures it may be suitable to take, and rest contentedly in the firm persuasion that we have not appealed in vain to its conscience and its loyalty."

Count Walewski's communication was not badly received in London at first. The chief of the Foreign Office, Lord Clarendon, wrote, January 23, to the English ambassador at Paris, Lord Cowley, that Parliament would never consent to pass a bill for the expulsion of foreigners; it would be as well worth while, said he, to propose to the House of Lords or the House of Commons the annexation of England to France; but, this reservation made, the counsellors of the Queen manifested no reluctance to examine the legislation in force and to cover its deficiencies if such existed. Count de Persigny felt quite reassured as to the dispositions of the English ministry. He wrote to Count Walewski, January 29: "In this country people do not run the risks of a terrible war through love of judicial subtleties and solely in the interest of a band of scoundrels."

Parliament, which was in vacation, was to reassemble February 8. The Prime Minister, Lord Palmerston, prepared what was called the Conspiracy Bill, which punished as high treason all plots formed in England for the assassination of a foreign prince, intending to submit it to Parliament by motion.

Things were at this point when, at the end of January, the unlucky idea of publishing in the *Moniteur* those of the colonels' addresses which contained real insults to England, occurred to somebody in Paris. As M. de Persigny wrote to Count Walewski, this was to weight the English government with a great difficulty. Nevertheless it was the general opinion that the Conspiracy Bill proposed by the Whigs would not be opposed by the Tories. " To-day," wrote the ambassador in a despatch of February 5, "I have been warmly congratulated by several of my colleagues who, considering the result already obtained, ascribe to me the merit of it. The truth is, that if I have done my duty, I have been singularly assisted by the political sympathies which the Emperor excites in the country and the respectful friendships he has been able to inspire. All the same, there must be no misapprehension. The discussion will be sharp and serious."

In presence of the disastrous effect produced by several of these addresses, Count Walewski addressed a despatch to Count de Persigny, February 6, in which he said: "If it has been possible to admit into the official journal among the enthusiastic manifestations of the devotion of the army to the Emperor words which seem in England to breathe another sentiment, they are too contrary to the language incessantly employed by the Emperor's government in this affair to that of Her Britannic Majesty for it to be possible to attribute them to anything but an inadvertence caused by the multitude of these addresses in the first moments. The Emperor charges you to say to Lord Clarendon how much he regrets it." Thanks to this retraction, Lord Palmerston obtained at the first reading of the Conspiracy Bill in the House of Commons a majority of two hundred votes. The Tories had voted with him, conformably to the promise they had made to Count de Persigny, and its final success seemed doubtful to nobody.

The second reading of the bill took place February 19. Several members of the House of Commons, not doubting the vote, were not present. The most unexpected incident occurred. Just when Lord Palmerston thought himself absolutely sure of victory, Mr. Milner Gibson proposed the following amendment: "The House expresses its horror of the attempt against the Emperor's life; it will lend its concurrence in order that remedies may be found for the faults which may exist in legislation. Nevertheless it can but regret that the Government, before asking the House to modify the law, did not think itself obliged to reply to the French despatch of January 20." This motion having been adopted by two hundred and thirty-four votes against two hundred and fifteen, Lord Palmerston and the other ministers resigned. The Tories went back to power, and Lord Derby formed a cabinet with Mr. Disraeli and Lord Malmesbury. By a strange result of parliamentary caprices and anomalies, it was the man of the *civis romanus*, the favorite minister of British patriotism, who fell under suspicion of not having sufficiently defended the national honor; it was the statesman so frequently accused of unchaining revolutionary tempests over Europe who was overthrown for having proposed an essentially conservative measure.

Count de Persigny said in a despatch of February 23 : "Lord Palmerston, with his customary liberty of spirit, has spoken to me about the situation as if it were a question of the resignation of a Chinese mandarin. Not a word of irritation against either men or things has found place in the conversation. . . . He remarked that this was the second time he had been turned out of the ministry on account of France and the Emperor; the first was under the ministry of Lord John Russell for having approved the *coup d'État;* and he made me observe that he would have the right to make this answer to those who have unjustly accused him of not being a sincere friend of France and the Emperor."

M. de Persigny had great hopes that the new cabinet would not withdraw the Conspiracy Bill. Lord Clarendon had been replaced as head of the Foreign Office by a personal friend of Napoleon III., Lord Malmesbury, who had visited him in the fortress of Ham. The ambassador neglected no means of convincing the English statesman and his colleagues. He spoke to them in the firmest and most eloquent language. But he could not persuade his own conscience that several of the criticisms which they made on certain faults of the imperial government were ill-founded. Lord Malmesbury said to him: "On every side, in all cities and municipalities, assemblies were convoked to prepare and vote addresses to the Emperor. All England, in a word, was afoot to testify its sympathy, when the *Moniteur* came to chill our hearts. The direct and official initiative of the French government has excited a sentiment which is all the more painful because it deprived England of the merit of the unofficial one."

Such was, in fact, the ambassador's own feeling. He considered that "the *Moniteur's* faculty of representing the Emperor was a danger with absolutely no compensation." He deplored that formal despatch of January 20 which had caused Lord Palmerston's downfall. Without fearing to wound Count Walewski, and possibly his sovereign as well, he had the candor and courage to write to the Minister of Foreign Affairs, February 28: "I have not to express myself concerning your despatch of January 20. All I can say is that had I been consulted about a proceeding of that character, as the usage of all Europe would probably demand and certainly ordinary human prudence, it would have been impossible for me, considering the way in which the question had already been posed and pressed forward by the English government, to do anything but advise that this communication should not be made, or, at least, should not be given the form of an official communication. . . . Here we are, through a series of incidents, faults, imprudences, or negligences, whatever one likes to call them, arrived at so deplorable a situation that a horrible event which should have roused the sympathies of all Europe, and of England in particular, in favor of the Emperor, has become the cause of a serious conflict between the two countries; that popular passions here, overexcited against France, seem to dominate the reason of the intelligent classes, and that at present a weak and undecided minister finds imposed upon him the passage of a bill which is nothing in itself, but which has inflamed against him all the passions of the country because it is supposed to have been imposed upon him by a foreign sovereign."

Count de Persigny had got as far as this in his despatch when he received a note from Lord Malmesbury inviting him to call at his house. To the great astonishment of the ambassador, the chief of the Foreign Office told him that the ministry declined to present the bill.

Matters thus assumed a very grave character, and there was room to fear that diplomatic relations between England and France might be broken off, when the Emperor suddenly caused the question to be settled directly between Count Walewski and Lord Cowley, without consulting and even without notifying Count de Persigny. The latter was deeply offended. " Last Tuesday," wrote he to M. Walewski, "March 16, Lord Derby called on me in the evening to congratulate me, as he said, on the great and fortunate news; and as, in my amazement at knowing nothing, I asked him what fortunate news he referred to, he told me with visible surprise at my ignorance what had passed between Your Excellency and Lord Cowley. Lord Derby's joy was very natural. The Tory party, after having broken its word to us three times, could hardly have expected that when presenting itself for the first time before the Emperor's Minister of Foreign Affairs it would receive nothing but felicitations and compliments. In the interest of the Emperor's dignity I ought to have been apprised before any one else whomsoever of the attitude taken by Your Excellency, for the ignorance in which you left me cannot but have disagreeable consequences. This, Monsieur le Comte, in the interest of our mutual responsibility, is what I have to say to you, and I am bound to say it."

Count Walewski having acted under the Emperor's order, the latter justified him and accepted the resignation of the ambassador, March 20, 1858.

And now to the communications which had been exchanged between the Minister of Foreign Affairs and Lord Cowley. In a despatch of March 4, addressed to the latter, Lord Malmesbury declared that all the offences enumerated by Count Walewski, if proved before a jury, would entail a condemnation, and that in view of the last outrage proceedings had been entered for complicity and for a publication which upheld assassination as a doctrine. Hence there was no further question of the Conspiracy Bill. But Lord Malmesbury, in the name of the Queen's government, expressed "the desire to maintain an alliance which, since the restoration of the Empire, had existed to the great advantage of both nations."

Count Walewski replied to Count de Persigny by a despatch bearing date March 11, inspired if not dictated by the Emperor; one finds in it the elevation of thought and style habitual with Napoleon III. It said that the government congratulated itself on the amicable assurances of the new English cabinet, and that His Majesty believed himself to have seized every occasion during the last six years of drawing closer the ties between the two peoples. . . . What had happened? Count Walewski had called the attention of the government of Her Britannic Majesty to the existence of a sect which in its publications and meetings erected assassination into a doctrine, and which, within the space of six years, had sent no less than eight assassins into France to murder the Emperor. "The character of our proceedings," added the Minister, "was outlined to you in the clearest manner by His Majesty, who wrote you towards the end of January: I am under no illusion as to the small efficacy of the measures that one could take, but that will always be a good proceeding which will successfully tranquillize irritations. It is not at present a question of saving my life, but of saving the alliance. . . . I need not tell you, moreover, that I have never thought of considering English legislation as knowingly protecting the guilty. My despatch of January had no other object than that of pointing out a deplorable state of things; but I carefully abstained from expressing any opinion as to the measures calculated to put an end to it. . . . In giving these assurances to Lord Malmesbury, kindly add that the Emperor's intentions having been misunderstood, His Majesty's government will refrain from continuing a discussion which, if prolonged, might injure the dignity and the good understanding of the two countries, and which it leaves purely and simply to the loyalty of the English people."

This despatch, whose only inconvenience was that of having arrived too late, was assuredly very fine both in substance and in form; but, one must confess, it was abnormal that the English ministers should have been made acquainted with its contents before the ambassador of France at London, to whom it was addressed.

CHAPTER XXXV

MARSHAL PÉLISSIER AS AMBASSADOR

BY a decree of March 23, 1858, Marshal Pélissier, Duc de Malakoff, was named ambassador of France at London, replacing Count de Persigny. The latter manifested on this occasion his patriotism and the loftiness of his sentiments. He wrote to Count Walewski, March 24: " The appointment of the Duc de Malakoff is made with intent to replace the policy of the Emperor's government on the level it occupied before the recent circumstances. In selecting as my successor an eminent man whose name is the symbol of a firm and dignified policy, while at the same time it reminds the two countries of the most glorious souvenir of their alliance, the Emperor's government gives, in a way, a striking adhesion to the observations I laid before it in offering my resignation. The double object to which my efforts and my counsels have incessantly tended, the preservation of the alliance and the maintenance of our dignity, are, in fact, admirably indicated by the choice of my successor, and thus I can applaud myself for not having appealed in vain to the just pride of my government. For the rest, I have never doubted for an instant the real views of the Emperor, and that is why I was not afraid, even at the risk of displeasing him, to tear away with violence the veil which concealed the truth. I have lost by this act of devotion a great and lofty situation which suited my tastes, but I have the conviction of having done my duty and served my country."

The meaning of the new appointment was at once comprehended in England, by official circles as well as by the public. Count de Persigny added: " Yesterday Lord Malmesbury, who came to spend the evening with me, told me that the Queen, who had received the Marshal's name with marked satisfaction, considered the choice as a testimony of high consideration towards England and at the same time of high dignity for France. That name pronounced last evening has produced in the first place what it is destined to produce everywhere — a certain salutary emotion, because reflection soon defines its real meaning."

In a despatch of April 17, 1858, the Marshal thus describes how he took possession of his embassy: " On my arrival in London, April 15, I was received with visible eagerness by the inhabitants of that city and the civil and military authorities. The troops formed in a double line along my path, and the municipality presented me with an address conceived in a good spirit, to which I replied by some cordial expressions which seemed to please those who understood them. I notified Lord Malmesbury at once of my arrival, and he appointed a meeting for the 16th at noon. I went there exactly on time, and we separated with mutual satisfaction at having met, and promising to meet again at three o'clock at the Queen's palace. I have had the honor of remitting my credentials to Her Majesty, who gave me a most gracious reception, but above all asked me several questions indicating an affectionate interest in the Emperor and the Empress. I dine this evening with Her Majesty, and I think that the principal generals of the Crimean army, who are in London, are also invited." Prince Albert wrote apropos of this dinner to Baron Stockmar: "The Duc de Malakoff has dined with us. He talks with the greatest frankness of the state of affairs in France, and blames several measures taken by his master. He is sorry to be obliged to go into society, which he detests, but it flatters him to be ambassador and to find himself so well received in England. As a diplomat he is ignorant of the details of affairs, but his influence as a man may be useful."

At the very time when the Marshal was congratulating himself on the brilliant and cordial reception given him, an incident occurred which came very near entailing new complications. One of Orsini's accomplices, Simon Bernard, being brought before a British jury, was acquitted April 17. Nevertheless his guilt was beyond doubt. He had taken part in ordering the bombs; he had them taken to Brussels and from there to Paris. He had given Rudio money, a false passport, a sign of recognition, and had sent him to Orsini. The English government was convinced that Bernard would be condemned, and was making ready to use that condemnation as a reply to those who accused it of either inertia or weakness. The ministers of the Queen possibly regretted the acquittal even more than those of the Emperor.

The Marshal-ambassador, preserving all his *sang-froid*, sought to reassure his government. "When I had the honor of dining with the Queen yesterday," he wrote to Count Walewski, April 18, "I had occasion to gather the impressions of Her Majesty and those of Lord Malmesbury concerning the result of the Bernard trial. The Queen and the principal Secretary of State expressed to me their fear lest this event should seem to justify the regrettable suspicions of which the English people and their government have recently been the object on the other side of the Channel, and also lest our own people should not sufficiently comprehend how faint an echo the applause with which certain refugees greeted the verdict of the jury met from the sounder portion of the people and genuine public opinion in England."

In the Marshal's opinion, the thing to do was to remain calm, practise patience, and procrastinate. "Resignation has its triviality at times," he said again in a despatch of April 23, "but this is a case of letting the water slip under the bridge, and a time to pass over many things which stricter prudence might have averted and which the English ministry is ready to avoid; for, no matter how sincere and honest its intentions may be with regard to the alliance, it suffers the penalty of having succeeded in seizing power on a question of foreign politics."

In Paris matters were less calmly considered. Count Walewski wrote to the Marshal, April 21: "Bernard's acquittal caused painful and general surprise in France, as might have been expected; public opinion was profoundly affected by it, and His Majesty's government learns that this impression is visible throughout the Empire. Under these circumstances, and without modifying in any wise your relations with the government of Her Britannic Majesty, whose sentiments you have been enabled to appreciate, the Emperor desires that your general attitude should evince a certain restraint, and particularly that you should refrain from appearing at public dinners where custom would place you under the obligation of responding to the toasts proposed."

The Marshal replied, April 23: "Monsieur le Comte, I can readily imagine the surprise created in France by the acquittal of Bernard; but the Queen, the English ministers, and the well-bred and reflecting portion of the population are not less painfully affected by it, and juries and their verdicts are spoken of disdainfully enough. But, in fine, there is force in *res judicata*, and any reprisal on that state of things seems to me difficult. I do not see what change I could make with respect to a government

x

as grieved over the situation as we are, if not more so, and hesitating, solely with intent to avoid a useless scandal, to proceed with trials which would necessarily lead to a new acquittal.

"As to dinners and meetings where speeches are made, I will avoid them as far as possible for the future; but it would have been difficult, somewhat discourteous, somewhat imprudent, to break an engagement to dine at the United Service Club, presided by H.R.H. the Duke of Cambridge, where unseasonable toasts are not to be dreaded, and where, should any occur, it would be easy, it seems, to put both men and things in their place. But nothing of the sort is to be feared, and, on the other hand, the remarks exchanged, the impressions communicated, were of a nature to inspire a conviction that in the army, the navy, in all classes of self-respecting society, keen sympathy with the Emperor and his government exists beyond all doubt, and sincere cordiality is manifested towards our army, our navy, and their commanders. If you had been present at this reunion, assuredly you would have borrowed no anxiety concerning these ranters, corrupted by the dregs of our refugees, who alone can have manifested a detestable adhesion to the acts of a familiar of Orsini." The Duc de Malakoff reached the following conclusion: "It is wise, prudent, and rational to leave to time the care of quieting an agitation which exists only in the lowest depths."

The London journals represented the banquet of

the United Service Club as a manifestation in favor of the Anglo-French alliance. The *Post*, in calling attention to the fact that the toast to the Emperor and Empress had been received with prolonged applause, added: "Notwithstanding that the two States may have different views in politics, yet there is not in England, excepting in those dregs of the population which are always ready for an upheaval at the slightest sign of a storm, a single man who does not see in the sovereign of France a sincere friend of our country, and who does not desire that Providence may long preserve him for the maintenance of peace and an affectionate alliance between two powerful nations." After the United Service Club, the Army and Navy Club likewise offered a dinner to the illustrious soldier. Then the great English families successively gave entertainments in his honor. The Marshal was the lion of the season, then in full swing.

Surrounded by demonstrations in favor of the alliance, the Tory ministry thought the Conspiracy Bill presented by Lord Palmerston might be allowed to sink into oblivion. Without officially withdrawing it, the same result was arrived at by not asking for its second reading before the expiration of the parliamentary session. The clouds were dispelled. One might have supposed himself back in the happy days of the "cordial understanding."

Napoleon III. had been well inspired when he confided the French embassy in England, under circumstances so difficult, to the hero of Malakoff. He was, in fact, a man of intelligence, who concealed an unerring judgment and extreme shrewdness under an affectation of frankness and sometimes of military rudeness. The Marshal had already practised diplomacy in the Crimea. Without getting into disgrace with the Emperor, he had set aside the sovereign's plan, which was to invest Sebastopol, and executed his own, which was the siege and nothing but the siege. The letters he wrote at the time to Napoleon III. prove his tact and ability. In London, he was discerning enough to comprehend that the acquittal of Bernard was the response to the unlucky addresses of the colonels, and no professional diplomatist could have taken a more circumspect and conciliatory attitude : the alliance which had been endangered owed its re-establishment to him.

Those of my colleagues who had the honor of serving under his orders during his embassy to London, which lasted from March 23, 1858, to May 9, 1859, have told me that they always found him a kindly chief, good and just. The Marshal chatted familiarly with them, and never displayed arrogance or pride. He was interested in literary matters, and, in his leisure moments, wrote poetry himself. He said one day to a distinguished young diplomat, Vicomte de Beaumont, afterwards consul general of France in Hungary and minister plenipotentiary: "See here, look at this piece of verse which I have just received; I think it execrable." M. de Beaumont made haste to read the lines; then he said prudently: "Monsieur le Maréchal, I beg pardon for differing with you. But these verses seem to me delightful." "You have a keen scent," replied the Marshal; "they are mine."

The Duc de Malakoff displayed a noble independence of character in his embassy. His meeting with the Duc d'Aumale was famous. M. Ernest Daudet has described it in an affecting way in the excellent work he has devoted to the memory of the illustrious prince academician. It was in Hyde Park. The carriage of the son of Louis Philippe was just passing another, the servants on which, like those of the Prince, wore the French cockade. The Duc d'Aumale recognized Marshal Pélissier, whom he had not seen since the time when he was his superior as governor-general of Algeria. On seeing the Prince, the Marshal rose and saluted. Leaving their carriages, they fell into each other's arms in presence of an astonished crowd. "Monseigneur," said the Duc de Malakoff, "I am serving France under Napoleon III. as I served her under your father; but I have forgotten nothing. Your portrait remains in my study. I always wear the cross of Saint Louis which the Bourbons gave me, and I take good care to put it in evidence when I am going to see my padishah. And he is not ignorant of the attachment I bear you. Now, I hope that we shall meet again."

Marshal Pélissier had a hand of iron and a heart of gold.

CHAPTER XXXVI

COUNT CAVOUR

JUNE 29, 1858, leaving the Empress and the Prince Imperial at Saint-Cloud, the Emperor set off for Plombières, in company with General de Béville, one of his aides-de-camp, Captain de La Tour d'Auvergne, one of his orderly officers, and M. Mocquard, chief of his cabinet. In the little city of the Vosges he had an interview with M. Cavour to which the public paid no attention. It passed almost unperceived, and yet it was to change many things in Europe. Before describing it, let us give a rapid glance at the antecedents of the Piedmontese statesman.

Camillo Benso, Count of Cavour, was born at Turin, August 10, 1810. By his father he was a Piedmontese, by his mother of French extraction, by his paternal grandfather he was connected with Switzerland and Savoy. His family gloried in a tie of kinship with Saint Francois de Sales. Entering the military school of Turin, young Cavour did well there in scientific studies, and was chosen among the cadets to form part of the corps of pages. Attached in this capacity to the household of the Prince of

Carignan, the future King Charles Albert, he showed from childhood a pride and independence unbefitting a page, and he was obliged to leave the service of the Prince, whom he displeased. An officer of engineers at sixteen, he was in garrison at Genoa when the French revolution of 1830 broke out. He avowed himself ardently in favor of this revolution, which in the court of Turin was exciting general condemnation. Charles Albert ascended the throne in 1831. He already distrusted the young officer of whom he afterwards said: "He is one of the most dangerous men in my kingdom." He sent him to the fortress of Bard to take part in the defensive works. M. de Cavour believed this to be a disgrace; six months later he gave in his resignation and entered private life. Not to be inactive, he undertook the direction of one of his father's estates, that of Leri, near Vercelli, and there devoted himself to business and agriculture, raising stock, cultivating beet root, studying all sorts of novelties, gas, the making of chemical manures, discounting banks, speculating in rice, wheat, maize, an innovator on economic ground as he was destined to be afterwards on one more vast. He made a great fortune in this way, and it permitted him to found a journal in 1847, *Il Risorgimento*.

During the long period of his abstention from politics, M. de Cavour had travelled much in Switzerland, England, and France. His relations with Baron de Barante, minister of King Louis Philippe at Turin, and with Count d'Haussonville, secretary of the legation, opened to him the doors of the principal salons of Paris, notably those of the Duc de Broglie, Madame de Circourt, and Madame de Castellane. As he spoke French better than Italian, he had great success. At that time he called himself a partisan of the *juste milieu*, the golden mean, and associated himself with the ideas of the Duc de Broglie, Count Molé, and M. Guizot. He professed a cult for England; but a secret instinct warned him that she would never seriously favor the Italian cause. "I am a great admirer of the English," he said at the time; "I feel a real sympathy with that nation, for I consider it the vanguard of civilization. But its policy does not inspire me with the slightest confidence. When I see it holding out one hand to Metternich, and with the other stirring up the ultra radicals in Portugal, Spain, and Greece, I confess that I do not feel disposed to believe in its political honesty." He had a presentiment that his country could rely only on France.

The Italian revolutions of 1848 at first disconcerted M. de Cavour. He condemned the provocations against Austria as untimely and dangerous, and did not believe in the programme of *Italia farà da se*. Elected deputy in June, 1848, by three departments, he took his seat in the Chamber among the moderates. In October 1850, he entered the cabinet presided by M. d'Azeglio as Minister of Agriculture, Commerce, and the Navy. At first,

King Victor Emmanuel hesitated to appoint him. "Understand," said he to his ministers, "that fellow will take all your portfolios." His consuming activity, his incessant successes in the tribune, his surprising capacity for work, his character, a curious blending of suppleness and energy, of prudence and audacity, soon gained for him a preponderating influence. In April, 1851, he added to his three portfolios that of Finances, and assured the material prosperity of the country before launching into adventures.

M. de Cavour may be considered the creator of the *Italian question*. Taking commercial liberty and political liberty as a double lever, he organized — thanks to the journals and the refugees established in Turin — a system of incessant propaganda. But he did not ignore the fact that the revolutionaries, unaided, could do nothing, and that without the armed assistance of some great power, it would always be absolutely impossible for Piedmont to free Milan and Venice. There was but one man who would and could aid him to accomplish that task. That man was Napoleon III.

There were great analogies between the Emperor and the minister. Both convinced apostles of free trade and the principle of nationalities, they pursued their object with inflexible obstinacy. Both had greater faith in the power of the press than in that of the tribune. Stage managers of the first rank, they excelled in directing and influencing public opinion; they availed themselves of secret agents, and simultaneously maintained an official and an occult policy. With the genius of conspiracy they combined the temperament of gamesters. Napoleon III. and Count Cavour could have done nothing against Austria without each other.

It was solely on account of Napoleon III. that the Piedmontese minister persuaded Victor Emmanuel to send troops to the Crimea. At first sight this seemed a more than singular proceeding. What grievance, one wondered, had little Piedmont against great Russia, which did not threaten it in any way? The policy of Count Cavour had but one excuse: the desire to posit the *Italian question* before a Congress after the war.

Had the Piedmontese politician at this epoch the idea of creating the political unity of the peninsula? One of the best informed in Italian matters of our diplomatists, Count Benedetti, does not think so. In his masterly study, *Le Comte de Cavour et le Prince de Bismarck*, he says: "To men whose genius has overcome the caprices of fortune, one easily ascribes calculations and a foresight which are hardly the attributes of human nature. Thoughtful study of Cavour's acts and sentiments at the time at which we have arrived (1856), inclines one to believe that his sole object then was the enfranchisement of Northern Italy; the state of Europe and even that of Italy did not admit of any other. . . . Never since his entry into public life had he formed another wish. He so little foresaw a fusion of all the Italian countries that up till then he had conceived and disclosed no combinations that were not exclusive of unity. During his stay in Paris, at the time of the Congress, he suggested several, notably in a note remitted to the plenipotentiaries of France and England, all of which comported with the territorial condition of the peninsula as it was at that period; they even guaranteed its maintenance." As to Napoleon III., we are convinced that in 1856 Italian unity was far from his mind. All he thought of then was wresting Lombardy and Venetia from the hand of Austria, and acquiring Savoy as the price of his armed assistance.

From the time of his arrival in Paris, Count Cavour ascertained that he could count absolutely upon the Emperor. February 21, he dined at the Tuileries in a sort of intimacy to which the Austrian plenipotentiaries were not admitted. The day before he had written to Chevalier Cibrario, apropos of a great lady celebrated for her beauty: " I notify you that I am enrolling the beautiful countess in the diplomatic lines, by inviting her to coquet with and if necessary to beguile the Emperor." February 22, he was visited by a close confidant of Napoleon III., Doctor Conneau, who said he was authorized to serve as intermediary for all secret information which the Sardinians thought it well to send to the Tuileries. A few days afterwards he learned that M. Mocquard, the Emperor's secretary, had recommended the Parisian correspondents of several English journals to support the cause of Piedmont. The only result Cavour obtained was that of stating, without solving, the Italian question before the Congress. He had planted a stake; that sufficed him for the moment, and he took back with him to Turin the memory that Napoleon III. had said to him at the time of his final audience: "I cannot enter into a conflict with Austria just now; but be tranquil, I have a notion that the existing peace will not last long." M. de Cavour was, in fact, tranquillized, and from that day he made ready for war, with the profound conviction that it would not be long delayed, and that the Emperor would be the ally of Victor Emmanuel. Piedmont had covered itself with macadamized roads. A magnificent military port had been created at Spezzia, Mont Cenis had been tunnelled as if to open a constantly accessible passage to the French troops who were one day to cross the Alps to the assistance of the Italians.

Meanwhile, the sympathies of Napoleon III. for the Italian cause remained as yet platonic. He found out at the Stuttgart interview that Czar Alexander I. was unfavorable to Austria, but would energetically support the King of Naples. A revolutionary policy in Italy could not be approved by Russia. Hence Count Cavour was obliged to moderate his claims and dissemble the greater part of his programme.

We have seen already that the crime of January 14, which for an instant seemed to endanger the alliance between France and Piedmont, resulted in strengthening it and in precipitating events. When the official *Gazette* of the kingdom published at Turin the two letters written, one from the Mazas and the other from the Roquette prison, in which Orsini made a final appeal to the Emperor in favor of the Italian cause, everybody believed that such a publication, an evident menace against Austria, could not have been made by the Piedmontese government without the consent of Napoleon III. Nevertheless Count Cavour's hopes still remained vague. They assumed precision only through the agreement which occurred between him and the Emperor in the interview at Plombières.

CHAPTER XXXVII

PLOMBIÈRES

LIKE Louis XV., Napoleon III. always had, beside his official diplomacy, an occult one which was often contrary to the first. Like Louis XV. he employed unknown agents, mysterious intermediaries. There was *the Emperor's secret*, as formerly there had been *the secret of the King*. "The Ministry of Foreign Affairs was often only a grand façade, behind which passed important things of which the ministers themselves were ignorant. At the time of the Crimean War and of the Vienna conferences, Napoleon III., at the moment when he seemed to agree with M. Drouyn de Lhuys, disagreed with him completely, the sovereign wishing the war to go on and the minister desiring it to come to an end. One may also say that the Emperor prepared the Italian war without Count Walewski's knowledge, and even in spite of him. The official journals frequently represented the ideas, not of the Emperor, but of his ministers, and it was sometimes the papers considered by the public as opposition journals, the *Siècle*, for example, in which it was necessary to look for the secret mind of the sovereign. As under the reign of Louis XV., the ministers had no confidence in their master, and were expecting to be disavowed at the very moment when they seemed to be enjoying his entire confidence and to possess his full approbation. Count Walewski was the declared adversary of Count Cavour's ideas, and it was during the ministry of Walewski that Cavour received the Emperor's encouragement and made ready, in concert with him, the war of 1859.

At the end of May, 1858, Doctor Conneau went to Turin on an absolutely secret mission. The situation of the doctor was apparently modest, but, at bottom, he was not merely the physician but the confidential friend of the Emperor, whom he had never quitted since the death of Queen Hortense, and he was more conversant than the ministers with the under side of the imperial diplomacy and the mental reservations of the sovereign. He saw Victor Emmanuel and Count Cavour, and after dwelling upon the sympathies of Napoleon III. for the court of Turin, he said that the Emperor proposed spending July at Plombières, where he would be pleased to meet the Piedmontese minister. M. de Cavour eagerly replied that he intended taking a vacation in Switzerland, and that from there he would go to pay his respects to the Emperor if he were authorized by His Majesty.

June 19, Count Cavour wrote to the Marquis Villamarina: "I am impatient to know whether the Emperor will give effect to Conneau's insinuations by inviting me to see him at Plombières." He added, as if to fortify himself: "Walewski and the majority of the political agents of France represent nothing but petty passions, and in nowise the great thoughts which the Emperor cherishes in his own mind."

When, on July 14, the Piedmontese statesman set out for Switzerland, he had as yet received no confirmation of Doctor Conneau's hints. But at Geneva he received the anxiously expected news in a letter from General de Béville, announcing that the Emperor would be charmed to see him at Plombières. "The drama approaches its solution," wrote Cavour at the time to his friend, confidant, and colleague, General de La Marmora; "pray heaven to inspire me that I make no blunder in this supreme moment. In spite of my usual confidence, I am not without great anxiety."

July 20, in the evening, Count Cavour arrived at Plombières. At eleven o'clock the next morning he was brought into the presence of Napoleon III.

Is it not curious to note, nowadays, how rapidly contemporaneous history discovers the most secret things? The mysteries of the Plombières interview were very soon revealed. The preliminaries have been made known by the letters of the Piedmontese statesman: *Letters published and unpublished of Camillo Cavour*. As to the interview itself, the least details of it were supplied by the publication of the report addressed by him to Victor Emmanuel, July

24, 1858, the contents of which we are about to analyze.

Napoleon III. opened the conversation by saying that he would be inclined to support Piedmont in a war with Austria, on the double condition that the struggle should not assume a revolutionary character, and that it might clothe itself with a pretext which diplomacy should find plausible. The minister having adduced Austria's failure to execute commercial treaties, and the abusive extension of her power in the duchies and the Romagna, the Emperor found the first pretext insufficient. As to the second, he said: "So long as my troops are at Rome, I cannot insist on Austria's withdrawing hers from Ancona and Bologna. I must be circumspect with Rome on account of the Catholics, and with Naples on account of the Czar, who makes it a sort of point of honor to protect King Ferdinand." "Well, then," replied Cavour, "let us abandon Rome to the Pope and Naples to its princes. It is sufficient to permit the Romagnols to make insurrections, and not to interfere with the subjects of King Ferdinand on the day when they feel like throwing off his yoke."

Then the two interlocutors examined the situation of the duchy of Modena, whose sovereign was the most ultra of all the princes, and where the Piedmontese propaganda, already very active, might at any moment kindle the spark desired. After considering the contingency of a war, they revolved the distribution of territories after peace. There was as yet no question of Italian unity. The peninsula might be divided into four States: 1, Piedmont, increased by Lombardy and Venetia, the duchy of Parma and Legations; 2, Tuscany, which with Umbria would form a kingdom of Central Italy, given perhaps to the house of Parma; 3, the Pontifical State, where the Pope would retain Rome, lose the Legations, and assume the title of President of the Italian Confederation; 4, the kingdom of the Two Sicilies, whose present sovereign would be maintained for a time in order to avoid offending Russia.

How was France to be rewarded for her armed concurrence? The Emperor demanded the cession of Savoy in exchange for the stipulated aggrandizement of Piedmont. M. Cavour, though suggesting that Savoy was the cradle of his master's family, made no absolute objection. But when the Emperor added that he would also be obliged to reclaim the seigniory of Nice, his interlocutor exclaimed: "Nice is Italian territory; if that is ceded, what becomes of the principle of nationalities?" Napoleon III. contented himself with replying: "Those are secondary questions, and there will be time enough to consider them hereafter," and the conversation closed; it had lasted from eleven o'clock in the morning until three in the afternoon.

An hour later, the Emperor drove out in a phaeton with M. de Cavour across the woods and valleys of the Vosges. It was during this drive that he expressed his desire that his cousin, Prince Napoleon, should marry the Princess Clotilde, daughter of King Victor Emmanuel. Cavour, whom the King had recommended to make no promise unless the marriage should be a *sine qua non* of the arrangements, alleged the youth of the Princess and made other objections, to which the Emperor replied by saying of his cousin: "He has often embarrassed and often irritated me; he is fond of contradiction and a faultfinder; but he has a great deal of intelligence, more judgment than people think, and a very good heart." Day was beginning to decline; the outing was nearly over. The Emperor insisted several times on the projected alliance: "I comprehend," said he, "that the youth of the Princess necessitates delays; but I want a positive answer, and I expect it." His last word as they parted was: "Have confidence in me as I have in you."

The Piedmontese minister left Plombières July 22. The 24th, at Baden, on an inn table, he wrote his report to his sovereign and despatched it at once, in all haste, by an attaché of the Sardinian legation in Switzerland. It is said that, after reading it, Victor Emmanuel exclaimed: "In a year I shall be King of Italy or simply M. de Savoy."

The Prince de La Tour d'Auvergne, minister of France in Sardinia, wrote to Count Walewski, August 15: "The comments, for the most part very improbable, occasioned by M. de Cavour's journey to Plombières, have given place to impressions more sensible and doubtless more correct. At present people are pretty generally persuaded — and in private conversation M. de Cavour confirms this opinion — that the Emperor strongly recommended prudence and moderation to King Victor Emmanuel's prime minister, and, I will add, it is hoped that this advice, coming from august lips, will bear fruit. M. de Cavour, none the less, shows himself fully satisfied and grateful for the reception he met with at Plombières. With me he has entered into minute details concerning it, which prove the deep and favorable impression made upon him by the cordiality with which he was treated. I think I may say that King Victor Emmanuel is not less willing to display the joy caused him by the letter of the Emperor."

This despatch seems to prove that even the minister of France at Turin was ignorant of what had passed at Plombières.

A characteristic detail is that the *Moniteur*, usually filled with accounts of the least acts and gestures of the Emperor, did not speak of the sovereign during the month he spent at Plombières. The official sheet never mentioned the visit of Count Cavour. During this visit, the bearing of Napoleon III. was rather that of a conspirator than a monarch. At a distance from his wife, he had arranged his bellicose plot in obscurity. He took care to concentrate public attention on the interview he was about to have with Queen Victoria at Cherbourg, and not upon that of Plombières. Well aware that the Queen and Prince were anything rather than favorable to his warlike schemes and the repartition of Italy, he forced himself to conceal them. On the other, he was especially careful, at a moment when he was preparing to receive the enthusiastic homage of pious Brittany, not to give an inkling in such a province of his recent interview with Cavour, the author of the law on convents, the adversary of the Pope's temporal power, the statesman most suspected by the Catholic party. In Brittany, Napoleon III. wanted to appear under an essentially religious and conservative aspect.

CHAPTER XXXVIII

THE CHERBOURG INTERVIEW

JULY 10, Count Walewski, Minister of Foreign Affairs, notified the Duc de Malakoff, ambassador of France at London, that Their Imperial Majesties would be at Cherbourg on August 5 to receive the visit of Queen Victoria and Prince Albert.

The Marshal replied July 11: "No doubt the Queen will be perfectly happy to meet the Emperor and Empress again, and to receive confirmation of the news that Their Majesties eagerly renounce all other cares in order to devote the entire 5th of August to their illustrious guests. In fact, I learned at Aldershot on July 5 what I have been somewhat tardily apprised of by your despatch of the 10th. The Queen did me the honor to say to me that I had won a good and peaceful victory there, on which I bowed respectfully and added: 'An easy victory, since the lofty benevolence of Your Majesty had smoothed away the asperities.'

"In an electric message from Plombières, July 7, 9h. 45m. the Emperor asked me: 'Is it the 5th of August that the Queen will be at Cherbourg? Answer at once.' — To which I replied without delay: 'The Queen has told me positively that she will arrive on the 4th and spend the 5th with Your Majesty.' — And the little electric current established by His Majesty with me ended, July 7, at six in the evening, with these expressions: 'I shall be happy to see the Queen again. We will be at Cherbourg between 4 and 5.'

"You doubtless recognize that with this series of informations before me, I need not excuse myself for finding your despatch a trifle tardy. I am not offended by it; be careful not to think so. But if I were, that sentiment, so foreign to me, would yield to the modest satisfaction I feel at having succeeded in putting the cap cordially on Cherbourg."

On August 5, in fact, at eight in the evening, the French and British Majesties met on board the royal yacht, the *Victoria and Albert*, which had sailed from Osborne at noon. The Emperor and Empress were received by Prince Albert at the foot of the ladder, and by Queen Victoria at the top. The Emperor ascended first; then the Empress in a white and lilac silk gown and a hat trimmed with white and black lace. The Queen embraced them both, and then she and Prince Albert led them into a salon where the conversation began. The Queen says of it in her Journal: "The Emperor seemed greatly embarrassed; the Empress less so, and very affable. The Emperor anxiously inquired whether the feeling against France was as keen as ever in England, and if people still expect an invasion. We smiled, and said that the irritation had greatly subsided, but that the unlucky addresses of the colonels had done incalculable harm. The Emperor replied that this was also his opinion, but that these addresses had been made without his knowledge, and that he had greatly regretted their publication." At nine o'clock Napoleon III. and the Empress left the royal yacht and returned to the maritime prefecture of Cherbourg. Their visit was returned there the next day at noon by the Queen and Prince Albert, accompanied by the Prince of Wales and the Duke of Cambridge. Breakfast was served. According to the Queen, the Emperor was *close;* he seemed indisposed to talk. After the repast, the Empress laid stress on the harm done by newspapers, and described in detail the Orsini outrage. There was a drawing-room afterwards, where Marshal Vaillant, Count Walewski, M. Rouher, Marshal Pélissier, and Generals Niel and MacMahon, whom the Queen thought "very amiable," were among those present. Among the ladies was a young Spanish girl, Mademoiselle Sophie Valera de La Paniega, by whose beauty the Queen was much impressed. She was a cousin of the Empress, who had brought her to Cherbourg to show her to the Duc de Malakoff. The old soldier found her charming. He wrote verses to her; according to General Fleury, he had "the gentle mania of composing quatrains." He asked the hand of the beautiful Spaniard, and within a few weeks Mademoiselle de La Paniega was the Marshal-Duchess of Malakoff.

In the evening the Emperor gave his guests a dinner on board the flagship *Bretagne*. When what the Queen calls the "terrible moment" of the toasts arrived, she found that proposed by the Emperor superb. "I drink," said he, "to the health of Her Majesty the Queen of England, and that of the Prince who shares her throne, and that of the royal family. In proposing this toast in their presence on board the flagship in the harbor of Cherbourg, I am happy to display our sentiments towards them. In fact, the facts speak for themselves, and prove that hostile passions, aided by certain unfortunate incidents, can change neither the friendship existing between the two crowns, nor the desire of the two peoples to remain at peace. Hence I firmly hope that if any one should seek to revive the rancors and passions of another epoch, they will be wrecked against public good sense, like waves against the dike which at this moment shelters the squadrons of the two empires from the violence of the sea."

Prince Albert was to respond, and before he began, the Queen experienced what she describes as "a moment of torture which I would not willingly pass through again." But she adds: "Albert got through his speech very well, though once he hesitated. In the cabin the Emperor shook hands with him, and we spoke of the emotion we had just experienced. The Emperor himself had changed color, and the Empress also was very nervous. As to me, I was trembling so that I could not swallow my coffee."

On the whole, the Cherbourg interview, which ended on Friday, August 6, was affectionate, but that of Osborne had been still more so. Prince Albert felt suspicious of Napoleon III. What might have been arranged at Plombières between the Emperor and Cavour awakened vague apprehensions in the Prince, who had remained German to the core. Two days after leaving Cherbourg he wrote to the Duchess of Kent: "The Emperor was preoccupied and sad. The Empress seemed to be suffering. The preparations of the French marine are immense. Ours are pitiable. Our ministers make fine speeches; but they do not act: my blood boils when I think of it." The bright days of the *entente cordiale* were over. Queen Victoria was still magnetized by Napoleon III. But the policy of "the extraordinary man," as she called the Emperor, disturbed Prince Albert and the ministers of Her Britannic Majesty.

CHAPTER XXXIX

THE TOUR IN BRITTANY

AFTER the festivities of Cherbourg, Their Imperial Majesties made a triumphant tour in Brittany. This province, which they had not yet visited, and whose inhabitants are essentially Catholics, had long been reputed the asylum of the white flag and of legitimacy. The ovations that a Napoleon went there to receive under the tricolor naturally had a special importance for the Emperor. The prefects set their wits to work to incite enthusiastic manifestations, and in the clergy they found auxiliaries as zealous and eager as themselves. For that matter, it must be admitted that no sovereigns had shown greater deference towards the Church. The Empress rejoiced in an excursion which, by its religious character, was transformed into a vast and long pilgrimage.

The *Bretagne*, with Their Majesties on board, quitted Cherbourg August 8, at two o'clock in the afternoon. It reached Brest the next day at one in the afternoon. The first visit of Their Majesties was to the church of St. Louis. Mgr. Sergent, Bishop of Quimper, addressed them in the following words: —

"Sire: Christians, and laborers, the Bretons are

grateful for your love for religion and the encouragements you give to agriculture; they applauded when a powerful arm replaced the pyramid on its base. . . . The children of Armorica, fitted for labors and dangers, do not content themselves with giving brave soldiers to your army, and to your fleets sailors whom all the world admire; at the same time they supply the Church with worthy priests and excellent missionaries. Your Majesty would be unable to take a step in their country without encountering heroic souvenirs, and every time you place confidence in them you will recognize the verity of what was said by one of their chevaliers when Mary Stuart went to Morlaix: *No Breton ever committed treason.*

"Madame, your gracious presence reminds this people of its dear duchess, whose royal spouse was also *the Father of the people.* A voice as eloquent as it is respected had apprised France that you were *Catholic and pious.* Your good works repeat this daily."

Leaving Brest, August 11, they went from there to Quimper, and thence, on the 13th, to Lorient. Their journey was a long ovation, a procession under triumphal arches. At Lorient there was a review. The Empress went to visit the orphan asylum and insisted on seeing the children at work. During the day Their Majesties set off for Port Louis in their yacht. Here they visited the fortifications, and Napoleon III. contemplated with emotion the citadel and led the Empress thither. It was a place which evoked souvenirs strangely in contrast with the present ovations. Condemned to deportation after the unsuccessful attempt of Strasburg, he had arrived at the citadel of Port Louis in the night of November 13-14, 1836, and until the 21st contrary winds had prevented the frigate *Andromeda*, which was to convey him to the United States, from leaving the port. During his stay at the citadel, the wife of a guard of engineers, Madame Perreaux, had lavished on him the most respectful attentions. He did not forget her. August 14, 1858, he met this dame again, happy, as she told him, to see him again before she died. The Emperor spoke kindly to her and assured the future of her family.

August 15, the Emperor and Empress quitted Lorient at eight in the morning and arrived at eleven at Sainte-Anne-d'Auray.

Sainte-Anne-d'Auray is classic Brittany, legendary Brittany. For centuries all old Armorica has come regularly to invoke there the *good saint*, the good mother of the Bretons. The *pardons* arrive there in procession and in long lines. All the populations, from Saint-Brieuc to Angers, from the Channel to the Loire, hasten eagerly to the venerated sanctuary. For the last two centuries the sailors of the neighborhood have come to make the rounds of the church in procession, bearing the model of a warship, and chanting an old hymn of thanksgiving in gratitude to St. Anne for having, in 1673, protected their forefathers in a fight against Ruyter's fleet. The walls of the sanctuary and of the cloister are hung with *ex votos*.

Almost opposite the church, in the middle of the field of Thorns, a barren space, with scanty grass, which a few scrawny trees shelter poorly from the sun, rises in open air the *Scala Sancta*, a double staircase by which one goes up to and comes down from a chapel. At the foot of it is an inscription in French and in Breton: "This staircase is ascended only on the knees." And the delegations of pilgrims are drawn up in echelons all along its steps, on each of which one should say a *Pater* and an *Ave*. The altar of this chapel is called the pilgrims' altar. Divine service is celebrated there but once a year, July 26, the feast of Saint Anne. But, by exception, it was going to be celebrated this year on the 15th of August, the Emperor's name day, but also the Feast of the Assumption.

On entering the city, Their Majesties passed under an arch of triumph, placed on the Blavet Bridge by the workmen of the port, and bearing the inscription: "The workmen of Auray to the Emperor and the Empress." A little further on, the imperial cortège met the Brothers of the Christian Schools taking their pupils to Mass. The little ones ranged themselves on either side of the road and chanted the *Domine salvum fac Imperatorem*, and the Emperor responded by a few kindly words. As they neared Saint Anne's the procession passed under a second triumphal arch, with the inscriptions: "August 15, 1858.

Rome and Crimea. *Fiat manus tua super virum dexteræ tuæ.*" On the threshold of the sanctuary Their Majesties were received by the bishop, the clergy, and the students of the Little Seminary. To the address of the bishop, invoking blessings on the imperial family, His Majesty replied: "Monseigneur, I am much affected by the words you have just spoken. There are days when sovereigns should set an example. There are others on which they should follow that of others. That is why, obeying the custom of the country, I have wished to come here on my feast day to ask of God that which is the object of all my efforts, all my hopes: the happiness of the people which has called me to govern it. I am happy to be received by a prelate so venerated, and I rely on your prayers to draw down upon me the Divine blessing."

At Rennes, where he arrived August 19, the Emperor's first visit was likewise to the cathedral. On its threshold, Mgr. Brossais-Saint-Marc, bishop of the city, said to him: "It is especially befitting for the clergy to offer a tribute of gratitude to you, Sire, the heir of the restorer of our holy religion; to you the supporter of the Papacy in the nineteenth century; to you, of all French monarchs since Saint Louis the most devoted to the Church and its work of civilization and progress."

Then turning towards the Empress, the Bishop of Rennes added: "And you, gentle, gracious Princess, who have wished to know the Bretons and make a pious pilgrimage to their glorious patroness, you in whose veins flows the blood of the Dominics and the Teresas, on whose forehead glows a nameless something which wins all hearts, and whose life is spent in making others happy, can you be forgotten in this concert of homage and prayer? No! no! Come; a throne is raised for you near that of your spouse, in that place where Anne of Brittany used to pray, she whom our peasants still call *the good duchess*, who was the wife of *the Father of the people*, the idol of her subjects, with whom Your Majesty has so many points of resemblance in grace and beauty."

So pleased was the Emperor by this language that on the instant he decided that the bishopric of Rennes should become an archbishopric. It was concerning this tour, which ended at Saint-Cloud August 21, that Louis Veuillot wrote in the *Univers:* "The journey is a religious event; it will have a considerable influence in the world. The Emperor has performed an act and spoken words which are worth more than a battle. We are reproached with our imperialist zeal; that zeal is in the first place for religion, next for civil peace, and finally for French glory — three things which will preserve liberty." It was at the moment when it was to be overclouded that the alliance between the Empire and the Church shed its most brilliant beams.

September of this year was spent by the imperial family at Biarritz. The early days of October were devoted to the camp of Châlons, and by the 12th the sovereigns had returned to Saint-Cloud, where, on that evening, the nuptial benediction was given by the Bishop of Nancy to the Duc de Malakoff and the charming Mademoiselle de La Paniega, cousin of the Empress. Here they remained until November, when they went to spend five weeks at Compiègne, inviting a different set of guests for each week. Among them were Lord and Lady Palmerston, Lord Clarendon, Lord Cowley, the English ambassador at Paris, and Lady Cowley. It was during these weeks of pleasure that certain disquietudes, very vague as yet, began to outline themselves, though no one dared to hint at their existence. Sagacious minds already divined that the Emperor was meditating some adventurous schemes. To Lord Palmerston, and especially to Lord Clarendon, he confided things that troubled them. He was careful to say nothing definite, so as not to affect them too seriously. He confined himself to generalities, but these generalities had a suspicious character. He talked of the principle of nationalities; but, even while admitting that the good relations between France and Russia prevented anything being done for Poland, he declared that he hoped to see Italy freed from Austrian domination. He flattered himself that England would befriend such a scheme and Russia likewise. Napoleon III. was encouraged by neither Lord Palmerston nor Lord Clarendon. The latter exclaimed, insisted on the dangers of the enterprise, on the scanty profit which France could derive from it, on the uncertainties of a struggle in which, as he said, Austria, attacked in her honor, would spend her last man and her last dollar.

The English ambassador, Lord Cowley, made haste to inform Queen Victoria of the confidences made by the Emperor to his guests. The Queen was so much alarmed that she wrote to an old friend of Napoleon III., Lord Malmesbury, to acquaint him with her apprehensions. "All that can be done to dissuade the Emperor from a war in Italy," she said in this letter, "must be done without delay. He does not reflect; he sees only what he wishes. If he makes war in Italy, he will be dragged, according to all probability, into a war with Germany; that war would include Belgium, and if, in consequence of our guarantees, we are mixed up in the quarrel, France might have all Europe against her, as in 1814–1815."

The tone taken by certain Parisian journals was not calculated to reassure the alarmists. An intimate of Prince Napoleon, M. Guéroult, wrote in the press: "We do not like war, and we hope it will disappear, some day, from the surface of Europe; but we should like to see one war, and to have it directed against Austria." As Napoleon III. and his cousin were not always of one mind, not much importance was at first attached to this article, but when an official sheet, the *Patrie*, talked in the same strain a few days later, the public became more anxious. This was so evident that, before leaving Compiègne, the Emperor, as yet unwilling to unmask his schemes, had the following note inserted in the *Moniteur:* "A discussion kept up with regrettable persistence by different Parisian journals seems to have caused an uneasiness which our relations with the foreign powers do not justify in the slightest degree. The government of the Emperor feels bound to caution the public against the effects of a discussion calculated to change our relations with a power allied to France."

The next day, December 5, the court quitted the château of Compiègne, and Their Majesties installed themselves with their son in the palace of the Tuileries. The close of the year was not marked by any incident. Apprehensions continued, but they still remained vague. They did not define themselves until January 1, 1859, when Napoleon III., receiving the diplomatic body, addressed to the Austrian ambassador, Baron Hübner, a phrase which was the signal for the war of Italy.

INDEX

Abd-ul-Medjid, Sultan, his interview with Thouvenel, after the breaking off of diplomatic relations with Turkey, 174.

Albert, Prince, objects to Prussia being represented at the Paris Congress, 33; writes Baron Stockmar his impressions of the Duc de Malakoff, 303.

Alexander II., of Russia, his relations with Morny, 85 et seq.; why he sent Kisseleff to France as ambassador, 86; his coronation, 92 et seq.; calls first on Napoleon III. at Stuttgart, 215; sends the Empress word to come immediately to Stuttgart, 217; his final interview with Napoleon III. at Stuttgart described in the *Revue des Deux Mondes* of Dec. 31, 1888, 220; his attitude toward Francis Joseph of Austria at the Weimar interview, 220 et seq.

Ali Pasha, Grand-Vizier, his letter to M. Thouvenel, 47; quoted concerning the question of the Principalities, 168.

Austria, objects to the union of the Danubian Principalities, 167, 168.

Barrot, Adolphe, French minister at Brussels, sends Saint-Amand to Paris ministry of Foreign Affairs with a despatch announcing a plot against the life of Napoleon III., 223.

Baudin, chargé d'affaires of France at St. Petersburg, his despatch concerning the Stuttgart interview, 227, 228.

Benedetti, director of political affairs in the French foreign office, his letters to Thouvenel concerning the results of the Osborne interview, 182; to the same concerning the Stuttgart interview, 229, 230; his opinion of Cavour, 314, 315.

Béranger, his death and funeral, 164.

Bernard, Simon, co-conspirator with Orsini, 236; tried and acquitted in England, 303; painful impression produced by his acquittal, 304, 305.

Bismarck, Prince, his policy a survival from the Middle Ages, 8.

Bocher, Captain Charles, letter quoted, 44.

Bonaparte, Jerome, presides at banquet to officers of the Crimean War, 123.

Borgo, Duchess Pozzo di, gives a legitimist fête in honor of the Paris Congress, 46.

Brigode, Countess de, her costume at the ball at the Foreign Affairs, 132.

Broglie, Duc de, pays formal visit to the Tuileries on being elected academician; what Napoleon III. said to him, 162.

Cambridge, Duke of, visits Napoleon III. at the camp of Châlons, 204, 205.

Cardigan, Lord, visits Napoleon III. at the camp of Châlons, 204, 205.

Castellane, Marshal de, describes Prince Frederic William, of Prussia, 118; describes Maxi-

milian II., of Bavaria, 142; describes Count Charles Tascher de La Pagerie, 142.
Castiglione, Countess de, account of, 133, 134.
Cavour, Camillo Benso, Count of, brings up the Italian question at the Paris Congress, 12; emphasizes Italian grievances, 41; sketch of his career, 310 et seq.; the creator of the Italian question, 313; why he induced Victor Emmanuel to send troops to the Crimea, 314.
Chaillou, Count Amelot de, Minister of France at Buenos Ayres and at Brazil, his costume at the Foreign Affairs ball, 134, 135.
Codrington, English commander-in-chief in the Crimea, 52.
Conches, Feuillet de, procures an eagle's quill for the signatures to the treaty of Paris, 36.
Conneau, Doctor, the confidant of Napoleon III. at Ham, and his secret messenger to Turin in 1858, 11, 315, 319.
Constantine, Russian Grand Duke, visits Napoleon III., 137 et seq.
Cornu, Madame, describes the Emperor as child and man, 4, 5; says he had dreamed from childhood of driving the Austrians out of Italy, 10, 11; that his temperament was, in many respects, feminine, 20.
Corps Législatif, new election to, 163, 164.

Damremont, Countess de, describes Paris at the time of the Congress, 34, 35.
Danubian Principalities, 166 et seq.
Darimon, Alfred, his opinion of the "law of general security," 284; his *Histoire de douze ans* quoted, 286.

Disraeli, Benjamin, what he thought of the peroration of the Emperor's speech after the Orsini outrage, 253.
Dufour, General, military preceptor of Napoleon III., 9.

England, averse to the union of the Danubian Principalities, 168, 171, 172; relations with France disturbed by the addresses of the French colonels, 281 et seq.
Espinasse, General, 279-288.
Eugénie, delighted that her child was the son of the Church and not merely the son of France, 13; more entertained by things of the mind than by those of art, 20; her beauty described, 21; presented with the Golden Rose, 68; her letter to Isabella of Spain before her marriage, 176; visits Saint Sebastian, Spanish soil, from Biarritz, 195.

Favre, Jules, Orsini's advocate, 272; his oratory described, 274, 275.
Fay, General, his *Souvenirs* quoted, 44, 53.
Figaro, The, its sale forbidden, 22; its ingenious letter to the Prince Imperial, 22, 23.
Filleul, Adèle, protectress of young de Morny, 73, 74.
Fleury, General, describes floods at Avignon, 56; his *Memoires* quoted, 59, 65, 72, 93, 201, 218; describes de Morny, 77, 78.
Francis Joseph, of Austria, seeks interview with Alexander II., of Russia, at Weimar, 222, 223.
Frederic William, Prince of Prussia, more cordially received than any other prince who visited Paris during the Second Empire, 115; described, 118.

INDEX 343

Gibson, Milner, his motion in the House of Commons on the second reading of the Conspiracy Bill, and its result, 294.

Gomez, co-conspirator with Orsini, 236; his arrest, 245; sentenced to compulsory labor for life, 276.

Gorce, de La, statistics of the Crimean War, 42, 43; his *Histoire du Second Empire* quoted, 52, 70; praises the Emperor's choice of words, 162; quoted on the transportations to Algeria, 286.

Gortchakoff, Russian Minister of Foreign Affairs, his sentiments towards France, 84; quoted by M. Baudin with regard to the Stuttgart interview, 227.

Guéronnière, Vicomte de La, describes Comte de Morny in his youth, 75.

Hatzfeldt, Prussian plenipotentiary at Paris Congress, 33; fêtes the members of the Congress at the Prussian embassy, 46.

Haussmann, Baron, prefect of Paris, admits that the transformation of that city was the personal work of Napoleon III., 6, 7.

Haussonville, Comte d', describes the manner in which legitimist society received young Walewski, 27.

Havrard, his *France artistique et monumentale*, quoted, 187.

Hebert, police officer, remembers Pieri, 225; recognizes and arrests him, 241.

Heine, Heinrich, 155.

Hélène, Grand-duchess of Russia, her interview with Vicomte de Serre, 225.

Hervé, Edouard, academician, describes a reigning beauty, 134.

Ideville, Comte Henri d', a tribute to the Comtesse de Castiglione quoted from his *Journal d'un Diplomate*, 134.

Isabella, Queen of Spain, her letter to Mademoiselle de Montijo before her marriage, 197.

Kherédine, General, envoy of the Bey of Tunis, afterwards Grand Vizier of the Sultan, 136.

La Tour d'Auvergne, Prince de, notifies Walewski of a projected attempt on the life of Napoleon III., 254; private letter to Walewski, 260, 261; despatch from, 266; letter on the interview at Plombières, 323, 324.

Lhuys, Drouyn de, resigns the Ministry of Foreign Affairs, 29.

Louvre, opening of the new, 186–191.

MacMahon, General, the only senator who opposed the law of general security, 286.

Manteuffel, Baron, Prussian plenipotentiary at Paris Congress, 33.

Maximilian II., of Bavaria, visits Napoleon III., 142 *et seq.*

Mehemet, Djemil Bey, Turkish ambassador to Paris Congress, 47; hint given him by Napoleon III. concerning the electoral frauds in Moldavia, 172–173.

Méloizes, Vicomte des, French minister at Weimar, despatch from, 223.

Méneval, Baron de, despatches to Walewski concerning the visit of the Bavarian king, 145 *et seq.*

Mesnard, Vice-President of Senate, twitted by the Empress with his opposition to her marriage, 20, 21.

Moldavia, union of, with Wallachia

proposed at the Congress of Paris by the French plenipotentiary, 167.

Moltke, General, visits Paris in 1856, 115.

Morny, Comte de, his origin and early career, 72 et seq.; ambassador extraordinary to Alexander II., 73; his first meeting with Napoleon III., 76; characterized, 80, 81; received coldly by the Empress Dowager of Russia, 82; his relations with Alexander II. and with Gortchakoff, 85 et seq.; did not brag of his origin in Paris but advertised it in Moscow, 92; despatch on Russian sentiment towards France, 108 et seq.; his foresight and steadiness of mind, 111 et seq.; his despatches of unsurpassed excellence, 112; his speech in the Corps Législatif after the Orsini outrage, 249.

Napoleon III., not a dreamer, but a man of action, 5; a cosmopolitan sovereign, 7; begins to conspire for the war of Italy in 1856, 8, 9; thought it his providential mission to cancel the treaties of 1815, 10; for a sovereign a very good husband, 19, 20; never hinted his ulterior schemes to his wife, 23; opens the parliamentary session, 126; demands the quashing of the Moldavian elections, 173; breaks off diplomatic relations with Turkey, 173, 174; visits Queen Victoria at Osborne and succeeds in inducing England to disavow the action of Lord Stratford de Redcliffe, 173 et seq.; his letter to Queen Victoria, 180, 181; his speech at the opening of the New Louvre, 190; initiates agricultural experiments in the Landes, 192, 193; his speech at the camp of Châlons, 202, 203; a fatalist and fearless, 232; appoints the Empress regent in case of his death, 255; in spite of the Orsini outrage retains his Italian sympathies, 261; goes to Cherbourg to meet Victoria and Prince Albert, 327 et seq.; meets Cavour by secret appointment at Plombières, 317-325; begins to show his hand, 337 et seq.

Napoleon, Prince, envoy to Berlin and Dresden, 149 et seq.; sends Humboldt the grand cross of the Legion of Honor, 153; his marriage with the Princess Clotilde urged by Napoleon III. at the Plombières interview, 323.

Ollivier, Émile, opposes the law of general security, 285.

Orloff, Count, Russian plenipotentiary at the Paris Congress, 85; his remark to Cavour concerning the Austrian plenipotentiary, 38.

Orsini, Félix, plans attempt on the life of Napoleon III., 235 et seq.; his arrest, 245; his letters to Napoleon III., 273, 274, 276, 277; sentenced, 276; executed, 277, 278.

Palmerston, Lord, prepares the Conspiracy Bill, 292; goes out of office after its second reading, 294; remarks to de Persigny that this was the second time he had been turned out of the ministry on account of France and the Emperor, 295; disturbed by the confidences made him by Napoleon III. at Saint-Cloud, 336.

INDEX 345

Patrizzi, Cardinal, Papal Legate, 61.
Pélissier, Marshal Duc de Malakoff, telegram from Sebastopol to Minister of War, 2; despatch from Sebastopol, 57; made ambassador to England, 302; his meeting with the Duc d'Aumale in Hyde Park, 309; his marriage, 337.
Persigny, Count de, 289 et seq.
Pieri, Italian conspirator, accomplice of Orsini, 234, 235; sentenced, 276; executed, 277, 278.
Pinard, Ernest, describes the Emperor's manner, 4, 6, 7; describes Walewski, 30; describes Morny, 78, 79.
Prince Imperial, Pio Nono's godson, 13; his baptism at Notre Dame, 60 et seq.

Redcliffe, Lord Stratford de, English ambassador at Constantinople, his attitude concerning the Principalities, 168; offends France by publicly celebrating the anniversary of Waterloo at Pera, 171; obliged to nullify his action at Constantinople, 182.
Ristori, Madame, describes the appearance of Napoleon III. just after the Orsini attempt, 243, 244.
Rothan, Gustave, describes the final interview at Stuttgart between Napoleon III. and the Czar, 220.
Rudio, Charles de, conspires with Orsini, 236; arrested, 246; sentenced, 276.

Serre, Vicomte de, minister of France at Carlsruhe, despatches from, 210, 224, 225, 226.
Sibour, Archbishop of Paris, assassinated, 120, 121.

Talleyrand-Périgord, Baron, represents France in the European commission, 172.
Thiers, buys the *Messager* newspaper from Walewski, 28; quoted, 32; homage paid him by Napoleon III., 127.
Thouvenel, French minister at Constantinople, 34; criticises the foreign policy of France, 169, 170; begins to understand the personal policy of Napoleon III., 170, 171; complains of the electoral methods of Vogorides, 172; his interview with Abd-ul-Medjid, 174; quoted on the resumption of diplomatic relations, 183.
Thouvenel, Louis, his *Three Years of the Oriental Question* quoted, 167 et seq.
Treaty of Paris, stipulations of the, 37 et seq.
Troplong, President of Senate, 248, 249.

Verger, assassin of Mgr. Sibour, 122.
Victor Emmanuel, sends Della Rocca to Paris, 258; Napoleon III. wished him to marry a Hohenzollern princess, 259; his little game with Della Rocca, 265; averse to marrying the Princess Clotilde to Prince Napoleon, 323.
Victoria, Queen, praises Eugénie and M. de Persigny, 178; describes the visit of Napoleon III. to Osborne as "politically a blessing from Heaven," 179; delighted by his praise of Prince Albert, 182; visits Cherbourg unannounced, 183; meets Napoleon III. at Cherbourg by appointment, 326 et seq.; writes to Malmesbury that she fears the Emperor may unite all Europe

against him in another war, 338.

Vogorides, Prince, lieutenant-governor at Yassy, employs force and fraud in the Moldavian elections, 172.

Walewski, Count, leader of French diplomacy in 1856, 25; reputed son of Napoleon I., 26; his career in France from 1829 to 1854, 27 *et seq.*; Saint-Amand owes his entry to diplomacy to him, 30; formulates the *Roman Question* at the Paris Congress, 40; a despatch from him to Persigny the beginning of complications with England, 291.

Zamoyski, Polish envoy to England, 27.

THE SECOND EMPIRE.
By IMBERT DE SAINT-AMAND.

CHARLES SCRIBNER'S SONS, PUBLISHERS.

THE COURT OF THE SECOND EMPIRE, 1856-1858.
With Four Portraits. Price, $1.50.

The three years bridging the time from the Crimean to the Italian war of 1859 form the epochs treated in the latest of M. de Saint-Amand's books. The author follows the course of public events in a brilliant chronicle of the treaty of Paris, the baptism of the Prince Imperial, the Coronation of the Czar Alexander II., the attempted assassination by Orsini and his fellow-conspirators of the Emperor Napoleon, and the diplomatic meetings which prepared the way for the war for Italian liberation. The secret history of this movement, contemplated by Napoleon as soon as the Crimean war had closed, and pursued by him with equal skill and success, is also strikingly unfolded.

LOUIS NAPOLEON AND MADEMOISELLE DE MONTIJO.
With Two Portraits. Price, $1.50.

This volume begins the author's elaborate study of the history of France during the reign of Napoleon III. The accession of the new dynasty marked a new era which in its own way and under the changed conditions of modern times, recalled the brilliancy of the First Empire. In this initial volume the author shows the development of Louis Napoleon's character from the days of his early childhood, through his varied experiences in Italy, Switzerland, England and America; his fiascos of Strasburg and Boulogne; his long imprisonment and escape; his return to France, and election, first to the Chamber of Deputies, then to the Presidency of the Republic, and finally the *coup d'état* and the proclamation anew of the Empire. The charming young Empress Eugénie makes a delightful companion portrait.

NAPOLEON III. AND HIS COURT.
With Four Portraits. Price, $1.50.

The second volume of the new Napoleonic series covers the period from the proclamation of the Second Empire to the birth of the Prince Imperial in 1856. It is the period of the alliance of France and England and the Crimean War, of which latter it is one of the most effective condensed accounts existing. The volume is full of striking historic portraits, Marshals Canrobert and Pélissier, the Emperor Nicholas, the Princess Mathilde, M. Drouyn de Lhuys and others, that agreeably vary the narrative, itself crowded with interesting and rapidly succeeding events.

FAMOUS WOMEN OF THE FRENCH COURT.

"*In these translations of this interesting series of sketches, we have found an unexpected amount of pleasure and profit. The author cites for us passages from forgotten diaries, hitherto unearthed letters, extracts from public proceedings, and the like, and contrives to combine and arrange his material so as to make a great many very vivid and pleasing pictures. Nor is this all. The material he lays before us is of real value, and much, if not most of it, must be unknown save to the special students of the period. We can, therefore, cordially commend these books to the attention of our readers. They will find them attractive in their arrangement, never dull, with much variety of scene and incident, and admirably translated.*" — THE NATION.

"*Indeed, a certain sanity of vision is one of M. de Saint-Amand's characteristics.... He evidently finds it no difficult task to do justice to Legitimist and Imperialist, to the old world that came to an end with the Revolution and to the new world that sprang from the old world's ashes. Nor do his qualifications as a popular historian end here. He has the gift of so marshalling his facts as to leave a definite impression. These are but short books on great subjects; for M. de Saint-Amand is not at all content to chronicle the court life of his three heroines, and writes almost more fully about their times than he does about themselves; but yet comparatively short as the books may be, they tell their story, in many respects, better than some histories of greater pretensions.*" — THE ACADEMY, London.

FOUR VOLUMES ON WOMEN OF THE VALOIS AND VERSAILLES COURTS.

Each with Portraits, $1.25. Price per set, in box, cloth, $5.00; half calf, $10.00.

    WOMEN OF THE VALOIS COURT.
    THE COURT OF LOUIS XIV.
    THE COURT OF LOUIS XV.
    THE LAST YEARS OF LOUIS XV.

The splendid pageantry of the court over which Catherine de' Medici presided and in which she intrigued, and the contrasting glories and shames of the long reigns of the "Sun King" and of Louis XV. are the subjects of these four volumes which depict the most brilliant days of the Valois and Bourbon dynasties.

FAMOUS WOMEN OF THE FRENCH COURT

THREE VOLUMES ON MARIE ANTOINETTE.

Each with Portrait, $1.25. *Price per set, in box, cloth,* $3.75; *half calf,* $7.50.

MARIE ANTOINETTE AND THE END OF THE OLD REGIME.
MARIE ANTOINETTE AT THE TUILERIES.
MARIE ANTOINETTE AND THE DOWNFALL OF ROYALTY.

In this series is unfolded the tremendous panorama of political events in which the unfortunate Queen had so influential a share, beginning with the days immediately preceding the Revolution, when court life at Versailles was so gay and unsuspecting, continuing with the enforced journey of the royal family to Paris, and the agitating months passed in the Tuileries, together with the ill-starred and unsuccessful attempt to escape from French territory, and concluding with the abolition of royalty, the proclamation of the Republic, and the imprisonment of the royal family, — the initial stage of their progress to the guillotine.

THREE VOLUMES ON THE EMPRESS JOSEPHINE.

Each with Portrait, $1.25. *Price per set, in box, cloth,* $3.75; *half calf,* $7.50.

CITIZENESS BONAPARTE.
THE WIFE OF THE FIRST CONSUL.
THE COURT OF THE EMPRESS JOSEPHINE.

The romantic and eventful period beginning with Josephine's marriage to the young commander whose "whiff of grapeshot" had just saved France from anarchy, and whose wonderful career was about to begin, comprises the astonishing Italian campaign, in which the power of Austria was so unexpectedly and completely humbled, the Egyptian expedition, the *coup d'état* of Brumaire, and is described in the first of the above volumes; while the second treats of the brilliant society which issued from the chaos of the Revolution, and over which Madame Bonaparte presided so charmingly; and the third, of the events between the assumption of the imperial title by Napoleon and the end of 1807, including, of course, the Austerlitz campaign.

FOUR VOLUMES ON THE EMPRESS MARIE LOUISE.

Each with Portrait, $1.25. *Price per set, in box, cloth,* $5.00; *half calf,* $10.00.

THE HAPPY DAYS OF MARIE LOUISE.
MARIE LOUISE AND THE DECADENCE OF THE EMPIRE.
MARIE LOUISE AND THE INVASION OF 1814.
MARIE LOUISE, THE RETURN FROM ELBA, AND THE HUNDRED DAYS.

The auspicious marriage of the Archduchess Marie Louise to the master of Europe; the Russian invasion, with its disastrous conclusion a few years later; the Dresden and Leipsic campaign; the invasion of France by the Allies, and the marvellous military strategy of Napoleon in 1814, ending only with his defeat and exile to Elba; his life in his little principality; his romantic escape and dramatic return to France; the preparations of the Hundred Days; Waterloo and the definitive restoration of Louis XVIII., closing the era begun in 1789, with "The End of the Old Régime," — are the subjects of the four volumes grouped around the personality of Marie Louise.

TWO VOLUMES ON THE DUCHESS OF ANGOULÊME.

Each with Portrait, $1.25. *Price per set, in box, cloth*, $2.50; *half calf*, $5.00.

THE YOUTH OF THE DUCHESS OF ANGOULÊME.
THE DUCHESS OF ANGOULÊME AND THE TWO RESTORATIONS.

The period covered in this first of these volumes begins with the life of the daughter of Louis XVI. and Marie Antoinette imprisoned in the Temple after the execution of her parents, and ends with the accession of Louis XVIII. after the abdication of Napoleon at Fontainebleau. The first Restoration, its illusions, the characters of Louis XVIII., of his brother, afterwards Charles X., of the Dukes of Angoulême and Berry, sons of the latter, the life of the Court, the feeling of the city, Napoleon's sudden return from Elba, the Hundred Days from the Royalist side, the second Restoration, and the vengeance taken by the new government on the Imperialists, form the subject-matter of the second volume.

THREE VOLUMES ON THE DUCHESS OF BERRY.

Each with Portrait, $1.25. *Price per set, in box, cloth*, $3.75; *half calf*, $7.50.

THE DUCHESS OF BERRY AND THE COURT OF LOUIS XVIII.
THE DUCHESS OF BERRY AND THE COURT OF CHARLES X.
THE DUCHESS OF BERRY AND THE REVOLUTION OF JULY, 1830.

The Princess Marie Caroline, of Naples, became, upon her marriage with the Duke of Berry, the central figure of the French Court during the reigns of both Louis XVIII. and Charles X. The former of these was rendered eventful by the assassination of her husband and the birth of her son, the Count of Chambord, and the latter was from the first marked by those reactionary tendencies which resulted in the dethronement and exile of the Bourbons. The dramatic Revolution which brought about the July monarchy of Louis Philippe, has never been more vividly and intelligently described than in the last volume devoted to the Duchess of Berry.

THE REVOLUTION OF 1848.

With Four Portraits. Price $1.25.

M. Imbert de Saint-Amand's volume on "The Duchess of Berry and the Revolution of 1830," which described the turbulent accession of Louis Philippe to the throne of France, is followed by the account of the Citizen King's equally agitated abdication and exile during the Revolution of 1848. As always, the historian writes from the inside, and his description of the exciting events of the February days that led to the overthrow of the Orleanist dynasty, the flight of the last king France has had, and the dramatically sudden establishment of the Second Republic is familiar and intimate rather than formal, and the reader gets a view of what passed behind the scenes as well as on the stage at that interesting and fateful moment.

www.ingramcontent.com/pod-product-compliance
Lightning Source LLC
Chambersburg PA
CBHW020236240426
43672CB00006B/542